VÉRA'S BUTTERFLIES

First editions by Vladimir Nabokov

inscribed to his wife

Моей Душечке
Октябрь 1967
Монтрэих

Colias lolita Nab.
♀

For Verochka
Jan 19, 1971
Montreux

Brenthis dozenita Nab.

NABOKOV'S DOZENITA
дозенитная перламутровка

NO. 103

Véra's Butterflies

First editions by Vladimir Nabokov

inscribed to his wife

By Sarah Funke

With contributions by Brian Boyd,
Stephen Jay Gould, Kurt Johnson,
James Salter, Stacy Schiff, Michael Wood

Edited by Glenn Horowitz

GLENN HOROWITZ BOOKSELLER, INC.

New York City / 1999

ACKNOWLEDGEMENTS

The translations of Nabokov's Russian inscriptions were prepared by Gavriel Shapiro; information on the sources of VN's imaginative Lepidoptera was provided by Kurt Johnson, who was assisted informally with the identification of moths by Frederick H. Rindge and Eric L. Quinter; Michael Juliar responded to bibliographic queries; Rodney Phillips, Curator of The Henry W. and Albert A. Berg Collection of English and American Literature at the New York Public Library, allowed us to examine their typescript of *Lolita: A Screenplay*, excerpts of which are published herein.

We are indebted to Brian Boyd and Dmitri Nabokov.

ISBN 0-9654020-1-0

CONTENTS

for Vera
Montreux, 1971

Maculinea
aurora
♂ Nab.

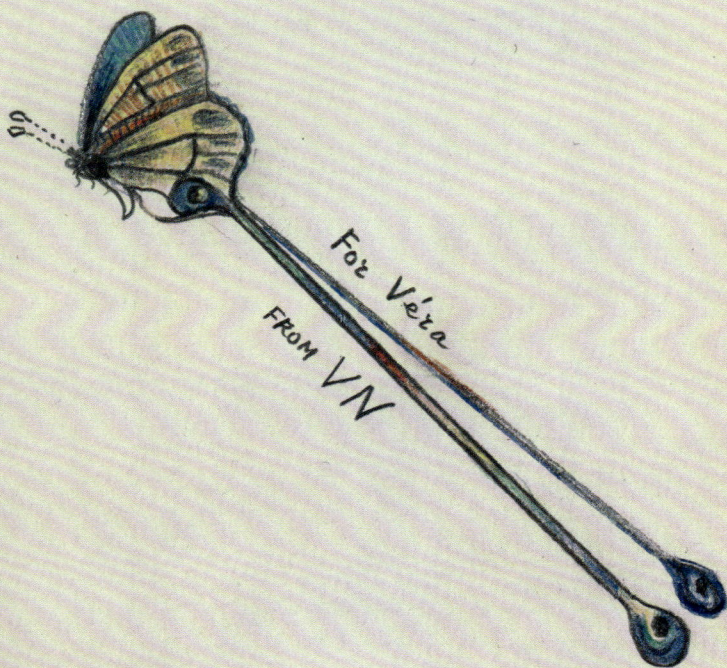

For Véra
From VN

Montreux
Xmas 1969

NO. 17

To Véra

Vanessa incognita

from V
Mont Reux
April 23 1962

NATURALLY PLAYFUL: AN INTRODUCTION

The first question many people will ask when they see the drawings reproduced in *Véra's Butterflies* is, "Are these renderings of real butterflies, or are they wholly imaginary?" The answer lies somewhere in between, for they are blends of fact and fiction, and fascinating ones at that.

In his scientific publications, which were meant for an audience of fellow lepidopterists and where accuracy was a requisite, Nabokov was a proficient illustrator of real butterflies. He was, after all, tutored in drawing as a boy by Mstislav Dobuzhinsky, one of Russia's foremost artists. At nine he first submitted to a distinguished Russian lepidopterist an aquarelle of what he thought was a new species, and at ten, as he records in his memoir, *Speak, Memory*, sent the description of a rarity he thought was another new species to the British journal, *The Entomologist*. After a search, the editor found that the butterfly had already been named, but he praised the boy's illustration.

Dedicated to butterflies even then, the young Nabokov made them his personal mark: in a formal photograph in childhood, in the first poem he had mimeographed for family and friends at fifteen, in his first published book of poems, at sixteen, in manuscript albums of his poetry, in his fiction and his verse, in letters and inscriptions. He signed one letter to his friend the critic Edmund Wilson with a drawing of two butterflies hovering over an abandoned pair of boots. To his friend the lepidopterist Cyril dos Passos he sent a Christmas card with an engraving of the Cornell campus in December, adding his own butterfly flitting above the snow. Even furnishings were not safe from his pen: he sketched one butterfly on the bathroom wall in the home of his Cornell friend, Morris Bishop, another flying along the leafy border of the lampshade above the lectern in his suite at the Montreux Palace Hotel on which he wrote his last novels and worked on his uncompleted *Butterflies of Europe* and *Butterflies in Art*.

Nabokov never signed books for strangers. Even the friends for whom he wrote inscriptions rarely received a butterfly drawing as well. Only for those closest to him, his wife's cousin, Anna Feigin, his sister, Elena, his son, Dmitri, and his wife, Véra, did Nabokov regularly embellish copies of his books with elaborate butterflies rendered in ink or colored pencil, never more spectacular or profuse than those he drew for Véra in the last twenty years of his life.

Vladimir and Véra Nabokov valued the intangibles of nature and art and imagination and memory much more than any accumulation of material possessions. Although when *Lolita* made him rich enough to retire from Cornell and even to afford spontaneously to buy Véra a string of pearls on his way back from picking up the bread and milk, Nabokov knew that for her birthday, for Christmas, for the anniversary of their first meeting or their marriage, she would appreciate much more than conventional gifts the butterfly drawings on copies of his work that he now had time to perfect for her. (Of course he also now realized the value his fame added to inscribed first editions of his work, and the legacy these inscriptions would one day leave for Dmitri.) Pencilled on the endpapers, half-title, or title page, his butterfly drawings were the perfect gift to a wife who was such a partner in all his literary efforts: they added a handwritten touch to the mechanically reproduced dedications "To Véra" in many of his published works; they took the form of *his* ludic logo, a butterfly, but were often labeled after some form of *her* name, and frequently executed in the rainbow hues that had some intimate private import for them as a couple (a major reason that the rainbow-spectrum theme looms so large in *Speak, Memory*, which ends with a chapter addressed to Véra). In these highly personal and affectionately playful drawings the scientific accuracy Nabokov needed in thousands of illustrations of the specimens he studied under the microscope was no longer relevant, and his imagination could take flight.

Yet Nabokov always insisted, as Stephen Jay Gould notes, that there is no science without fancy and no art without facts. In the butterflies he devised and labeled for Véra he mingles fact and fancy even more sportively than in his fiction. He assigns each invented butterfly a name that follows the standard two-word (or "binomial") form for Latin scientific names, first a capitalized"genus" (which typically would contain a number of species) and, second, the species itself. In some cases he ascribes a new species name within a genuine genus; in others, he invents both genus and species names. But to what extent do any of the drawings represent recognizable butterflies? Does Nabokov intend specific references or does his imagination randomly recombine and reshuffle and redesign features he remembers from a lifetime of investigating Lepidoptera?

When Nabokov appends to his drawings real generic names – those of butterflies like the North American and European *Colias* or *Vanessa*, the African *Charaxes*, or even the lesser known group of colorful wasp-mimicking moths known as *Aegeria*–he portrays accurately the wing shapes and pattern markings typical of the genera he has chosen, but he adds resplendent new markings and colors, always more luxuriant than in any of the genus's actual butterflies, or combining the most visually vibrant traits of various of its real species.

What then of the butterflies with not only specific but even generic names that are fanciful or personalized, like *Paradisia, Iridula, Adorata adorata, Vladimiria,* or *Verina*? Many of the drawings in this category are quite extraordinary, showing fantastic wing shapes and colors. Being an entomologist who has worked closely with the groups of butterflies in which Nabokov was an expert, Johnson explored this question with the help of two colleagues well-versed in moths, Eric L. Quinter and Frederick H. Rindge, both of the American Museum of Natural History. (Rindge, who has been at the American Museum for over fifty years, well remembers when Nabokov first began working in the early 1940s as a volunteer assistant to his first American mentor, the renowned lepidopterist William Phillips Comstock.) Close study of the "Véra" drawings revealed that nearly all work could be identified within particular, distinctive groups of butterflies and moths.

In some cases, Nabokov's insect model was so well known (to an entomologist) as to leave no question about its precise identity: one, for instance, an improbable-looking Australian Lacewing whose elongate tails are tipped with bulbous eye-spots, another with its transparent wings drawn so clearly it could belong only to one group of Satyr butterflies known from South America. In all cases, knowledgeable lepidopterists had little difficulty in quickly recognizing clues to the Lepidoptera that let Nabokov's inspiration take wing.

But although an expert eye can recognize the allusion behind even a new generic name, Nabokov's sketches of these butterflies always reflect something grander than the reality. In some ways, it might not be far off the mark to think of the drawings as particularly affectionate caricatures. As in all good caricatures, the intent is obviously not to produce a "realistic" drawing, yet the subject will be instantly recognizable beneath– or even because of– the exaggeration. And of course, Nabokov's intent is not to poke fun at his subjects but to celebrate them, to festoon them in flamboyant new finery.

In thinking of his wife, what kinds of butterflies and moths did Nabokov choose to portray? Appropriately, many caricature species that would have been familiar to him from the woods and fields around Vyra, the Nabokov family estate near St. Petersburg, where he collected as a child– *Vanessa atalurticae*, *Vanessa incognita*, even *Colias verae* and *Colias lolita*.

Others suggest species he may have first seen in the lavish color illustrations of the Lepidoptera books given to him by his mother or among the tropical specimens offered for sale by the butterfly dealers he would visit in his childhood on trips to Germany. Such exotic butterflies helped inspire those he described in his Russian fiction, in his evocations and imaginings of the tropics in stories like "The Aurelian" or "Terra Incognita," or as part of the fictional expeditions in his novel, *The Gift*. Once he reached the United States and began to work as a volunteer at the American Museum of Natural History in New York and as a paid research fellow at the Museum of Comparative Zoology at Harvard University, he no doubt, like any dedicated lepidopterist, spent hours "pulling drawers" to marvel at the incredible diversity of butterflies and moths and see the originals of what he had known only from illustrations. The bold shapes and shades of the world's most exuberant and colorful butterflies gave him the cue for such of his exotic inventions as *Adorata adorata*, *Adorina verae* and *Paradisia radugaleta*.

As one might expect, many of the drawings Nabokov presented to his wife portray imagined butterflies within the lycaenids, the group in which he specialized. These include the Blue *Maculinea aurora* and the Hairstreak *Thecla vera* (both imaginary species placed in real genera), and at least a dozen fantastically colored Metalmarks. Although Nabokov was an acknowledged expert on one of these groups, the Blues, he clearly had considerable familiarity with the other lycaenid groups as well. One of Nabokov's close friends at Harvard was Harry Kendon Clench, later the curator of butterflies at the Carnegie Museum of Natural History and a world authority on the Hairstreaks. The collegiality of Nabokov and Clench as fellow "lycaenidologists" is well known – their early papers on Blues and Hairstreaks appeared in the same issues of the Harvard entomological journal *Psyche* in the 1940s. As a prank, now famous among lepidopterists, Nabokov created a fake Hairstreak to puzzle Clench: "*Thecla caramba*" Nabokov called it (the species name means something like 'Wow!' in Spanish). Clench was not fooled, but later retained the name in his own work and today *caramba* still survives as the name of a brilliant blue and green Hairstreak butterfly from southeastern Brazil.

The equally dazzling Metalmark butterflies are close relatives of the Blues and Hairstreaks and Nabokov no doubt knew of their astonishing variety in the tropical regions of the world. Some of Nabokov's drawings of Blues, Hairstreaks and Metalmarks in the "Véra" series are extravagant renderings, resembling rainbows or stained glass – a personal motif for Nabokov, associated with both creativity and love in his autobiography, *Speak, Memory*, and its novelistic mirror-reversal, *Look at the Harlequins!* Yet nearly every wing shape Nabokov portrays actually exists in nature, and the colors, while brazen, are not always that far beyond their real counterparts.

When Nabokov provided clues in his Latin names, or in certain wing shapes and colors, does that mean that we can specifically identify each butterfly or moth he used as a model? Are the butterflies and moths suggested by us in the captions the precise subjects he was drawing? Sometimes, but not always. What *is* certain is that no matter how grand or imaginative Nabokov's drawing appears to be, there is something in nature which it closely resembles, sometimes in nearly every detail.

Nabokov loved playful deception, partly because he thought nature did: as he writes in his autobiography, "The mysteries of mimicry had a special attraction for me. Its phenomena showed an artistic perfection usually associated with man-wrought things. . . . I discovered in nature the nonutilitarian delights that I sought in art. Both were a form of magic, both were a game of intricate enchantment and deception." In the 1950s he was even ready to undertake writing a major book on natural mimicry until the ambitious scope of his plans scared the publisher away. Throughout his art he tries to find equivalents for the detail, the playfulness, the deceptiveness, and the invitation to discovery he found in nature. Just as in his novels the most fantastic details of his most fantastic worlds, such as *Pale Fire*'s Zembla or *Ada*'s Antiterra, often turn out to refract obscure facts of our real world, so his butterflies often feign to be impossible in the very details where he knows he has drawn on nature.

Ten of Nabokov's drawings assign the species name "*verae*" – the Latinization appropriate in rendering his wife's name into the language of taxonomy– to either a real or fanciful genus of butterflies. Another name used more than once in the drawings is "*lolita*", as a species belonging to both a real butterfly genus, *Colias*, and an imaginary one, *Verina*, itself derived (via Russian this time) from his wife's name. The Russo-Latin "*Verina verae*" even doubles up to create a species name meaning "Véra's véra's."

Many taxonomists name species after loved ones, but in his scientific work Nabokov never did. Nor did he ever name butterflies after characters from his fiction. That privilege fell to the lepidopterists who over the last fifteen years have completed much of his pioneering work on the Blue butterflies of Latin America. In tribute to the astute grasp he showed of the natural generic divisions in neotropical Blues, despite having to work in war-time conditions from a limited number of specimens, these lepidopterists two or three generations younger than him have bestowed on the scores of new species they have recently identified a series of names from Nabokov's family and from his novels and stories, such as *vera*, *lolita*, *humbert*, and many more.

When they were naming these butterflies in Nabokov's honor, none of these lepidopterists had an inkling of the existence of the "Véra" drawings and *their* new names. But Véra's butterflies are now a part of the Nabokov legacy in lepidoptery. With the publication of this book, those who have admired Nabokov's literary art will be able to see in these intimate and sportive labors of love yet another side of this multitalented man. Perhaps viewing these drawings will also bring them to a deeper appreciation of the beauty and complexity of the butterflies and moths whose magic enchanted Vladimir Nabokov for a lifetime.

Kurt Johnson

Research Associate, Lepidoptera
The Florida State Collection of Arthropods
Gainesville, Florida 32614-1210

Brian Boyd

Professor of English
University of Auckland
Auckland, New Zealand

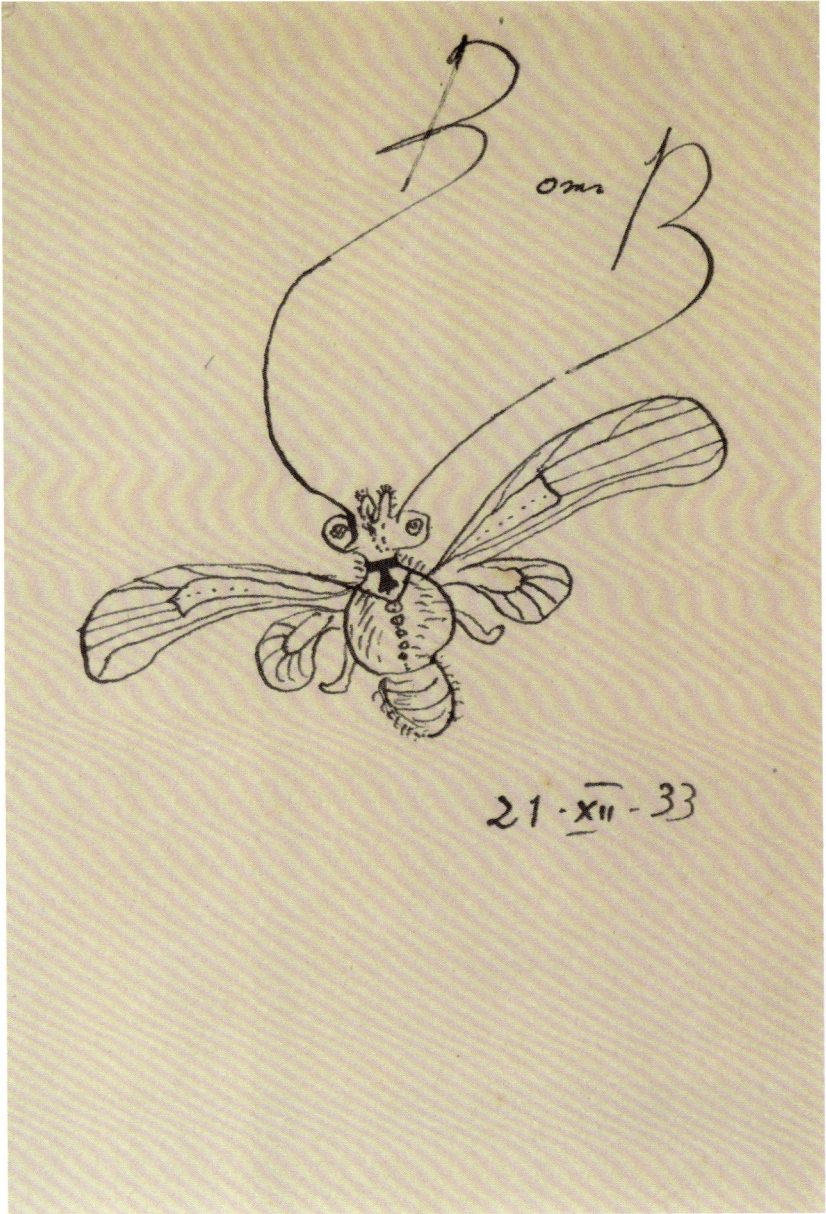

21·XII·33

NO. 29

Thecla verae Nab.

Christmas 1971

NO. 127

THE EYE

Colias verae
NABOKOV

голубых колиасов
не бывает.

Oct. 1, 1965

Montreux

VANESSA
VERAE

Миленькой моей

от

Ƀ

8 · II · 1957

Ithaca

1 **Poems [Stikhi].** [St. Petersburg: Privately Printed], 1916.

Slim 12mo.; front hinge weakened; two Russian stamps inside rear cover ("The Writer's Bookstore" and "Price"); cream printed wrappers; light overall wear.

First edition of VN's first documentable publication: a collection of 68 love poems in Russian he composed between August 1915 and May 1916 to Valentina "Lyussa" Shulgin; 500 press-numbered copies (this is copy #335). Copies are readily located in American research institutions, and in a 1969 *Vogue* interview VN claimed that "several copies of it still lurk in my native country" (Tallmey interview, *Strong Opinions* (hereafter SO) p. 154). Preceded by an elusive poem which VN's parents had printed in 1914 in an edition of a couple of dozen copies for distribution to friends and family. Boyd notes: "To judge from the one line Nabokov remembers (*Nad rododendronom v'yotsya ona,* Over the rhododendron it hovers), lepidoptera emerge already in this spring of his long publishing career" (*The Russian Years* (hereafter TRY) p. 111). Juliar A2.1.

One of VN's copies, annotated by him, with a hand-labeled spine; publication information added to the poem on page 17; minor emendations to pages 29 (letter change) and 40 ("?" to *!*); and a curious giraffe stamp on the title page. The bookstore stamp in the rear suggests that this volume was acquired rather than retained by VN—and might also explain the presence of the giraffe. The Nabokovs were perpetually on the look-out for the bibliographic rarities, once even placing ads in a European Russian weekly in the hope of filling in the holes in their collection. (A second family copy, #344, was sold by this firm to the Houghton Library at Harvard University in the early 1990s.)

VN printed *Stikhi* at his own expense in June 1916; by the end of the summer, however, he had labeled it "a misfortune" (TRY p. 120), and critics were in agreement. Having previously published only in his school paper and once in *Vestnik evropy,* a prestigious journal of liberal political commentary and somewhat conservative literature, VN was unprepared for the critical thrashing *Stikhi* received. He later assessed: "the versification is fair, the lack of originality complete..." (Tallmey interview, 1969, SO p. 154). Boyd recounts more than one "unfortunate" related incident: VN's Russian literature teacher Vladimir Gippius "brought a copy to class and had his students delirious with mirth as he fired his sarcasm at Nabokov's most romantic lines." The children's poet and literary critic Korney Chukovsky sent VN "a polite letter of praise but enclosed in the envelope, as if by mistake, a rough draft outlining a franker judgment. Zinaida Gippius, a major Symbolist poet and sharp-tongued hostess of the capital's leading literary salon, told V. D. Nabokov at a session of the Literary Fund to tell his son, please, that he would never, never be a writer." The only positive review came from a writer hoping to curry favor with VDN. VN later recalled: "The whole business cured me permanently of all interest in literary fame and was probably the cause of that almost pathological and not always justified indifference to reviews which in later years deprived me of the emotions most authors are said to experience" (TRY pp. 120–21).

VN used his father's printer to produce this volume, which bore his own name ("V. V. Nabokov"). Once he began publishing in Berlin and Paris after the Revolution, he would use the pseudonym, "V. Sirin," to distinguish himself from his father, who was a prominent Russian journalist, editor and contributor to *Rech'*, "St. Petersburg's leading liberal daily" (Boyd, "Chronology of Nabokov's Life and Works," p. xxxi) and, after his emigration to Berlin, the founding editor of the most influential Russian émigré daily, *Rul'*. (He also had a hand in setting up Slovo, the largest émigré press in Berlin.) It was during the years that both VN and VDN were contributing regularly to *Rul'* that VN opted for a pen-name to prevent confusion.

VDN had a history of writing and speaking out against the government oppression his son would so vehemently deride in interviews, letters, and even in some of his poetry and fiction throughout his career. His contrarian views lost him his appointment at the Imperial School of Jurisprudence, his court title, and, after he signed "a manifesto calling the country to resist conscription and taxes," his panoply of political rights. After serving a three-month prison sentence – during which he wrote to his son of the butterflies and moths in the prison yard – he championed the constitutional democracy as a journalist and editor. As VN was readying *Stikhi*, VDN brought out *From England At War,* his report on his mission to England as a representative of the Russian press. In 1917 he finally rejoined the established political ranks, first as Chancellor in the first Provisional Government and, after he resigned, as a member of the Constituent Assembly. Fearing his two oldest sons – VN, 18, and Sergei, 17 – would be drafted into the Red Army, he sent his family to the Crimea, where he later joined them and became Minister of Justice in the Crimean Provisional Regional Government set up primarily by the Russian Constitutional Democrats and Tartar nationalists. The Crimea was evacuated in the spring of 1919, and that fall VN began Michaelmas term at Cambridge. The family was soon ensconced in Berlin, where the Russian émigré population would reach nearly half a million before moving, almost *en masse,* to Paris by the middle of the decade. On March 28, 1922 VDN was killed shielding CD leader Paul Miliukov from the bullets of right-wing assassins. "Easter," the poem VN wrote to commemorate his father, was published in *Rul'* on Easter Sunday that year; it appeared in his next collection, *The Cluster* [*Grozd'*], in December. (ibid pp. xxx–xxxvi)

2 **A Shropshire Lad.** By A. E. Housman. London: Grant Richards, (1912).

32mo.; French censor's stamp on rear endpaper; red cloth; very light wear; a lovely survival.

Together with:

Last Poems. By A. E. Housman. London: Grant Richards, MDCCCCXXII.

8vo.; a few pages lightly soiled; cigarette burn through pp. 77–78; French censor's stamp on rear pastedown; top edge gilt; navy cloth, lightly rubbed.

A late, modest edition of *A Shropshire Lad*, with VN's note indicating that it was a gift from his mother, Elena Nabokov, during his student years at Trinity College: *V. Nabokov/from E. N./7 Dec. 1919;* and his evaluation of Housman's poetry in his minute Cyrillic script on the rear endpaper: *Delightful, and delicate, and tender… The English Kol'tsov* … Shapiro notes: "Alexei Kol'tsov [1809–42], a Russian 'peasant' poet who wrote in the genre of the folk song; his poetry is often compared to that of Robert Burns, his Scottish predecessor."

Last Poems is a first edition, second printing, inscribed to VN (with his single pencil "x" on page 41, "In the midnights of November") by Count Robert Louis Magawly-Cerati de Calry: "With my love & best wishes for Xmas Bobby: 21/xii/22." Calry, Russian "only by blood" (TRY p. 168), was one of VN's closest friends and, at times, roommate, at Trinity College, Cambridge, where VN began in Zoology and French and Russian, eventually dropping Zoology (though he published his first lepidopteral paper in 1920). At the end of first term in 1921 Calry invited VN on a ski-ing excursion to Switzerland. "They went ice-skating at Champéry, were photographed in riding breeches at the top of the Dents du Midi, and skied at St. Moritz. Nabokov not only used the skis de Calry provided, but slept in the same bed, unaware that de Calry was homosexual" (TRY p. 188). VN graduated in June 1922 and returned to Berlin; this Christmas gift from Calry of one of VN's favorite poets is evidence that they contin-ued to correspond. In 1943 VN wrote to Wilson, who had recently met Calry: "He is quite a character (a passive pansy, to be exact) with a pathetic fondness for titled Russians. He has haunted various nooks of my life like a mild ghost. I rather like him, although he does not really exist. I notice that his stories about me greatly improve with time. He is something of an indifferent imitation of Proust. But still I like him" ([July 1943], *Nabokov-Wilson Letters* (hereafter NWL) p. 106).

Calry's memory is preserved in the penultimate paragraph of chapter thirteen of *Speak, Memory*. In retrieving his college reminiscences, VN collects several "fragmentary little pictures." One is "R.C. charmingly inviting me to join him on a trip to the Swiss Alps." Another is of "T., a very old and fragile waiter, spilling the soup in Hall on Professor A.E. Housman, who then abruptly stood up as one shooting out of a trance..." (pp. 272–73).

Both these books bear the censor's stamp, testifying to the fact that these were among the very small number of books that VN chose to take with him when he left France in May 1940. In *Speak, Memory*, when contemplating the chess problem he wrote his last night in Paris before leaving for America, he describes this stamp—found not just on that leaf, but on many books in this collection, as well:

In one corner of the sheet with the diagram, I notice a certain stamped mark that also adorns other papers and books I took out of France to America in May 1940. It is a circular imprint, in the ultimate tint of the spectrum—*vio-let de bureau*. In its center there are two capital letters of pica size, *R.F.*, meaning of course *République Française*. Other letters in lesser type, run-ning peripherally, spell *Contrôle des Informations*. (p. 293)

In a 1964 *Playboy* interview, VN, aged 65, claimed Housman had been among his favorite writers during his twenties and thirties, and that his esteem for him was likely to "remain intact" (Toffler interview, SO p. 43). Boyd offers an interesting contrast between the two, in light of the fact that VN spent as much time in scholarly pursuit of the ideal translation of *Eugene Onegin* as Pushkin had spent writing it. In 1964, his four-volume edition had just come out: "Almost a century ago A.E.

Housman held his melancholy at bay in the long gaps between unexpected creative bursts by devoting his whole scholarly career to editing Manilius, a writer barely read even by Latin scholars. Nabokov, on the other hand, consecrated more than four years of intense effort, at a time when he was at the height of his inventive powers – in the years he wrote *Lolita* and *Pnin* and was itching to start *Pale Fire* – to the greatest of Russian poets" (*The American Years* (hereafter TAY) p. 354).

These two slim volumes are the sole literary survivals from VN's Cambridge years not yet in institutional hands.

3   **"Wanderings [Strantsviia]" and "Russia [Rossiia]."** In *Russian Thought [Russkaia mysl']*. No. V–VII, and No. IV. Sofia: May–July, 1921; Prague: April, 1922.

8vo.; pages evenly browned; one page mended with tape; binder's label; green cloth, original wrappers trimmed and bound-in.

A pair of early periodical appearances that VN had bound together; this and other items in the library in similar inexpensive pebbled cloth hail from the 1950s and '60s – one was inscribed in Cambridge, two in Ithaca, and the rest in Montreux, and three bear a binder's label: "Reliure-encadrements/Vuichoud/1820 Montreux." They contrast starkly with the three-quarter and full morocco presentation copies specially bound for him by his publishers. The earlier of these volumes prints two poems: "Wanderings" and "Russia." Both have been reprinted only once to date: "Wanderings" in *The Empyrean Path* [*Gorniy put'*] and "Russia" just after VN's death, when Ardis Press issued a massive collection of his poems in Russian; VN had begun to select poems for this volume in the '70s, but he died before making a final choice (*Stikhi*, Ann Arbor, 1979; Juliar A50). The April issue prints two memorial tributes to VDN, who had been assassinated on March 28. Juliar C30, 31. VN marked the table of contents in each volume noting his own contributions, and made a single spelling correction to one of his poems. VN had made a single earlier appearance in this journal, with his poem "Winter Night" (No. III–IV, March–April 1917).

4   **"Childhood [Detstvo]," and "Rupert Brooke [Rupert Bruk]."** In *Literary Almanac: Facets [Literaturnyi al'-manakh: Grani]*. Volume one. Berlin: (Russkaia Tipografiia), 1922.

8vo.; some leaves loose in the first signature; others unopened at center; glue repair in rear gutter; printed wrappers, browned and nicked, closed tear to head, chip to heel; ink of rear panel text uneven, faded.

Two early periodical appearances: "Childhood [Detstvo]," a poem subsequently reprinted only in the collection *The Empyrean Path* [*Gorniy put'*]; and "Rupert Brooke [Rupert Bruk]," a lengthy and impassioned essay on the English poet, with Russian translations of his work by VN, which was never reprinted. Juliar B5.1. VN drew a pencil arrow from his name ("V. Sirin") on the list of contributors printed on the cover, where he added the title of the essay on Brooke in Russian. In a 1964 interview for *Playboy* he counted Brooke among his favorite writers of his Western European period, "between the ages of 20 and 40," but claimed that Brooke, as well as the others, had "lost the glamour and thrill they held for me" (Toffler interview, SO p. 43).

5   **Nikolka the Peach [Nikolka Persik].** Translated from Romain Rolland's French (*Colas Breugnon*) by Vladimir Sirin. (Berlin): Slovo, 1922.

8vo.; grey pictorially printed paper-covered boards, grey cloth spine; blue topstain; censor's stamp on rear panel; covers slightly bowed.

First Russian translation of Rolland's 1919 French novel; excerpted in *Rul'*; variant A, in grey boards without the English printing notice on the copyright page; issued without a dust-jacket. Juliar A4.1. Slovo was founded in part through VDN's negotiations with Ullstein, the "mammoth and liberally inclined" press that he also convinced to underwrite *Rul'*, the Berlin Russian-language daily newspaper he edited until his March 1922 assassination (TRY p. 177). Slovo provided VN his first publishing contract, complete with advance, and went on to issue *Mary* [*Mashen'ka*], *King, Queen, Knave* [*Korol', dama, valet*], *The Defense* [*Zashchita Luzhina*], and *The Return of Chorb* [*Vozvrashchenie Chorba*]. An informal census of American research institutions locates six copies.

A presentation copy, inscribed to Véra's cousin Anna Feigin in Russian on the front endpaper: *To [my] darling* [lit. little soul] *wandering, tender...V. Sirin 23-xii st. st.* [Old Style] *Berlin*. Shapiro notes that VN's inscription contains a wordplay also employed in some of the presentations to Véra: "*dushen'ka*, a diminutive form of *dusha* that means 'soul' in Russian. We may recall that according to popular belief in ancient Greece and Rome, the soul, respectively, *psyche* and *anima*, was thought of as a butterfly." This inscription was made on Véra's

Julian calendar birthday, just before the Nabokovs' first Christmas together as a married couple, December 23, 1925 — though in Berlin in 1925 it was in fact already January 5 by the Gregorian calendar. (During the 19th century the Julian calendar lagged 12 days behind the Gregorian; in the 20th century, 13 days.)

By 1922 VN had long experimented with translation, bringing Mayne Reid's *The Headless Horseman* into French Alexandrines as early as 1910; and Alfred de Musset's *La Nuit de Décembre* into Russian in 1916. He undertook the translation of Rolland's tale on a bet with his father that he could scale the "Vesuvius of words," master the manifold "puns, proverbs and jokes, flourishes and refrains, sayings and charms" it contained, win the "uninterrupted game of rhythmic figures, assonances and internal rhymes, chains of alliterations, rows of synonyms" (quoted in TRY p. 176). However, VDN didn't get a chance to pay on the wager: he was assassinated more than seven months before its November publication.

In retrospect *Colas Breugnon* would prove an appropriate model for VN. Rolland waited for over five years to see his finished work in print, enduring delays caused by narrow-minded publishers who objected to the "'freethinking' posture of the book" and to Rolland's exhibition of "clear individual intelligence,' rather than 'confused collective thought'" (Beaujour p. 561). VN would engage in similar confrontations in his struggle to get *Dar*, the Russian original of *The Gift*, published in its entirety in the 1930s.

In this translation, as in his "adaptation" of Lewis Carroll's *Alice in Wonderland* published the following year, VN revealed not just a desire to do justice to the tone and spirit of the original work but also a prodigal competence to do so. In later years he would follow a plan of literal translation, insisting that the strict definition of each word of an original must be preserved at the cost of rhyme and occasionally of immediate sense — Boyd writes that this tends "to occasion a delay in perceiving the meaning, but then a more exact perception of it." This philosophy yielded three volumes of commentary complementing his translation of *Eugene Onegin* in 1964. But in the instance of *Colas Breugnon*, VN "includes no notes at all, and he uses those provided in the French edition to create substitute formulations. He frequently drops classical allusions... When he cannot find easy Russian equivalents, Nabokov also sometimes omits French expressions which, although still generally understood are no longer in common use... [he] successfully, even ingeniously, transposes *Colas Breugnon's* French cadences into Russian" (Beaujour p. 558). If *Nikolka the Peach* embodies a principle

[31]

VN would later refute, its publication is equally evidence of his need for complete authorial control, which he never abandoned: the 23-year-old translator "quietly rubbed out" all the editor's corrections in proof (TRY p. 189).

This book was likely inscribed in the very two-room flat Véra had rented with her cousin Anna Feigin from a German family until two weeks after she married VN on April 15, 1925; after Anna left for Leipzig, VN took her place in the apartment (the Nabokovs would remain in Berlin, off and on, until they finally left for Paris in the mid-'20s, in 1937). This would not be the last time Anna would live with one or both of them. In 1929 they jointly bought land just east of Berlin in the hope of eventually building a house; though their plan never came to fruition, VN did use the landscape as the setting for the murder in *Despair*. In 1932 the Nabokovs moved into a room vacated by Anna's co-tenant in still another Berlin flat, and in 1939 they dispatched their son Dmitri from Paris to Deauville to remain in comparative safety with Anna. Long after VN had helped settle Anna in New York—he was instrumental in securing her emigration—he and Véra briefly shared her Upper West Side apartment. Boyd describes Anna as "a talented pianist who never had the chance to pursue her studies," stating that she "was no intellectual, but VN would value her friendship highly over the fifty years he knew her, and come to think her 'a marvelous example of humanity'" (TRY p. 382). Boyd does not overstate VN's esteem for his cousin-in-law. In 1926 he allowed her to prepare the first typescript of *Mary*, his first novel, from his fair copy notebooks, and later benefited from her agent-like efforts in negotiating an advance from *Sovremennye zapiski*.

Throughout their lifelong friendship Véra and Anna repeatedly lavished counsel and care on one another. In 1934 Anna was one of only two people—besides Véra and VN—to know that Véra was pregnant with Dmitri. Boyd notes: "Even to Nabokov's mother it came as a complete surprise" (TRY p. 407). In the late sixties, as Anna's health began to fail, Véra returned to New York to convince her to join them in Montreux. In 1967, "almost eighty and nearly blind, Anna Feigin, once so altruistic and accommodating, could be nervous, impatient, and demanding, and still refused to make the move Véra had been urging all year . . . on March 8, Véra's sister Sonia cabled from New York that Anna Feigin's faculties were rapidly deteriorating and she needed urgent care. Two weeks later Véra flew across the Atlantic and brought her cousin back to Montreux, where she found her an apartment and live-in help . . . [her] condition would keep them where they were . . . " (TAY pp. 528, 531).

Until Anna's death in 1972, the Nabokovs provided her with apartments and nursing care, curtailing their travels to allow to her to accompany them and vacationing closer to Montreux to be near her when she could not travel.

6   The Cluster [Grozd']. Poems. Berlin: (Gamaiun), 1923 [December 1922].

16mo.; two-tone full morocco; light general wear.

First edition of VN's first commercially published collection of verse, including 36 poems – primarily love poems – seven of which would be included in *Stikhi* (Ardis Press, 1979); Juliar speculates that "possibly 1000 copies" were printed. Juliar A5.1. VN wrote the love poems, of somewhat dubious merit, to Svetlana Siewert, his fiancée, in over ten months, and presented a copy of the volume to her just before Christmas; within weeks her parents called off the engagement because VN lacked gainful employment. The most significant of these fundamentally inconsequential early works was a heartfelt reflection on his father's recent assassination, "Easter," which had appeared on Easter Sunday in 1922 in *Rul'*.

A presentation copy, specially bound (lacking the wrappers) for his mother in two-tone full morocco with the author, title and Elena Nabokov's initials stamped in gilt on the cover. Inscribed, in Russian: *To Mummy from the grateful author. 23.xii 1922.* With a small icon drawn in ink on the following leaf.

By the end of 1921, VN's poetry was still deemed technically proficient but fairly trite. *The Cluster* was not his finest showing during his formative years, and was certainly outdone by *The Empyrean Path [Gorniy put']* which came out a month later. "Nabokov simply included too much of his poetic output at a time when most of the poems did not rise above the proficiency of a dextrous apprentice. But [*The Cluster*] does at least mark a decisive move on Nabokov's part toward the discipline – though not the majesty and sweep – of Pushkin: its meters remarkably echo those of *Eugene Onegin*" (TRY p. 201). But 1922–23 marked VN's entry into the world of émigré book publishing, and *The Cluster* was his first step. From mid-June 1916 through mid-July 1917, he wrote 172 poems; over a third were love poems to "Lyussya" (31) and "Eva" (39). Over the course of the next six years, he averaged a poem every other day, and began publishing in earnest at the end of 1922 when he brought out four books in as many months: two translations (of Romain Rolland's *Colas Breugnon* and Lewis Carroll's *Alice in*

Wonderland) and two collections of poetry (*The Cluster* and *The Empyrean Path*). These publications came out in the nick of time. By the end of 1923 – when, it is rumored, he had a third collection of poetry and an assemblage of stories on the way – émigré publishing was in crisis. "Berlin's Russian publishing market had started to crash, and over the coming months hundreds of thousands of books would have to be pulped" (TRY p. 220).

Though VN's poetry was less well-received than his translations, it did garner some notices:

The few reviews the verse books attracted conceded Sirin's promise and technical polish but wondered at the poems' lack of freshness and substance...his lines are more often poetesque than poetry. But perceptive reviewers discerned already some of the first signs of the Nabokov we know: the bold sound play (*"V Nazarete, na zare,"* "In Nazareth, at dawn"), the acute vision (a footprint in sand filling up with gleaming water), the unexpected details (Christ on the cross, remembering the wood-shavings beneath his father's workbench). On the strength of such qualities Aykhenvald, author of the best review, recommended Sirin to Khodasevich as a promising young poet. (TRY p. 201)

With these four publications, VN established "Sirin," the authorial identity behind all of his Russian works. Initially he took the name to avoid confusion with his father, who also published prolifically. However, after VDN's assassination in March 1922, VN continued to use it. He later explained:

In modern times *sirin* is one of the popular Russian names of the Snowy Owl, the terror of tundra rodents, and is also applied to the handsome Hawk Owl, but in old Russian mythology it is a multicolored bird, with a woman's face and bust, no doubt identical with the "siren," a Greek deity, transporter of souls and teaser of sailors. In 1920, when casting about for a pseudonym and settling for that fabulous fowl, I still had not shaken off the false glamour of Byzantine imagery that attracted young Russian poets of the Blokian era. (Appel interview, 1970, SO p. 161)

Several years later, he claimed: "my occasional English prose, shorn of its long Russian shadow, seems to reflect an altogether more agreeable person than the 'V. Sirin,' evoked with mixed feelings by émigré memoirists, politicians, poets, and mystics, who still remember our skirmishes of the nineteen-thirties in Paris..." (foreword to SO, 1973, p. xvii).

7 The Cluster [Grozd']. Berlin: [Privately Printed], 1923 [December 1922].

16mo.; cream printed wrappers; trimmed.

Bound in blue cloth with:

Stikhotvoreniia 1929–1951 [Poems 1929–1951]. Paris: Rifma, 1952.

16mo.; cream printed wrappers; trimmed, flaps excised.

First editions; Juliar A5.1 and A27.1. As a testament to the first three decades of their marriage, VN had these two volumes specially bound together (they were trimmed for binding, with the result that *Poems* lost its flaps) in inexpensive blue pebbled cloth in Montreux–the same cloth used to bind *Two Paths* with *The Empyrean Path* for Véra (item #8). At his death, dozens of copies of *Poems 1929–1951* remained in his library; it is not a difficult item to find in American libraries. Boyd relates that this volume was solicited by Irina Yassen, the head of the small Parisian firm whose name means "rhyme" in Russian. It prints 15 Russian poems, and VN's prefatory note, in which he established 1929 as the start of his mature poetical period: "The first of them concludes the period of my youthful art... [They] were published in émigré journals and newspapers, and nine of them appeared under pseudonyms: 'V. Sirin' (the first seven) and 'Vasilii Shishkov' (the following two)" (quoted in Juliar, p. 213).

   The Cluster is inscribed twice: once in 1948, in Ithaca, with a companion inscription to that found in *The Empyrean Path* (see next entry); it alludes to their anniversary two months earlier: [In Russian:] *Better latish* [in English:] *than never! To my darling. 15.vi.1948. V. Ithaca, N.Y.* ("Ithaca, N.Y." is clearly in the ink used for the second, 1969, inscription.) VN took up his position at Cornell University–in Ithaca–on July 1, 1948, and began teaching that fall. He remained there, off and on, until January 19, 1959, when he and Véra left for an extended visit to Europe, which, after a sojourn in Los Angeles in 1960 (while VN worked on his *Lolita* screenplay), became permanent when they settled into the Montreux Palace Hotel, where the second inscription was made on Véra's birthday: [In Russian:] *and even better,* [in English:] *my darling. 5.i.1969 Montreux.* The small butterfly that appears with this inscription is reminiscent of the metallic and iridescent Metalmarks because of its wing shape and colors. "This group has a fantastic diversity in the tropics," Kurt Johnson tells us. "The wing shape and the eyespot below the pointed hindwing suggest the colorful *Abisara* group; however, Nabokov has rendered the eyespot far larger and more grandiose than occur in the real butterflies."

   Poems is inscribed in Russian: *To my dear darling. V. 1952;* with a three-word Russian annotation on page 41, and VN's autograph insertion of a title, *L'Inconnue de la Seine,* in the table of contents. It is likely that this title—the only non-Russian one in the book—was supposed to have been added with a non-Cyrillic machine before binding and was inadvertantly omitted. On the page where the poem appears, this has been done.

VN took up the pen-name "Shishkov" in response to the unfair treatment both he and the more established poet Vladislav Khodasevich had been receiving at the hands of critics. Georgy Adamovich, an influential editor of the leading conservative poetry journal in Paris, boycotted both of them. By the late '30s VN had stopped publishing poetry altogether, though he continued to write verse. In 1936 Khodasevich had published a piece under the pseudonym "Vasily Travnikov" (TRY p. 509); at his death in 1939, VN published a poem of tribute, "Poets," about the silencing and eventual disappearance of poets. To protect his identity VN wrote it in a completely new meter, as "Vasily Shishkov," playing off Khodasevich's *nom de plume,* according to Boyd, in both sound and sense (TRY p. 509). Adamovich published a glowing review which repeatedly posed the question: "Who is Vasily Shishkov?" VN's reply was embodied by the story he wrote and published soon after under his own name, entitled "Vasily Shishkov"; the story has only two characters: Vasily Shishkov and Sirin.

VN has long been considered "a prose writer who happened to write verse" (Scherr p. 623) but clearly he saw himself differently. Scherr writes that "Nabokov began his career as a poet, and of his published poems over 400 were written before he completed his first novel, *Mary,* at the end of 1925" (p. 608); he also notes that the over 500 Russian and 20 known English poems "represent only some fraction of his total output" (ibid.). In 1971 VN included all fifteen poems from *Poems 1929–1951* in *Poems and Problems,* in which he attempts to define, in his foreword, the different periods of his craft; and at his death in 1977 he was compiling a voluminous tome of Russian poetry spanning his entire career, to include the poetry from *The Gift*; the fifteen poems included here; all but one poem from *The Return of Chorb*; 120 previously uncollected; and 50 others previously unpublished. (He died before making a final selection; it was brought out by Ardis Press in 1979.) Still, critics almost unanimously agree that VN's poetry "does not stand comparison with his prose in terms of artistic accomplishment" (Scherr p. 609).

Лучше поздноватенько than never !

Душеньки моей

15 . VI . 1948

Ithaca, N.Y

V.

и еще лучше,
my darling

5 . I . 1969

Montreux

NO. 7

GLORY

to Véra

Montreux
Dec 1970

TO VÉRA: A FEW THOUGHTS ON THE WOMAN IN THE FRONT MATTER

Véra Nabokov signed a vast number of pages in her husband's name; often enough she signed with his name. Her handwriting invades his diaries. But she knew well the weight of an inscription. She steered clear of the front matter of his books, sacred territory, perhaps more so to her mind than to anyone else's.

From the moment she met Vladimir Nabokov in 1923, she believed he was the greatest writer of his generation; to that single truth she held firm for 68 years, as if to compensate for all the loss and turmoil, the accidents of history. While this was convenient for Nabokov, the dedication was no less essential to Véra. As one relative observed, she had a need to do something great with her life. The ambition Zina expresses for Fyodor in *The Gift* was entirely Véra's for Vladimir: She knew he could, and would, "Write something huge to make everyone gasp." She was rarely so confident of the rest of the literary world. Apart from Evelyn Waugh and Alain Robbe-Grillet, few prose writers met with her unqualified enthusiasm. Robert Musil bored her to tears; Virginia Woolf gave her the creeps; Saul Bellow struck her as tasteless. She was a tough grader. When her husband expressed his admiration for George Eliot her response was immediate. "Now why did I marry you?" she wailed.

One shivers to think what would have happened if she had not. For 52 years Véra Slonim Nabokov served variously, and without complaint, as her husband's chauffeur, typist, researcher, and teaching assistant; his chess partner, translator, agent, stockbroker, and legal counsel; his alias, understudy, and accomplice; his occasional editor, his ideal reader, his muse. She has been described in many ways, not all of them flattering, but perhaps best of all by Saul Steinberg, whose work won high marks from both Nabokovs. Steinberg saw Véra as central both to Vladimir's art and to his well-being. "She was his gyroscope," he avers.

She was also his front-man, as anyone who requested a signed book would discover. On December 7, 1958, "Hurricane Lolita" was at its height; the telephone rang frequently at the Nabokovs' home on Highland Road in Ithaca, New York. Véra was detailed to answer it; her husband had no fondness for tangling with "space spooks." On that winter Sunday, the caller was a Lehigh College student, phoning to ask if Nabokov might sign his copy of the novel the entire country was talking about. Plainly, Véra answered that her husband did not give autographs. That evening the Nabokovs heard a violent knocking at the front door; the young man had driven to Ithaca to plead his case in person. His was not the insistence of a simple fan; his fraternity had assigned him the task of procuring the autograph. He was adamant. Would Mrs. Nabokov at least sign the book for him? "Of course not, I did not write it," she replied. Then a revelation occurred: "Suddenly it dawned on me that what he needed was a tangible proof that he had driven to our house and asked for an autograph. And he was almost in tears! I offered to give him a note certifying that Mr. Nabokov gives no autographs. And he was consoled, happy and thankful!," Véra reported, delighted to have settled on a solution that worked for all parties. Generally Nabokov signed books only for relatives and close friends, who had the good grace not to apply for inscriptions. He—and Véra—reminded others that the signed copies bestowed upon them were genuine rarities. His principles remained inviolable. He could not affix his name to a petition for a very simple reason: "I never sign anything I have not written (except traveler's checks)."

He did inscribe at least one book he did not write, a volume that speaks loudly to the inscriptions to Véra in the books he did write. In 1971, Nabokov acquired a handsome, copper-red notebook, standard Swiss issue. On the cover he sketched a butterfly, hovering over the line, "Véra's notebook." Inside he inscribed the volume in four rhyming Russian lines: "To Verochka, for comments, for notes, for order, for stories." What follows are columns after columns of Véra's renderings of her husband's complicated income, in a medley of currencies. She could have filled that volume any number of ways; she had been a published translator when she met her future husband; she occasionally tried her hand at poetry; she enjoyed scholarly research. She had countless opportunities to answer the phone as Diana Trilling did, offering herself up for a reviewing stint in her husband's stead. She never did; the life was equal parts passion and restraint.

As early as 1930, in Berlin, Vladimir was inscribing books to Véra. He did so periodically throughout the American years, and with greater frequency—sometimes on the receipt of a new edition, more often on special occasions—after *Lolita* had swept the Nabokovs back to Europe. Often he did so retroactively. His 1918 and 1923 poetry collections went to Véra just before the 1948 move to Ithaca with similar Russian inscriptions, variations on "Better late than never." There was little ceremony in the presentation; there was no gift paper, no curling ribbon. As Nabokov had explained when the manager of the Scribners bookstore kindly offered the insolvent immigrant a clerking job in the fall of 1940, "One of the few things that I decidedly do not know how to do is to wrap anything." Generally he would leave the volume for his wife to stumble upon—a kind of Easter Egg surprise—when she opened her eyes in the morning, when she ambled in for breakfast. (He was an early-riser. She was not, or at least preferred not to be.) Véra took enormous delight in the minutely-worked creations, in the faux-but-plausible Lepidoptera and the faux-Latin nomenclature. She exclaimed over her husband's artistry, as she had not over the landscapes he had painted for her in the early days of their relationship. Those, she had informed him, were perfectly undistinguished.

The signed copy can turn out to be the cursed copy, the merits of its text sapped by its front matter: It can be condemned to an unread future. A different fate befell the books in which Nabokov created elaborate breeds of phosphorescent butterflies for his wife, into which he inserted the most dedicated dedications imaginable. Many of these works made their home in a glass-fronted case next to her bed, others on the shelves of her room. She read and reread these volumes, of which she knew whole passages by heart, having smoothed the prose when it was "still warm and wet"; having typed the bulk of the works, countless times; having collaborated on their translations; having checked the texts in multiple editions in multiple languages over the course of decades. Together those shimmering volumes seem to point to a line uttered offhandedly by a delusional hero in the work, a declaration to which Véra Nabokov's life can be read as one taut ribbon of luminous testimony: "To begin with, let us take the following motto (not especially for this chapter, but generally): Literature is Love. Now we can continue."

Stacy Schiff

Adorina verae Nab.

VN
Xmas
montreuX
1974

NO. 133

Paradisia radugaleta

from V
to V

5. I. 1969
Montreux

NO. 8

8   Nabokov, V. V. and Andrei Balashov. **An Almanac: Two Paths [Al'Manakh: Dva puti].** St. Petersburg: Published privately by the authors, (1918).

12mo.; cream printed wrappers; censor's stamp on rear panel.

Bound in blue cloth with:

The Empyrean Path [Gorniy put']. Berlin: Grani, 1923.

12mo.; cream printed wrappers, trimmed; censor's stamp on rear panel.

First editions; 500 copies of *Two Paths*, the second of VN's volumes published as a student, were printed; this is the only known copy. The press run of *The Empyrean Path*, the most significant of VN's first serious collections, is unknown, but was likely larger; copies are readily available in research institutions. Juliar A3.1 and A6.1. With light pencil underlining and two one-word marginal notations to Balashov's works.

VN had these two early volumes of poetry inexpensively bound together for Véra (his discrete pencil *1* and *2* are on the respective covers; *The Empyrean Path* has been trimmed to approximate the dimensions of *Two Paths*), with "Poems" stamped on the spine, and inscribed the set: *from V/to V/5.i.1969/Montreux* with a spectacular butterfly, *Paradisia radugaleta*, laying eggs on a green stem. Boyd explains that it is named "after 'Ardis,' Ada Veen's paradisal family home in *Ada*, and 'Radugalet,' the 'other Ardis,' where Van's father and uncle share an estate. (*Radgua* means 'rainbow' in Russian, and -let is the English diminutive, although *raduga lets* would mean 'rainbow of summer.') Nabokov had finished composing *Ada* just ten weeks prior to drawing this butterfly." Of the dozens of lepidopteral images he drew for Véra in his books, this is among the most striking: the upper and lower wings have distinct rainbow patterns of a dozen colors, detailed in pencil and ink. The forewing is, in reality, typical of many tropical Metalmarks, butterflies often showing spectacular colors. The unusual hindwing, with a bulbous, curvate tail and eyespot, also has a counterpart in nature. Johnson wonders if Nabokov actually modeled this beautiful image on "the African *Abisara* Metalmarks, butterflies which have a tail like his drawing and also an eyespot. Perhaps he had seen this genus and admired it," he speculates, "however, the eyespot in *Abisara* most often occurs above the tail, not below it as shown on Nabokov's *Paradisia*."

The second volume is separately inscribed, nicely echoing the inscription of the same date found in *The Cluster* (entry #7): *Better late* [in Russian:] *than later/ to my dear love/ VI.1948/ V.* With several significant annotations. In addition to three word changes, a translation of one line of the poem on page 154, and a citation for the poem on page 174, VN mapped out the stresses of the seven-line poem on page 33 with a series of dashes, dots and lines, and added a note of approximately a dozen words in Russian, dated March 23, 1919, to the poem on page 63.

Two Paths, VN's second published book – but rarer by far than *Stikhi* – is comprised of twelve poems impetuously written for Svetlana Siewert in the summer 1917 at Vyra, his family estate, at the age of 18, and released, along with an additional eight works by a companion at Tenishev School – the "elite but liberal" institution where he and his brother Sergei were educated from 1911 until their 1917 departure from St. Petersburg – and was printed the following year in the Crimea.

The Empyrean Path is a more mature and substantial work, published nearly five years after *Two Paths*, during a publication binge when four Sirin works came out in as many months. This volume, printing 128 Russian poems (Juliar notes: "153, counting parts of poem groups separately"; and two translations, of Byron and Keats) – was VN's first major publication, and was esteemed by critics and later, by the author himself, as the better of the two volumes from this period. When assembling his collected poetry for projected publication by Ardis Press in 1979, VN pulled 32 of the 153 works from *The Empyrean Path*, but only 7 from the 37 of *The Cluster*. Like *The Cluster*, it was brought out under the aegis of his father, VDN, who took some liberties with his son's intended title. VN had suggested two possibilities: "*Svetlitsa* (a clean bright room, and intended as 'a symbol of light, height, solitude,' but chiefly a play on Svetlana's name) or *Tropinki Bozhiya* (*The Tracks of God*)" (TRY p. 189). His father, with the collusion of the editor of the almanac *Grani*, in which VN's poem "Childhood [Detstvo]" had appeared earlier that year, adapted this second suggestion into the final title. Boyd recounts: "They gave [it] a punning twist. ..: retaining both the path and its transcendental dust, they altered *gornyy put'* (mountain trail) to *Gorniy put'* (*Empyrean Path*, a trail mounting [to] the highest heavens). VDN teased his son by withholding the title 'to avoid the caprices peculiar to young authors'" (ibid.). VDN was assassinated before the volume came out in January 1923, and VN added a dedication: "In memory of my father."

9 **Alice in Wonderland [Ania v strane chudes].** By Lewis
Carroll. With drawings by S. Zalshupin. Berlin: Gamaiun,
1923.

8vo.; pages evenly browned; rear endpaper mildly offset; colorfully
illustrated paper-covered boards, lightly rubbed with some edgewear;
censor's stamp on rear panel.

First edition of VN's translation; variant A, in illustrated boards; a second variant is also known, in "plain heavy green wrappers" and with an
illustrated dust-jacket in imitation of these boards. Juliar A7.1.
Gamaiun secured their commission of this translation with a five-dollar
bill in the summer of 1922, a princely sum considering the year and the
fact that, coming on the heels of VN's arduous labors on *Nikolka the
Peach*, Lewis Carroll's work offered him a relatively small challenge.
Both translations display VN's linguistic and cultural knowledge, put to
use in a manner that VN would later deride when he had decided that
fidelity to the text took precedence over "fidelity to the tone" and to the
"spirit" of the originals (Connolly p. 23). Nearly 50 years later he
reflected: "How much better I could have done it fifteen years later! The
only good bits are the poems and the word-play" (*Anniversary Notes*,
p. 3). But in a survey of Russian editions of Lewis Carroll's tale, VN's
version emerges as "one of the most ingenious and delightful," more as
an "adaptation" or "transposition" than as a translation (Connolly
p. 19). VN frequently transfers Lewis Carroll's allusions and models into
Russian analogues: pounds, shillings, and pence become kopecks;
"Speak English!" becomes "Speak Russian!"; William the Conqueror
becomes Vladimir Monomakh; the original parody of Robert Southey
becomes a parody of Lermontov (ibid.) (Dmitri Nabokov notes that "his
famous patriotic verse "'Borodino'...cries out for parody"). Within
twenty years of its publication, copies of VN's translation of *Alice in
Wonderland* would be deemed rarities. He later attributed his invitation to teach at Wellesley in 1941 in part to the fact that they had this
edition in their Lewis Carroll collection.

VN had a lifelong relationship with Lewis Carroll's works. He had
first read *Alice in Wonderland* in English at the age of 7 – he had begun
learning English at the age of two, and French, at six. In fact, English,
not Russian, was the first language VN learned to read. In 1971, in
response to Paul Sufrin's question of the connection between VN's
"*Alice-in-Wonderland* world of unreality and illusion" and his "real

struggle with the world," he described *Alice* as "a specific book by a definite author with its own quaintness, its own quirks, its own quiddity. If read very carefully, it will be seen to imply, by humorous juxtaposition, the presence of a quite solid, and rather sentimental, world, behind the semi-detached dream" (*Swiss Broadcast* interview, SO pp. 183–84). He uses *Alice*'s sequel, *Through the Looking Glass*, as a prop in *Pale Fire* (TAY p. 452), and as a defense against editor Katharine White's complaint that the chess allusions in "Exile" (a section of his autobiography serially published in *The New Yorker*) were too complex for her readers: he noted that Lewis Carroll included "a very subtle and difficult chess problem" as the frontispiece for his children's tale (March 24, 1950, *Selected Letters* (hereafter, SL) p. 99). On a list composed in 1965 of "scenes one would like to have filmed" he included "Lewis Carroll's picnics" (Howard interview, SO pp. 60–61). One scholar writes that "the insane and logical voice of Lewis Carroll permeates his works" (Lee quoted in Sisson, p. 637). Many parallels have been drawn between *Alice in Wonderland* and *The Real Life of Sebastian Knight*, VN's first novel composed in English, and others as well. In interviews VN addressed such parallels, noting: "I have been always very fond of Carroll...I do not think that his invented language shares any roots with mine [in relation to *Bend Sinister* and *Pale Fire*]" (Appel interview, 1966, SO p. 81). And the obvious irony, the "real-life farce" of Lewis Carroll's status as "the greatest children's story writer of all time" (Garnham interview, 1968, SO p. 119), was not lost on him:

He has a pathetic affinity with H. H. [Humbert Humbert, the notorious romantic pedophile of *Lolita*] but some odd scruple prevented me from alluding in *Lolita* to his perversion and to those ambiguous photographs he took in dim rooms. He got away with it, as so many other Victorians got away with pederasty and nympholepsy. His were sad scrawny little nymphets, bedraggled and half-undressed, or rather semi-undraped, as if participating in some dusty and dreadful charade. (Appel interview, 1966, SO p. 81)

10 Mary [Mashen'ka]. Berlin: Slovo, 1926.

8vo.; a few leaves lightly soiled; abrasions to pages 139–40, 141–42, obscuring several characters; trimmed; three-quarter cloth, extremities frayed and spine worn.

First edition of VN's first novel; excerpted in *Vozrozhdenie*, Paris, March 2, 1926, and in *Slovo*, Riga, March 27–28, 1926; *Mary* derived in part from an earlier, abandoned novel entitled "Happiness," a title VN retained right up until publication. It did not appear in the States until 1970, brought out by McGraw-Hill. Juliar A8.1. VN's Russian novels from the 1920s and '30s—printed, Juliar speculates, in single runs of 1500–2000 copies, though Boyd notes in his review of Juliar that this theory, though likely true, is untested—are readily located in American institutions, and are occasionally seen in commerce. Our informal census locates between one and two dozen copies, sometimes more, of each. The poetry and translations are less common, though not unknown. Even *Stikhi*, VN's first documentable publication, is not impossible to procure. The only VN title that can be legitimately called rare is *Two Paths*, of which only the copy described herein is known. That there are so many survivals of such fragile productions can only be attributed to the continued Russian emigration to the United States in the 1940s after Hitler invaded Paris. In 1991 Boyd wrote: "By the time Paris fell to the Germans on June 14 [1940], the Nabokovs' former apartment on rue Boileau was already a heap of rubble and the first Russian emigration was in much the same state. New York would become a publishing capital for Russian émigrés—as it is to this day..." (TAY p. 13).

A presentation copy, specially bound without the green wrappers, by VN for his mother. Inscribed in large, flowing letters across the first blank, in Russian: *To Mummy.... V. 19-iii-26 Berlin.* With minor emendations to six pages and nearly two dozen lines of translation spanning pages 135–139; with this note on page 133: *English translation of pp. 135 to top of 139 entirely my own/ VN.* Upon Elena's death in May 1939, this volume devolved to VN's sister, also named Elena; it bears her husband's ownership stamp on the half-title and its verso: "Dr. J. Sikorska/ Nusle II., Viktorinova 6."

Despite some murmuring that VN's nostalgia was somewhat "old-fashioned" (TRY p. 246)—this was the first of several novels which contained very realistic descriptions of his childhood haunts at Vyra, the family's country estate fifty miles outside St. Petersburg—*Mary* received accolades for its unusual structure and vibrant, if occasionally unpalatable, detail. At a complete reading on January 23, 1926, the émigré critic Yuli Aykhenvald, at all times VN's most enthusiastic admirer, called him "a new Turgenev." VN signed a contract with Slovo on February 15, and *Mary* was in book stalls a month later. Slovo promoted it as "a novel of émigré life." Its action takes place during the week in April 1924 "when the rush to leave Berlin peaked" (TRY p. 246), in a pension inspired by his mother's squalid quarters in Prague. He later reflected: "The émigré characters I had collected in [*Mary*] were so transparent to the eye of the era that one could easily make out the labels behind them..." (foreword to *King, Queen, Knave*, NY: McGraw-Hill, 1968). VN did not make any money to speak of from *Mary*'s Russian publications—little from its serial appearance, nothing from the book (he did, however, realize some profit in 1928 from the German translation); he was, at this time, supporting himself with reviews in *Rul'*, the émigré daily.

Mary marks several important beginnings for VN. It is his first novel; his first work dedicated to Véra; and it marks a stylistic leap into new structures, designed to support his nearly obsessive focus on, as Boyd succinctly puts it, "the gap between revisitable space or retainable matter and inaccessible time" (TRY p. 252). It was his first extended fictional treatment of autobiographical material, which he would refine throughout his career. In mid-October, in the midst of composition, he wrote to his mother of his progress:

My hero is not a very likeable person, but amongst the others there are very sweet people. I am getting to know them better and better, and it already begins to seem that my Ganin, my Alfyorov, my dancers Kolin and Gornotsvetov, my old Podtyagin, Klara, a Kiev Jewess, Kunitsyn, Mme Dorn and so on—least but not last—my Mary—are real people, and not my inventions. I know how each one smells, walks, eats, and I understand how God as he created the world found this a pure, thrilling joy. *We* are translators of God's creation, his little plagiarists and imitators, we dress up what he wrote, as a charmed commentator sometimes gives an extra grace to a line of genius. (TRY pp. 244–45)

When VN calls his characters "real people" he is not being merely rhetorical. The title character of this novel, Mary, who never physically appears during the action of the story, is based on Valentina "Lyussa" Shulgin, the "Tamara" in VN's memoirs. "The girl really existed," he wrote to Edmund Wilson twenty years later (January 20, 1945, NWL p. 148), and five of her love letters were transcribed in the novel. In the foreword to the English translation, written forty-five years later, VN reflects on this and other autobiographical touches in Mary:

The beginner's well-known propensity for obtruding upon his own privacy, by introducing himself, or a vicar, into his first novel, owes less to the attraction of a ready theme than to the relief of getting rid of oneself, before going on to better things. It is one of the very few common rules I have accepted...[Ganin's] Mary is a twin sister of my Tamara, the ancestral avenues are there, the Oredezh flows through both books, and the actual photograph of the Rozhestveno house as it is today...could well be a picture of the pillared porch in the "Voskresensk" of the novel.

This is the first of many works VN would dedicate to Véra—the Russian dedications always read "Dedicated to my wife"; the English, "To Véra." Boyd posits that the turn of events in *Mary*—and the subsequent innovation of naming a novel for a character who never appears —may be a direct reflection of Véra's influence:

> Only when Ganin changes his mind on the last page of the book does he in fact turn his story toward triumph, when he realizes he has all his past already with him and need not befoul the present. The Nabokov who had chosen his own new route in life and felt secure enough in his love for Véra to be haunted no longer by his dream of a past love could feel kinship with Ganin only at this final moment of the novel...[H]is marriage itself provided the other of the major themes that would shape his work. In later years he would often bemoan the very meager artistic results of his frenetic love-life in his late teens and early twenties. One inescapable implication is that by contrast his marriage *did* contribute to his art... (TRY p. 283).

11 **Mary.** Translated from the Russian by Michael Glenny in collaboration with the author. New York: McGraw-Hill, (1970).

8vo.; fore-edge lightly foxed; black cloth; purple topstain; dust-jacket, lightly used.

First edition of the first English translation; with a foreword written specially for this edition. Juliar A8.2. VN's corrected copy, with his discreet underlining and pencil ticking to nearly two dozen pages, all listed on the front endpaper; on page 57 he left a question mark, and on pages 34 and 50 suggested new words—*sprocket* for "big gear" and *broom?* instead of "floor brush." Dmitri Nabokov had been trained from an early age to become his father's primary translator. When his operatic career diverted his attentions, however, VN hoped to find competent translators: "I need a man who knows English better than Russian...I would revise every sentence myself and keep in touch with him all the time, but I *must* have somebody to do the basic work and then to polish my corrections" (to James Laughlin, July 16, 1942, SL p. 41). This is the only Glenny translation of a VN work.

Mary was, ironically, the penultimate of his Russian works translated into English in his lifetime. VN recognized several risks in undertaking its translation: it dealt more heavily with autobiographical material than any of his other fiction; almost 50 years separated the original from its translation, during which he had not just changed his language of composition and refined his skills, but had also recycled much of the same material fairly recently in his autobiography: "Mary" was, in fact, the "Tamara" who had enchanted VN's American audience in 1949 (in *The New Yorker*), in 1951 (in *Conclusive Evidence*), and in 1967 (in *Speak, Memory*). By 1970 it had become his habit to preface the English-language editions of his Russian works with a discussion of each book's composition, translation and publication. Boyd has asserted that these forewords offered as "clues what turned out to be new puzzles, or disclose[d] genuine clues to subtly camouflaged patterns while feigning irrelevant patter or obstructive pronouncements. His forewords formed part of the irascible and arrogant Nabokov persona" (TAY p. 477). In this preface VN wrote that the translation was "as faithful to the text as I would have insisted on its being had that text not been mine...The only adjustments I deemed necessary are limited to brief utilitarian phrases in three or four passages alluding to routine Russian matters (obvious to fellow-émigrés but incomprehensible to foreign readers) and to the switch of seasonal dates in Ganin's Julian Calendar to those of the Gregorian style in general use (e.g., his end of July is our second week of August, etc.)." He also explains the title: "The Russian title of the present novel, *Mashenka*, a secondary diminutive of *Maria*, defies rational transliteration (the accent is on the first syllable with the 'a' pronounced as in 'ask' and a palatalized 'n' as in 'mignon'). In casting around for a suitable substitute (*Mariette?, May?*) I settled for *Mary*, which seemed to match best the neutral simplicity of the Russian title name." (VN frequently wrestled with many alternative English translations before settling on a final title.)

Revisiting this English translation the following year, VN lamented that because he had treated his first love in depth so recently the translation process had lost "some of its thrill...Yet I do feel another, more abstract though no less grateful, tingle when I tell myself that destiny not only preserved a fragile find from decay and oblivion, but allowed me to last long enough to supervise the unwrapping of the mummy" (Whitman interview, 1971, SO pp. 179–80).

12 **Mary.** Translated from the Russian by Michael Glenny in collaboration with the author. London: Weidenfeld and Nicolson, (1971).

8vo.; purple cloth; front cover bowed; dust-jacket, spine gently bumped.

First English edition, printed from the McGraw-Hill plates with a new title page; slightly taller than the American edition and with a different photograph on the jacket: the English edition shot dates to 1925, the publication year of the first edition; McGraw-Hill's photo is more recent. Juliar A8.3. One of two dedication copies, inscribed on the front endpaper: *For Véra/Montreux, 1971;* with one of the largest butterflies in the collection, from the Blue genus *Maculinea* with a ficticious species name, *Maculinea aurora* Nab. (female). "Nabokov creates a species with a bold aurora of orange along both the upper and under-side of the hindwings. In Blues, this might happen on the undersurface but would be quite rare on the upper surface of the hind-wings...Nabokov probably wishes he could find a Blue with such a bold display of marginal orange of the upper surface—so, here it is." VN added *January* on the verso of the title page next to the copyright date, presumably the month in which it arrived in Montreux; Juliar names February 18 as publication day, and VN added that date on the second dedication copy (see next entry).

13 **Mary.** Translated from the Russian by Michael Glenny in collaboration with the author. London: Weidenfeld and Nicolson, (1971).

8vo.; purple cloth; front cover bowed; dust-jacket, spine gently bumped.

First English edition. Juliar A8.3. A second dedication copy, inscribed on the dedication page, *Montreux/Jan. 1971* (though VN added the "official" publication date, *February 18*, on the verso of the title page), with an imaginative moth with translucent wings and a rainbow-arrayed body, *Aegeria iridulaeformis* Nab. Boyd explicates this name:

"Iridule" is a word Nabokov's character Shade coins in *Pale Fire* ("and that rare phenomenon/The iridule—when, beautiful and strange,/In a bright sky above a mountain range/One opal cloudlet in an oval form/Reflects the rainbow of a thunderstorm/Which in a distant valley has been staged"), where Kinbote glosses it: "An iridescent cloudlet, Zemblan muderperl-welk. The term 'iridule' is, I believe, Shade's own invention." Véra Nabokov explains it herself: "We have often had the occasion to watch it at Telluride. It is single, fairly rarely seen and most attractive." (to Igor Yefimov, March 21, 1980)

Johnson explains the name in light of the moth's legitimate model: "The genus is accurate and the transparent wings are drawn very precisely. The fanciful part is the abdominal colors which would, in nature, be iri-descent blue, green or red but not all three colors together."

14 King, Queen, Knave [Korol', dama, valet]. Berlin: Slovo, 1928.

8vo.; pages evenly browned and occasionally brittle; grey wrappers, edgeworn with a single crease and stray ink mark to the cover; small chip to rear; an attractive copy.

First edition; excerpted in *Rul'*, September 23, 1928. Juliar A9.1. A presentation copy, inscribed to Anna Feigin on the first blank in Russian: *To dear, loved Anyuta, from the author. Berlin 1928.*

VN's second novel was an unqualified success, engendering positive reviews, an evening of public debate in Berlin, and the first financial rewards he received for his writing. Ullstein, the largest liberal German publisher, offered 2500 marks that fall for serialization and 5000 marks for German book rights—in contrast with the 300 marks Slovo had paid for this first edition. Ullstein's purchase allowed VN and Véra to settle their debts—Véra had taken up German stenography towards this end—and left enough of a balance to finance their first butterfly excursion together, to the Pyrenées.

King, Queen, Knave was, like *Mary*, conceived, executed and published in just over a year. It departed from *Mary* and other, shorter works in theme and style, leaving off from VN's obsessive observation of émigré living to focus instead on the lives of three Germans. In his survey of Russian reviews Julian Connolly notes that these changes did not go unnoticed, and writes that one 1928 critic "remarked that the novel seems at times to read like a translation from German, although he finds no traces of 'Germanisms' in the text" (p. 203). Boyd reflected over a half-century later that "adultery and murder freed Nabokov not only from a specifically émigré milieu but also from the personal, the lyrical, from any temptation to direct statement of his own philosophical position" (TRY p. 279).

VN later realized that this novel inaugurated what would come to be seen as the "familiar pattern of his inspiration: two or three days of tingly foreglow, then the sudden flash of a new novel, more or less complete, after which there would follow a long process of mental sorting that could last six months or more, until every detail seemed right. Only then would he begin writing. *King, Queen, Knave* followed that pattern perfectly" (TRY p. 274). In his 1968 preface to the McGraw-Hill edition, he looked back on its composition, partially addressing its reception 40 years earlier:

Of all my novels this bright brute is the gayest. Expatriation, destitution, nostalgia had no effect on its elaborate and rapturous composition.... I had been living in Berlin, on and off, for half a dozen years. I was absolutely sure, with a number of other intelligent people, that sometime in the next decade we would all be back in a hospitable, remorseful, racemosa-blossoming Russia...One might readily conjecture that a Russian writer in choosing a set of exclusively German characters (the appearances of my wife and me in the last two chapters are merely visits of inspection) was creating for himself insurmountable difficulties. I spoke no German, had no German friends, had not read a single German novel either in the original, or in translation. But in art, as in nature, a glaring disadvantage may turn out to be a subtle protective device... I might have staged *KQK* in Rumania or Holland. Familiarity with the map and weather of Berlin settled my choice.

15 **King, Queen, Knave.** Translated by Dmitri Nabokov in collaboration with the author. New York: McGraw-Hill, (1968).

8vo.; black and grey cloth; dust-jacket.

First edition of the first English translation. Juliar A9.2. With VN's hastily drawn pencil butterfly outline on the half-title, and his bibliographical note to the front endpaper: *Mailed April 22, 1928* [the year of the Russian first edition]. *One of three 'unique' first edition copies (with short page at the beginning of every signature).* In fact, the short pages occur less regularly than that, though they do indeed constitute an important point of issue. This printing was suppressed because of the defective trimming and many, if not most, copies were destroyed. While sources vary as to the number of surviving copies, there are to our knowledge substantially more than three. In the wake of the suppression, the stated "second printing" became the first published edition. Juliar notes in his 1991 update:

Field says that the first English language edition "was defective and was destroyed except for a few copies." Contrary to Field, more than a few copies were distributed; they are not difficult to find. In addition, some book club copies with the defects were issued...The defects were four short leaves (the 2nd, 6th, 11th, and 15th) in each of the nine 16-leaf signatures, and a roughly trimmed bottom edge...For this edition the U.S. Copyright Office shows a publication date of 29-Apr-68; for the same edition, A9.4 states 13-May-68 on its copyright-page as does the review copy, F9.2. The former date was probably the intended publication date of what became the defective first state; the latter date was probably the actual publication date of the corrected second state. Except for the physical defects noted, there are no other production differences between the two states; nor are there any textual differences. (1991 update, p. 6)

Boyd claims that of all VN's works, possibly only *Camera Obscura* (1933) was more substantially changed in translation (*Laughter in the Dark*, 1938) than *King, Queen, Knave*, of which he writes:

Nabokov altered the novel at every level. In its texture: imagery, psychological shimmer, physical detail, incidental characters. In its structure: preparation for later events; internal reflections (the mannequin motif, the playing-card motif, the new motif of the *King, Queen, Knave* movie); external reflections of "Mr. Vivian Badlook," Nabokov and Véra, and "Blavdak Vinomori" [anagrams for Vladimir Nabokov]. In its characterization: Franz's lone lyrical recollections of his hometown river; Martha's relentlessly conventional soul; Dreyer's rich fantasy. And, finally, in its narrative technique: plot conventions unconsciously adopted by a young novelist and too deeply embedded in the story to discard were now rescued by an explicit twist of self-conscious irony. (TAY p. 522)

Boyd also notes that the mannequin in Dreyer's department store is named "Ronald" in the English translation in honor of Ronald Hingley, who had reviewed *Speak, Memory* unfavorably in 1967. Julian Connolly's comparison of the two versions reveals that the English translation "contains more erotic material and more references to bodily functions" and "also discloses a sadistic streak within [Franz's] character...In revising the novel, Nabokov even suggests that Franz would become a participant in Nazi atrocities later in life" (p. 205). He also notes that VN "charges the English version...with pointed literary allusions" (ibid. p. 212). Connolly's conclusion summarizes those of several prominent critics: "[VN's] revisions not only tighten the work in terms of plot and characterization, they significantly expand the richness of its literary and metaliterary allusiveness" (ibid. p. 213).

After Dmitri completed the literal translation, VN took a break from *Ada* to revise it over the course of three months, taking just one week off to review the galleys for Andrew Field's critical study. He defends his alterations in the foreword: "Very soon I asserted [ascertained] that the original sagged considerably more than I had expected...[M]y main purpose in making [the "little changes"] was not to beautify a corpse but rather to permit a still breathing body to enjoy certain innate capacities which inexperience and eagerness, the haste of thought and the sloth of word had denied it formerly. Within the texture of the creature, those possibilities were practically crying to be developed or teased out."

This is the first American novel VN published with McGraw-Hill. He had left Putnam's, disgruntled by president Walter Minton's lackadaisical attitude towards advertising his post-*Lolita* works despite his and Véra's repeated suggestions and exhortations. He was especially fearful that *Ada*, once complete, would suffer in Putnam's care. (In addition, he wanted additional compensation for his translations and revisions of translations.) After a dissatisfying meeting Véra had with Minton on the subject of *King, Queen, Knave* and further fruitless negotiations, VN found an enthusiastic adorant in McGraw-Hill's Peter Kemeny: "We regard you as the greatest writer of fiction at work today, the most profound and inventive master of the English language, the novelist whose work one must be most convinced will endure. I and my colleagues ask you to allow the most successful and powerful book publisher in America to place its resources in your service…Our financial agreements would be the most generous possible" (quoted in TAY p. 524).

Two weeks later he wrote again, offering to publish each of VN's works separately and, eventually, to publish a collected edition as well, though the complete works never came to pass. VN later explained his switch: "Putnam's position was that Mr. Nabokov was much too good a writer to fuss about such sordid trifles as more money for more books and Mr. Nabokov's position was that no matter how good he was he should get enough to buy pencil sharpeners and support his family" (quoted in TAY p. 530).

16 **King, Queen, Knave.** Translated by Dmitri Nabokov in collaboration with the author. New York: McGraw-Hill, (1968).

8vo.; marbled endpapers; top edge gilt; three-quarter red morocco, stamped in gilt.

First edition, second printing; Juliar A9.2. The publisher's year-end presentation copy, bound in morocco and gifted to VN; inscribed by VN in Russian on the first blank: *To Vérochka from the author Xmas 1968.* With an elegant butterfly rendered in pencil and gently colored in reds and blues. VN's American publishers made a habit of presenting him with specially bound copies of his books; these were usually made as holiday gifts at the end of the year with sheets on hand, with the result that several of them were not first printings. That this copy is a second printing should not be attributed to the false perception, often repeated, that the first printing was destroyed.

17 **King, Queen, Knave [Korol', dama, valet].** New York: McGraw-Hill, (1969).

8vo.; marbled endpapers; top edge silver; three-quarter red morocco, stamped in silver.

Second Russian-language edition, first published on American soil; photographically reproduced from the 1928 first Russian edition; with VN's 1967 foreword to the first English translation, his list of works, and the copyright page all printed in English. Juliar A9.5.

The dedication copy of the only edition of *King, Queen, Knave* dedicated to Vera, in the publisher's presentation binding, inscribed on the binder's first blank: *For Véra From VN Montreux Xmas 1969*, with a spectacular Hairstreak with eyespots on the bulbous tail ends. Johnson notes that "the Australian Lacewing with this characteristic is famous among entomologists and was also used as a logo for a time by the Xerces Society to which Nabokov 'belonged' – at least their publications were in his archives (Boyd). But these Neuropteran tails are here attached to a Hairstreak butterfly of the 'Coronata group' which, as shown by Nabokov, are vivid sky blue on their upperface and green beneath with large spots at the base of the tails. Nabokov's good friend Harry Clench was the world's authority at the time on the Hairstreak butterflies."

In a letter to McGraw-Hill's president Edward Booher Véra hit on two of the problems in reviving émigré works: copyright and orthography:

[*King, Queen, Knave*] was published more than 28 years ago and was never copyrighted. It is, of course, protected by the Bern Convention in Europe. It was written at a time when VN was stateless and a resident of an European country. The Copyright Office *may* decide that for these reasons it still could be copyrighted on publication, but this is not certain. Also: the original version was set in accordance with the rules of the "old orthography." During the revolution some of those rules were modified, three then currently used letters were scrapped (actually, five but two had not been much used anyway), certain case endings were changed, so were certain rules governing the use of prefixes. All these changes don't bother an educated Russian of the new formation but would they not put off American students? The Russian publishers who published VN's Russian books have long ceased to exist. I doubt they would have had any claims in any case since the books have been out of print for more than twenty years, and all the publishing houses had been liquidated before or during the war. (SL, p. 427)

VN found this Russian-language edition, published by McGraw-Hill simultaneously with the English translation in celebration of their acquisition of VN and his writings, "perfectly enchanting" (to Frank E. Taylor, September 17, 1969, SL p. 458). He was equally thrilled – "absolutely delighted" – with the publisher's gifts, "the beautifully appetizing bound copies of *Ada* and *King, Queen, Knave*" presented to him for Christmas 1969 (to Taylor, December 20, 1969, SL p. 466; for that copy of *Ada* see item #122). The irony of McGraw-Hill's offer to publish *King, Queen, Knave* in Russian was not lost on VN: "In the twenty years between Nabokov's switching to English in 1938 and the American publication of *Lolita*, he had had to take his first four English novels from publisher to publisher, and to abandon altogether the attempt to have his Russian novels translated, let alone republished in the unprofitable Russian. How different things were now!" (TAY p. 530). McGraw-Hill's response to the commercial failure of this Russian edition was to co-publish Russian-language editions of *Mary* and *Glory* with Ardis Press, drawing on their ability to market Russian-language books to a wider audience.

18 The Defense [Zashchita Luzhina]. Berlin: Slovo, 1930.

8vo.; largely unopened; hinges weakened; censor's stamp on page [236]; black wrappers, few light chips to spine and edges.

First edition; lacking the final blanks [237] – [238]; serialized in *Sovremennye zapiski*, November 1929–April 1930; excerpted in *Rul'*, September 1929–January 1930; and in *Poslednie novosti*, April 6, 1930. Juliar A10.1, 1991 update. The first English translation would not be published until 1964, at which point VN claimed this first edition was "now rare and may grow even rarer" (p. 7); it is, in fact, no less common than his other novels, though attractive copies are difficult to find.

A presentation copy, inscribed to Véra on the first blank in Russian: *Here it is for you, my love, from the author. Berlin ix–30*. With a note card, both sides covered with Véra's pencil notes in French, apparently quoting text from another volume.

Sovremennye zapiski, "without question the best journal in the emigration" (TRY p. 341), appeared three or four times a year, containing works by well-established authors, with each issue running close to 500 pages. Despite the fact that its four editors were all Socialist Revolutionaries, it "kept itself independent of party politics" (TRY p. 342). The Nazi occupation ended its 20-year intellectual domination of the émigré community in 1940. Though by 1930 VN had been publishing for several years, he had been infrequently published in *Sovremennye zapiski* ("short lyrics" in 1921 and 1922; the more substantial "A University Poem" and a story, "Terror," in 1927) until he showed them *The Defense*, the "story of a chess player who was crushed by his genius" (to James Laughlin, November 27, 1941, SL p. 39). All of VN's subsequent Russian works of substance would appear between this journal's covers, "sometimes in chunks more than eighty pages long" (TRY p. 342).

VN seems to have anticipated in more than one story from this period the success he would achieve with *The Defense.* Just a few months after he had begun, in August 1929, he wrote to his mother that it was "high time to kill Luzhin and give his corpse to Ullstein so they can buy it to dissect and translate" (quoted in TRY p. 341). (Ullstein had provided his first significant publishing revenues in the fall of 1928 when they purchased the German rights to *King, Queen, Knave.*) Though reviews were mixed, the foremost literati were all wild with praise. Nina Berberova, in her now oft-repeated encomium, saw in VN's work validation for the entire generation of émigré writers; she wrote: "A tremendous, mature, sophisticated modern writer was before me, a great Russian writer, like a Phoenix, was born from the fire and ashes of revolution and exile. Our existence from now on acquired a meaning. All my generation were justified. We were saved" (quoted in TRY p. 343). Bunin, whom VN had earlier named among the best living poets (he much preferred Bunin's poetry to his prose), wrote: "This kid has snatched a gun and done away with the whole older generation, myself included" (quoted in TRY p. 343). The few nay-sayers—as usual, Georgy Adamovich was the most vocal dissenter—were proved wrong by the quickness with which *The Defense* was picked up by both German and French publishers (Ullstein and Fayard); Fayard approached VN even before serialization was complete. By the end of 1929 VN was performing lepidopterological research at the Dahlem museum (TRY p. 345), and finishing up his first collection of stories and poems, *The Return of Chorb* [*Vozvraschenie Chorba*].

The publication of *The Defense* represented a milestone for VN, and occasioned a review of his growing ouevre. Boyd asserts that Sirin had been "amused" by the "disparities of judgment" reflected in an assessment by a bitter contemporary, Georgy Ivanov, and the spray of responses it drew:

Ivanov accused him of imitating the hacks who wrote for an old Russian illustrated weekly and then of copying what everyone was writing in French; Levinson on the other hand, a Russian deeply imbued with French culture, found Sirin's work startlingly new and his style "very individual in spite of its Tolstoyan base." In a Warsaw newspaper one writer found Ivanov's review dazzling, while another called its author a Salieri. One Paris critic declared Sirin unable to create characters in whom we can live [believe?], another rated Luzhin on a par with Tolstoy's Natasha or Pierre.

Some reviewers found VN non-Russian, others declared that he had suddenly answered the question whether Russian literature, émigré or Soviet, could carry on at the high level of the nineteenth century. (TRY p. 351)

In *Mary*, the title character's love letters were copied from Lyussa's. In *King, Queen, Knave*, VN and Véra appear on a beach with a butterfly net. In *The Defense*, VN loaned to his hero "Mademoiselle O.," his own French governess to whom he would later devote an entire chapter in his memoir (TRY p. 69); a St. Petersburg rental he shared with his family in 1906 (TRY p. 70); an episode from Véra's life, when in Petrograd at the Obolensky school she "witnessed the visit of the lame commissar for education depicted in *The Defense*" (TRY p. 214); and Vyra, his family estate, which appears as vividly here as it does in *Mary*. During the novel's composition Véra wrote to VN's mother: "Russian literature has not seen its like" (quoted in TRY p. 291). VN himself wrote to Elena: "...In three or four days I'll add the last full stop. After that I won't struggle again for a long time with such monstrously difficult themes, but will write something quiet and smooth-flowing. All the same I'm pleased with my Luzhin, but what a complicated, complicated thing!" (ibid.).

19 The Defense [Zashchita Luzhina]. Berlin: Slovo, 1930.

8vo.; two-line pencil note on the binder's front pastedown; pages evenly browned, many lightly soiled; brown cloth.

First edition; lacking the wrappers, the first and final blanks. Juliar A10.1. With a colorful butterfly drawn for Véra, named *Veraedes prelestna Nab.*, docketed *holotype/ Sept. 21, 1967/ Montreux.* (Boyd comments: *Veraedes*, "Véra-like (Latin)" and *prelestna*, "charming (Russian).") Véra labeled the cover "V. Sirin/ The Defense" in Cyrillic in ink, and noted on the title page in pencil: *bought from a bookstand as dirty as it is. Second hand.* Presumably the erasures throughout indicate the previous owner's markings; the marginal pencil ticking and underlining on a dozen pages is likely VN's. VN and Véra made a concerted effort, especially in later years, to locate copies of his earliest Russian publications in the hope of cobbling together a bibliographically complete collection.

20 The Defense [Lushins Verteidigung]. (Translated from the Russian by Deitmar Schulte. Frankfurt, Vienna, and Zurich: Buchergilde Gutenberg, 1965.)

8vo.; purple cloth stamped in black with a chess piece; dust-jacket, lightly rubbed, minor wear to top edge.

Second edition of the first German translation; preceded by Rowohlt's 1961 edition. Juliar D10.3. A presentation copy, inscribed to Véra in Russian on the front endpaper: *To Vérochka from V 1965 Gardone R*[iviera] *Garda L*[ake], with a brightly toned butterfly. VN had expected a German edition to bring in some ready cash in 1930. Unfortunately, Boyd notes, it "ran afoul of the Depression" which had overwhelmed that country, dashing VN's hopes for deriving a reasonable income there; in 1931 there were only 30,000 Russians left in Berlin, compared to 400,000 in France, where the Paris-based *Sovremennye zapiski* continued to pay well. (TRY p. 355)

21 **The Defense.** Translated by Michael Scammell in collaboration with the author. New York: Putnam's, (1964).

8vo.; black cloth; green topstain faded; dust-jacket, spine bumped and spotted, edges lightly browned.

First edition of the first English translation, completed by Scammell and aggressively revised by VN; with a foreword specially written for this edition; serialized in *The New Yorker* in two installments, "the first time the magazine had ever accepted a complete novel" (TAY p. 472). Juliar A10.2. Broken type in first line of page 75, as noted by VN on his list of faults in the edition. VN's corrected copy, with his two-line autograph note in Russian and an errata list of 28 page numbers on the half-title, 11 of these with a few words explaining the correction to be made; most of the corresponding pages (and an additional one, page 46) bear his pencil emendations to spelling and punctuation—ten of these page numbers are crossed out on the list and the alterations have been erased.

In 1952 New York's Chekhov House published VN's finest Russian novel, *The Gift* [*Dar*], never before published in its entirety, and asked for additional works. VN had hoped they'd agree to bring out his earliest Russian novels—especially *The Defense*—in English, but they held fast to their mission of Russian-language publication, and insisted on either translations of his English works or previously unpublished Russian works. He would have to wait until 1967 for a French edition of the original Russian text (Paris, Editions de la Seine, posited by Boyd as "as fictional as Editions Victor"; this was the second title to be distributed in the USSR by Radio Liberty in the '60s under this bogus imprint (TAY p. 504–5); it was not brought out in Russian in the States until after VN's death (Ann Arbor: Ardis, 1979). However, the success of *Lolita* paved the way for further English translations such as this—as of

1964, only *Laughter in the Dark*, *Invitation to a Beheading*, and *The Gift* had been published in translation.

The Defense prompted one of John Updike's best-known pronouncements, causing him to declare VN "distinctly...the best writer of English prose at present holding American citizenship...He writes prose the only way it should be written–that is, ecstatically. In the intensity of its intelligence and reflective irony, his fiction is unique in this decade and scarcely precedented in American literature" (quoted in TAY p. 485).

22 **The Defense.** Translated by Michael Scammell in collaboration with the author. New York: Putnam's, (1964).

8vo.; marbled endpapers; top edge gilt; full green morocco, stamped in gilt; stamped "V. N." on the cover.

First edition of the first English translation; line of broken type on page 75, intact in some copies. The publisher's specially bound presentation copy, with Putnam's original mailing label–addressed to VN at the Palace Hotel, Montreux–loosely inserted. Juliar A10.2.

23 **The Defense [Zashchita Luzhina].** Paris: Editions de la Seine, (1967).

8vo.; red and white wrappers, lightly rubbed.

Ostensibly the first French edition of the Russian text, with an unascribed Russian translation of VN's 1963 English foreword, a translation he revised heavily before publication; "reputedly 1000 copies." Like Editions Victor, Editions de la Seine was a front for a CIA-sponsored publication project. Juliar A10.6, noting that the 1967 publication date is derived from "an uncorroborated citation." With a Metalmark, rendered in pencil greys and red and most reminiscent of the genus *Necyria*, named *Obloshka obloshkensis* (according to Shapiro, "Cover coverensis," a pseudo-Latinized Russian which Boyd translates as "to 'cover in the place of cover' (which makes the espionage element still clearer)." Considering this, Johnson notes that "striped 'ruptive' colors as in this Metalmark serve as protective camouflage in nature, breaking the visual image of predators, perhaps significant to this overall theme." Signed three times: *V. Sirin 1929*; *V. Nabokov*; *Vladimir Nabokov 1973*. Though the signatures are all obviously of the same moment, the first is docketed with the publication year of the first edition, and the third, *1973*, presumably the date of this butterfly's pupation. The cover is labeled in thick black marker, *Signed*, and VN noted on the title page in pencil, *1967*. This edition prints a preface by émigré critic Georgy Adamovich, the leader of VN's aesthetic adversaries throughout the 1920s and '30s in Paris.

With a nine-page typescript translation of the foreword, copiously emended by VN in pencil. The fact that VN rewrote nearly every word suggests that the first round was completed by another translator, but Juliar, in his 1991 update, was unable to discover that person's identity.

24 **The Return of Chorb [Vozvrashchenie Chorba].** Berlin: Slovo, 1930.

8vo.; pages evenly browned; edges fragile and crumbling; cream wrappers, darkened, with a few small chips and stains.

First edition of VN's first collection, published on the heels of the success of *The Defense*; 15 stories and 24 poems. Juliar A11.1. Of the poems, VN included only one from 1923; three from 1924; less than a third of those published in 1925; and half of his output from 1926–28; nearly all feature the theme of Russia and its exiles. All but one would be included in the 1979 collection brought out by Ardis Press. By the time he stopped writing stories in Russian – his last was penned in 1939 – VN had published approximately fifty: "1924 was marked by the publication of nine stories; for 1925 the number amounted to five. Over the next fourteen years he continued to publish an average of one to three stories per year..." (Tolstaia and Meilakh, "Russian Short Stories," p. 644).

A presentation copy, inscribed to Anna Feigin on the first blank in Russian in December of 1929: *To Anyuta, I give my little book with delight. The author. Berlin xii–29.*

Tolstaia and Meilakh offers a balanced perspective on the critical reception VN received for his Russian stories:

One reviewer noted that "Sirin's short stories are somewhat weaker than his novels," while another concluded after comparing the short stories with the novels, that "in [the former] one finds the same pointedness of language and narration, structured on the principle of renewing material, the same intentionally chance nature of the point of departure [...] the same refined power of observation of a man who loves life because it is the sole splendid material for creative transformations." (ibid. p. 648)

25 **Glory [Podvig].** [Paris: Sovremennye zapiski], 1932.

8vo.; minor stains to pages 145–148, not obscuring text; hinges weakened; cream printed wrappers; light stains on first blank and covers;

front hinge and upper joint reinforced with tape; edgeworn, with a few small chips to spine; censor's stamp on rear panel.

First edition; 1000 copies; serialized in *Sovremennye zapiski*, February–December 1931; *Sovremennye zapiski* bought the rights to book publication before composition was complete. Excerpted in *Poslednie novosti*, January 1931–January 1932; *Rossiia i Slavianstvo*, Paris, January–October 1931; and *Segodnia*, Riga, February 1931. Juliar notes: "Contrary to Zimmer, there was in 1932 neither a Paris Rodnik edition nor a Berlin Petropolis edition. This is the only book publication of *Glory* in Russian until 1974." Juliar A13.1.

A presentation copy, inscribed to Véra on the first blank with a Russian term of endearment, translated literally: *To the Doggie from the author. Berlin viii–32.* With VN's minor emendations and pencil ticks to several pages and two ephemeral pieces clipped to pages 195 and 223. The first is a small leaf torn from a German recipe pamphlet, labeled in ink (in an unidentified hand): "English beefsteaks/macaroni Duce/Compote d'Apricot." VN penciled a few page references on the top and verso. The second is a comparably small leaf from a notebook, headed by either Véra or DN in pencil, *Glory*, with a list of a few dozen page numbers and an "NB": *'Cornice' overhangs or a snow cornice at top of steep windblown slope. A rock shelf is a ledge.*

By the time of publication VN had debated several titles: *Voploshchenie* ("the 'realization' of a plan, the 'embodiment' of a dream"); *Zolotoy vek*, ("golden age"); and others (TRY p. 353); he wrote in the foreword to his English translation:

... The book's—certainly very attractive—working title (later discarded in favor of the pithier *Podvig*, 'gallant feat,' 'high deed') was *Romanticheskiy vek*, 'romantic times,' which I had chosen partly because I had had enough of hearing Western journalists call our era 'materialistic,' 'practical,' 'utilitarian,' etc., but mainly because the purpose of my novel, my only one with a purpose, lay in stressing the thrill and the glamour that my young expatriate finds in the most ordinary pleasures as well as in the seemingly meaningless adventures of a lonely life... after all but lapsing into false exotism [exoticism] or commonplace comedy, [the novel] soars to heights of purity and melancholy that I have only attained in the much later *Ada*.

In an ensuing review of the characters and "political types" of *Glory*, VN admits that two characters—Vadim and Teddy—were drawn from his days at Trinity College at Cambridge: "they are mentioned under their initials, N. R. and R. C., respectively, in my *Speak Memory*, 1966, Chapter Thirteen, penult paragraph...." Boyd identifies "N. R." as Prince Nikita Romanov; "R. C" is Robert de Calry, whose gift copy of A. E. Housman's *Last Poems* is described in entry #2.

26 Glory [Podvig]. [Paris: Sovremennye zapiski], 1932.

8vo.; binder's label; blue pebbled cloth, original wrappers bound-in.

First edition; lacking the first blank. Juliar A13.1. A specially, if modestly, bound presentation copy, preserving the front wrapper in incredibly fresh condition, inscribed 38 years after its publication, on the binder's front endpaper: *Glory/to Véra/Montreux/Dec 1970*. With an energetic butterfly of the *Parnassius* species, ornamented in white, blue, and red. Johnson notes:

Nabokov sought and caught Parnassians in both Europe and America, and also as a youth purchased them from Otto Staudinger, a famous German collector-dealer (see *Speak, Memory* and *The Gift*). They are unmistakable, very primitive, white butterflies of the Swallowtail family (although lacking tails). They inhabit the high mountains where Nabokov collected both in the Old and New World. In reality Parnassians are white, red, and black. If the blue spots here were either black or red they would be accurate. Perhaps the blue was put in for a "red, white and blue" motif re Nabokov's note '[Old?] Glory.' Who knows?

VN's corrected copy, with annotations to several pages: on the front cover he transliterated the Cyrillic title into *Podvig*; on the half-title he explained two misprints (each indicated on its page) and called attention to page 38, where he added a lengthy annotation in Russian. Shapiro notes that it parodies an Ivanov verse, and states that "[a] stanza from his other, considerably earlier, poem, is quoted in *The Gift*, p. 146." On page 235, the last page of text, VN translated the final two sentences into English, in a version matching verbatim the McGraw-Hill edition of the first English translation. Several other pages bear his light pencil "x" and emendations, and clipped to two pages are lepidopteral ephemera – a stamp and an unopened sugar packet.

27 Glory. New York: McGraw-Hill, (1971).

8vo.; discoloration from tape (now removed) on copyright page, showing through to the title page; black cloth; goldenrod dust-jacket.

First edition of the first English translation, with a specially written foreword; the last of VN's Russian novels to be translated into English. Juliar A13.2. The dust-jacket on this copy – as on every copy we have examined – is nearly .5 cm shorter than the book, and bears the 1933 Nachman-Acharya pastel sketch of VN.

The dedication copy, inscribed with a beautiful rainbow-colored butterfly perched on a green stem, named for Véra – *Neovanessa verochka*

Nab.—on the dedication page, *3.xii.1971 Montreux*. On the copyright page VN added *November* in red ink before "1971," and made a marginal note (subsequently erased) on page 70. "With this butterfly," Johnson opines, "Nabokov may be playing a trick.

Neovanessa ("New Vanessa") would indeed represent something very new among these common butterflies from the family Nymphalidae (Nabokov's "Brushfoot" family discussed in *Speak, Memory* and other works) known as Painted Ladies. The wing shape would be readily recognized by lepidopterists as that not of Vanessa but its sister group of butterflies, Polygonia—or Anglewings. Yet, rainbow colors occur in none of these. But is the butterfly a complete ruse? Perhaps not, because there is a South American group of rainbow colored Metalmarks with a wing shape looking much like Polygonia—it is called Amphiselenis and its species, chama, fits this profile quite closely. It is possible Nabokov remembered these odd little Metalmarks looking quite like miniatures of the more well-known northern Anglewings.

The 1971 translation into English of VN's only remaining Russian novel, Glory, was a family affair. Dmitri had undertaken it in good faith but, after several months of continual interruptions from the world of opera—his primary career—he had been unable to finish. Véra undertook the final third, and VN revised the entirety to make it "meticulously true to the text" (TAY p. 578). Having nearly finished the final read-through, he wrote in his diary: "Two pages left!... the entire thing corrected by me, an excruciating task that took three months to complete with a few interruptions. Last Russian novel, thank God" (quoted in TAY p. 580). In his foreword he discusses his choice of "Glory" as the English title, referring to himself in the third person:

Nabokov cannot be unaware that the obvious translation of *podvig* is 'exploit,' and, indeed, it is under that title that his *Podvig* is listed by bibliographers; but if you once perceive in 'exploit' the verb 'utilize,' gone is the podvig, the inutile deed of renown. The author chose therefore the oblique 'glory,' which is a less literal but much richer rendering of the original title with all its natural associations branching in the bronze sun. It is the glory of high adventure and disinterested achievement; the glory of this earth and its patchy paradise; the glory of personal pluck; the glory of a radiant martyr...

In a 1966 interview VN put the reason for the retitling even more concisely: "It is the story of a Russian expatriate, a romantic young man of my set and time, a lover of adventure for adventure's sake, proud flaunter of peril, climber of unnecessary mountains, who merely for the pure thrill of it decides one day to cross illegally into Soviet Russia, and then cross back to exile. Its main theme is the overcoming of fear, the glory and rapture of that victory" (Appel interview, SO p. 88).

28 **Glory.** Translated from the Russian by Dmitri Nabokov in collaboration with the author. New York: McGraw-Hill, (1971).

8vo.; fore-edge foxed; black cloth; water spots to topstain; dust-jacket, lightly used, front flap creased.

First edition of the first English translation. Juliar A13.2. With two annotations by VN to his foreword – adding three clarifying phrases to page xi and a quote and citation to page xiii – both noted on the front endpaper.

29 **Camera Obscura [Kamera obskura].** (Berlin): Sovremennye zapiski and Parabola, [1933].

8vo.; two chips to page 106 not affecting text; grey cloth, original wrappers bound-in.

First edition; serialized in *Sovremennye zapiski*, May 1932–May 1933; excerpted in *Russkii invalid*, Paris, May 22, 1931; in *Nash vek*, Berlin, November 8, 1931; and in *Poslednie novosti*, April–September 1932. Though the title page is in Russian and the verso, in German, the copyright notice is in English: "Copyright by V. Nabokoff-Sirin" – VN's first use of the hyphenated name *en route* to the final "Nabokov." Juliar A14.1. Uncommon in trade, but easily found in American research institutions.

A specially bound presentation copy, preserving the cream wrappers printed with a film motif; inscribed on the front endpaper in Russian, *To V from V 21.xii.33*, with an ink drawing of a "monstrous-looking insect" that Johnson notes "resembles butterflies that have emerged from their chrysalid and have been unable to 'blow-up' their wings for flight. Their bodies appear huge and their wings, shriveled and dangling. Nabokov was fascinated with butterfly rearing and recounted it in both *Speak, Memory* as well as *Ada*."

Of the three books in the collection preserved in a modest grey pebbled cloth binding, this is the earliest. VN added *x.1933*, the month of publication, in pencil to the title page. The others are *The Gift* [*Dar*] inscribed to Véra in Cambridge in 1952 (item #71); and *Other Shores* [*Drugie berega*], inscribed to her in Ithaca in 1955 (item #63).

Boyd notes that *Camera Obscura* was "the shortest of all his novels in conception: a mere six months, he later thought, between the image and its transfer to paper" (TRY p. 363). It had grown from the ashes of *Bird Of Paradise*, a novel he completed, then completely rewrote, eventually preserving only the essential plot of "the blind man betrayed" (TRY p. 362). Boyd describes VN as "already dissatisfied" with his final Russian version even before a word had been published (TRY p. 378), even in the face of public enthusiasm: he read to a packed auditorium in the fall of 1931, though the number of Russian residents in Berlin had severely waned, and was able to charge for an invitation-only reading the following spring in an effort to raise funds for his mother in Prague, despite the fragile German economy. In 1936 it was badly translated into English by Winifred Roy for Hutchinson's John Long imprint. In 1938 VN seized upon the opportunity to supplant Roy's disastrous attempt, ironing out many of *Camera Obscura*'s flaws in the process by altering the text—in spots, radically—in his own English translation. However, Boyd concludes, "as a novel, *Camera Obscura* is too thin in texture and too hasty in structure to satisfy on the level of Nabokov's other works" (TRY p. 368).

In discussing sources for his movie-themed, camera-ready novel, Boyd explores VN's connection to 1930s cinema. In Berlin the Nabokovs went to the movies every couple of weeks; he "loved the comedy of Buster Keaton, Harold Lloyd, Chaplin, Laurel and Hardy, and the Marx brothers...he admired a few serious features...but most of all he enjoyed the grotesqueness of cinematic cliché." One Berlin companion wrote: "For Sirin there seemed no greater pleasure than to single out intentionally an inept American film. The more casually stupid it was, the more he would choke and literally shake with laughter, to the point where on occasion he would have to leave the hall" (TRY p. 363).

30 **Camera Obscura.** Translated by Winifred Roy. London: John Long, 1935 [1936].

8vo.; black cloth, lightly rubbed.

First edition of the first English translation; the first of VN's novels to be translated into English; with the publisher's 1935 summer ads in the rear. Although many other foreign language editions were based on this version, it was the only appearance of Roy's botched English text. It is not unheard of in research institutions, but is scarce in trade with the dust-jacket (which this copy lacks). Juliar claims that a "'cheap edition' in wrappers was published in Jan38," and quotes Howard Woolmer in *Malcolm Lowry: A Bibliography*, p. 5: "Apparently, it was common practice in Britain in the 30's [*sic*] for publishers to sell off their remaining first edition copies at a reduced price, which they called a 'cheap edition.'" Still, he admits that he has "no physical evidence or firm citation to show that this translation was actually released in wrappers." Juliar D14.4.

In VN's eagerness to see his work published in English—a goal since his earliest days at Cambridge—he let pass this miserable translation which he later confessed he had "insufficiently revised" (Appel interview, 1967, SO p. 82), calling it "inexact and full of hackneyed expressions meant to tone down all the tricky passages" (to Hutchinson & Co., August 28, 1936, SL p. 15). This was a pithy encapsulation of his assessment of Roy's first attempt, which he had taken time off from *Invitation to a Beheading* to review:

It was loose, shapeless, sloppy, full of blunders and gaps, lacking vigour and spring, and plumped down in such dull, flat English that I could not read it to the end; all of which is rather hard on an author who aims in his work at absolute precision, takes the utmost trouble to attain it, and then finds the translator calmly undoing every blessed phrase. Please believe that had the translation been in the least acceptable I would have passed it...a good translation is most important for the success of a book...I hope that it has now been thoroughly improved and that it will not give rise to any objections of the above kind. (to Hutchinson & Co., May 22, 1935, SL p. 13)

He learned his lesson: the next English translation of a VN work—*Despair* (1937)—would be his own. Soon after Roy's revised but still fairly miserable adaptation was released, VN retranslated the novel himself for the first American edition, substantially rewriting along the way, and retitling it *Laughter In The Dark*. Though he later deemed that translation "not quite successful" (Appel interview, 1966, SO p. 82), it was far superior to Roy's version. Bobbs-Merrill published it in 1938. When both *Camera Obscura* and *Despair* failed to lure an audience, VN blamed his publisher, Hutchinson, for bringing out his challenging prose under the John Long imprint which generally catered to a less sophisticated audience than VN's works, perhaps, demanded.

31 Camera Obscura [Camera Oscura]. [Translated by Alessandra Iljina.] Milan: Muggiani, (1947).

8vo.; publisher's price-tag on rear pastedown; orange paper-covered boards, orange cloth spine; colorful illustrated dust-jacket, rubbed and edgeworn.

First edition of the first Italian translation. Juliar D14.5 A presentation copy, inscribed in Italian with one of several diminutives by which VN called Véra: *To my Verinka with the love of the author i.iv.1948.* Shapiro notes that "author" bears "the Georgian ending -dze, apparently alluding to the Stalin-ruled Russia."

32 **Laughter in the Dark.** (New York): Signet, the New American Library, (1950).

12mo.; illustrated wrappers, light wear. In a specially built full leather slipcase.

First paperback edition, reproduced from his 1938 translation; VN's first mass-market paperback. Juliar A14.3. A presentation copy, inscribed to Véra in Russian on the title page: *To my darling–the same, after a quarter of a century. V. iii.1950 Ithaca N.Y.* In 1938 VN's agent, Altagracia de Jannelli, secured him a $300 advance from Bobbs-Merrill to correct the travesty perpetrated by Winifred Roy in her 1935 translation for John Long. With just over half that amount in his pocket after taxes and fees, VN "set about rewriting the novel to appeal more to himself and America and Hollywood," considering among possible new titles "Blind Man's Buff," "Colored Ghost," "The Magic Lantern," "The Clumsy Moth," and "The Blind Moth."

He altered names to make them less German [Kretschmar to Albert Albinus, Magda to Margot, Horn to Axel Rex, Anneliese to Elisabeth, Max to Paul]. He revamped the opening, stressing the movieland banality of the story, as if to lure an unimaginative producer. He introduced villain and hero not via the villain's static comic strips but by way of the hero's plan to make old master paintings spring to life as animated cartoons–as if in this case he wished to introduce the novel's cinema theme right from the start and to inspire an imaginative director. He improved the mechanism by which hero meets villain, he redesigned the means by which hero discovers the villainy of villain and heroine. There were some losses in the revision–the "Cheepy" comic strip of the Russian version, and a fine parody of Proust– but far more gains. (TRY p. 445)

The *New York Times* review of VN's 1938 translation identifies the novel as a "slight but expertly fashioned ... psychological novel" but faults VN for his lack of "real sympathy for any of his characters," offering a conclusion he must have appreciated: "it is a pity that so polished and graceful a novel should have to go out into a hard and cynical world with a comparison to Dostoievsky on its dust wrapper" (Harold Strauss, May 8, 1938).

33 **Despair [Otchaianie].** Berlin: Petropolis, (1936).

8vo.; virtually unopened; pages bright; printed wrappers, lightly rubbed; minor wear to bottom edge; tiny chip and small closed tear; censor's stamp on rear panel.

First edition; serialized in *Sovremennye zapiski*, February–October 1934; excerpted in *Poslednie novosti*, December 1932–November 1933. Juliar A15.1. Uncommon in this superb condition. A presentation copy, inscribed on the first leaf to Véra and Dmitri, in Russian: *To my darlings. V. iv–36.*

VN's first reading in Paris, a public triumph, included the first two chapters of *Despair*, which he had originally titled "Notes of a Hoaxer" ["Zapiski mistifikatora"]. In his assessment of this novel, whose plot revolves around a man who tries to fake his own death by murdering a vagrant he believes could pass for his double, Boyd is more critical than VN's contemporary readers:

Nabokov's sheer intelligence crackles in every line of *Despair*, but for all the brio of the book's style something seems sadly lacking in its structure. Hermann allows Nabokov to parody his own sense of art as a step beyond the self and toward a sympathy for others perhaps even richer than life allows. Nabokov has never inverted values he holds dear with more gusto or glee, but Hermann's unwarranted supposition that another face looks like his remains a brittle and meager basis for a whole novel. It never quite convinces, and page after page that would make one tingle with excitement in another context can here only intermittently overcome one's remoteness from a story whose central premise fails to merit the suspension of disbelief. (TRY p. 389)

VN himself refers to *Despair* as "something more than an essay on the psychology of crime" but admits that it "turns out to be a half-baked thriller–even when I translate it myself!" (to Altagracia de Jannelli, 1938?, SL, p. 29). He had asked "a grumpy Englishman" to proof his first attempt, but his would-be editor returned the manuscript after reading just a chapter, according to VN, "saying he disapproved of the book; I suspect he wondered if it might not have been a true confession" (foreword to VN's English translation). Despite this jest, the only clearly autobiographical element of the novel is the setting for the murder, which takes place on the German property VN and Véra had purchased jointly with Véra's cousin, Anna Feigin, with a plan to build on it one day. Ultimately the only useful purpose the land would serve VN was this fictional one.

34 **Despair.** New York: Putnam's, (1966).

8vo.; marbled endpapers; top edge gilt; satin ribbon; full red morocco, front panel stamped "V. N." in gilt.

First American edition, second English translation, with a foreword by VN specially written for this edition; serialized in *Playboy* (December 1965 through April 1966), and winner of their Best Fiction award that year, along with a $1000 cash prize. Juliar A15.3. A specially bound publisher's presentation copy, with the calling card of Putnam's president Walter Minton loosely inserted.

For this version VN overhauled his 1937 translation for Hutchinson's John Long imprint, his first attempt at translating any of his own works. He later referred to the 1937 experience as his "first serious attempt . . . to use English for what may be loosely termed an artistic purpose," though that is debatable. Despite the unfavorable "reader reports" (to Hutchinson & Co., August 28, 1936, SL p. 15) they received, Long had paid VN 15/- per 1000 words, and ultimately published the novel to the sound of one hand clapping. VN blamed his commercial failure on Hutchinson's insistence that *Despair*, like *Camera Obscura* the year before, be brought out under the John Long imprint, which he saw catering to the audience for mindless thrillers.

For this retranslation, VN claims in his foreword, he rewrote much of the original text, and added "an important passage which had been stupidly omitted in more timid times." Boyd accounts for the changes in VN's revised translation: "Although he had anticipated that he would have to make major changes, he found less to do than he expected . . . He added some fresh images, some vivid local details, some fictional preparations for later events, and the brilliantly comic final paragraph in which Hermann bellows down to the crowd and the police below as if he were the director of a movie in which the crowd is required to hold the police and allow the archcriminal about to emerge to make a clean escape" (TAY p. 489).

VN's foreword includes his translation of a Pushkin poem, "with the retention of measure and rhyme, a course that is seldom advisable – nay, admissible – except at a very special conjunction of stars in the firmament of the poem." This is especially interesting in light of the timing of its publication: it appeared while the ruckus about VN's unmetered, unrhymed translation of Pushkin's *Eugene Onegin* was still reverberating. (Boyd notes that the brouhaha "continues quite vociferously even to 1997, in Hofstadter's *Le Tombeau de Marot*.)

35 **The Eye [Sogliadatai].** Paris: Russkiia zapiski, 1938.

8vo.; crease to top corner of first 24 pages; printed wrappers, lightly foxed and well worn; rear panel creased; front panel stained; no chips or tears to edges.

First edition of *The Eye*; with 12 short stories; with a leaf (pages [255–256]) of publisher's ads in the rear unnoted by Juliar; serially published in *Sovremennye zapiski*, November 1930; excerpted in *Poslednie novosti*, October 12, 1930. Juliar suggests that book publication was "apparently...originally scheduled to be published in the early 30's [*sic*], after its periodical appearances." Juliar A12.1. A presentation copy, with a pencil butterfly colored in red and blue drawn for Véra – the cover is labeled in pencil *Véra's* – on the first blank.

By 1924 most of Berlin's Russian émigré community had fled to Paris; by 1930, even fewer remained. VN's public reading of the first chapter of *The Eye* "was the first Union of Russian Writers evening for months" (TRY pp. 349–50). The "classless narrator" and early '20s Berlin setting of the novel were completely familiar to his audience, who must have appreciated the protagonist's position among the "representatives of the many-faceted Russian intelligentsia," as VN deemed them in the foreword to Phaedra's 1965 edition almost 30 years later, "the favorite characters of my literary youth: Russian expatriates living in Berlin, Paris, or London." (When Phaedra brought out *The Eye* they dropped the stories that had originally accompanied the Russian text, and promoted it for its range of expatriate characters, though VN countered: "they might just as well have been Norwegians in Naples or Ambracians in Ambridge: I have always been indifferent to social problems, merely using the material that happened to be near.")

The Eye was VN's first novel written in the first person – his protagonist, we are led to believe, has committed suicide before he begins to tell the story. The novel prefigures the unique manipulation of narrative devices that would mark later works such as *Pale Fire*, told as the commentary to a poem; *The Gift* and *Ada*, incorporating literary works by their protagonists; and even *Speak, Memory*, in which the final chapter is directed to "you." He wrote in 1965 that "the texture of the tale mimics that of detective fiction but actually the author disclaims all intention to trick, puzzle, fool, or otherwise deceive the reader. In fact, only that reader who catches on at once will derive genuine satisfaction from *The Eye* ..."

36 **The Eye.** (Translated by Dmitri Nabokov in collaboration with the author.) New York: Phaedra, 1965.

8vo.; tan cloth; dust-jacket, lightly rubbed with one small closed tear to the rear panel and a couple of faint pencil marks.

First edition, state A, of the first English translation, with the publisher's address on the copyright page; in the state A dust-jacket with the photo of VN cropped below the neck instead of below the chin; the jacket is 2 mm. shorter than the book on every copy we have examined. In 1991 Juliar changed his designation of these states from "variants," on the following grounds: "two of Nabokov's own copies were with a variant a cloth binding and a variant b dust jacket. The fact that the advance copy (see E12.1) is similar to variant a implies that 'variant' could be changed to 'state.'" He further notes: "The publication date according to the U. S. Copyright Office is 30Oct65; according to the copyright-page, it is 1Aug65; and according to a preview copy and its enclosed material, it was changed from Oct65 to 15Sep65." Serialized in *Playboy* (January–March 1965). Juliar A12.2.

The dedication copy, inscribed on the half-title in Russian for Véra (the jacket is labeled *Véra* in pencil): *Blue Colias's do not exist. October 1, 1965, Montreux*. The inscription refers to a drawing of a marvelously attired butterfly, *Colias verae* Nabokov, from the *Colias* genus of Sulphur or Yellow butterflies known from throughout much of the world. "In the high mountains, where VN loved to collect both in North America and Europe, and also in the tundras of the far north, many Sulphurs become more darkly colored, some even tending toward dusky shades of green." Johnson notes that this example is "accurate in wing shape and pattern. However, the blue hue adopted here by Nabokov is fanciful." VN's hand-pressure was so great that the butterfly is ghosted onto the title page by the transfer of ink from the facing page, which is black with white text dropped out; and there is a simple pencil outline of a butterfly on the front endpaper. VN numbered the pages of the foreword at the top, and left marginal ticks on four pages.

VN's relationships with his two publishers of *The Eye*—*Playboy* and Phaedra—took opposite turns. Despite some preliminary misgivings about appearing in *Playboy*, VN became "grateful for their generous remuneration, the complete freedom they allowed him, and their ready consultation with him over publishing conditions." They sent him the proofs for their serialization nearly six months before the projected publication date, "in the hope that he might make extensive revisions...Since they offered a $1,000 bonus as an inducement, he spent the last weeks of June adding 'some rainbow patches'" (TAY p. 484). Boyd offers one example: "And what do I care if she marries another? She and I have had heart-rending meetings by night, and her husband shall never find out about these dreams I've had of her." This became: "And what do I care if she marries another? Every other night I dream of her dresses and things on an endless clothesline of bliss, in a ceaseless wind of possession, and her husband shall never learn what I do to the silks and fleece of the dancing witch" (TAY pp. 484–85).

VN's reaction to Phaedra went in another direction. Initially he was full of appreciation for the attention they paid him: their generous advances and publicity budgets contrasted starkly with the paltry sums Putnam's had bestowed on him for more significant titles. Boyd relates that "Phaedra published only books Minton [at Putnam's] was not prepared to take," and were glad to have them (TAY p. 510). Unfortunately, their first undertaking for VN was a commercial circus, and displayed their "naked hope of profit but little publishing acumen and less taste" in comparing him to Ian Fleming and John Le Carré. After a cable from an exasperated VN, they substituted Turgenev, Fitzgerald, and Conrad for the American masters of action and suspense. Véra wrote back: "He does not want to be compared to anyone in the advertisements because you should realise that you are publishing the work of a completely individual writer...If you want to compare, please compare the present work to his other publications...recommend his books as just that: his books" (quoted in TAY p. 501).

As usual, one of VN's greatest challenges was in choosing an English title. The Russian *sogliadatai*, he explains in his foreword to this edition, "is an ancient military term meaning 'spy' or 'watcher,' neither of which extends as flexibly as the Russian word. After toying with 'emissary' and 'gladiator,' I gave up trying to blend sound and sense, and contented myself with matching the 'eye' at the end of the long stalk." Boyd presents an interesting perspective on this decision: "Nabokov could well have called its English translation *I Spy*, but went one better with *The Eye* and its pun on 'I.' By diverting attention from the 'I' that persists and tells his story, Smurov thinks he escapes the relentless eye of others...Since all the attention is on Smurov, the sensitive narrating eye watching Smurov and watching others watching Smurov can feel safe from anyone else's gaze...Smurov *is* a spy, of course, but only on himself, or rather on other people's sense of himself" (TRY pp. 348–49). VN continues in his foreword to reflect on the effect that the distancing elements of time – 35 years – and language may have on his audience: "Tracking down Smurov remains, I believe, excellent sport despite the passing of time and books, and the shift from the mirage of one language to the oasis of another." Still, he acknowledges the inevitable result:

...the social group casually swept into artistic focus acquires a falsely permanent air; it is taken for granted at a certain time in a certain place, by the émigré writer and his émigré readers. The Ivan Ivanovich and Lev Osipovich of 1930 have long been replaced by non-Russian readers who are puzzled and irritated today by having to imagine a society they know nothing about; for I do not mind repeating again and again that bunches of pages have been torn out of the past by the destroyers of freedom ever since Soviet propaganda, almost half a century ago, misled foreign opinion into ignoring or denigrating the importance of Russian emigration (which still awaits its chronicler).

37 The Eye [Silmä]. Translated by Juhani Jaskari. Jyvaskyla: K. J. Gummerus, (1968).

8vo.; stiff white wrappers; dust-jacket.

First edition of the first Finnish translation. Juliar D12.7. A presentation copy, inscribed for Véra – VN labeled the cover *Véra* twice, incorporated a butterfly into the illustration, and initialed the spine – on the title page in Russian on their 43rd wedding anniversary: *Here is an iridescent butterfly for my iridescent darling! V. 15–iv–1968. Montreux.* With a pert, colorful butterfly.

38 Invitation to a Beheading [Priglashenie na kazn']. Paris: Dom Knigi, (1938).

8vo.; unopened; front endpaper lightly soiled, with two pin holes; cream wrappers printed in red and black.

First edition of VN's "grim fantasy" (to George Weidenfeld, January 12, 1958, [1959], SL p. 273); serialized two years before book publication in *Sovremennye zapiski*, June 1935–March 1936. Juliar A16.1. According to Juliar, contemporary advertisements priced this work at $.75 and $1.00; the ads in the rear of this copy, integrally printed with the text, list the price as $1.00. A presentation copy, inscribed to Véra in Russian: *To my Vérushka.*

VN wrote this novel in "a burst of spontaneous generation," taking time off from *The Gift* to set it to paper (Appel interview, 1966, SO p. 74). He composed the first draft in two weeks during the summer of

1934, and then set it aside to resume *The Gift*. After the summer he looked it over again and, as Véra began to type it, made revisions into December. As late as 1967 – after *Lolita*, *Pale Fire*, *The Gift*, and *Speak, Memory* had all been published – VN considered *Invitation to a Beheading* the book for which he reserved "the greatest esteem" – though he reserved the "most affection" for *Lolita* (ibid., SO p. 92).

In 1969 he wrote that, along with *Bend, Sinister*, *Invitation to a Beheading* served as an "absolutely final indictment of Russian and German totalitarianism" (Talmey interview, SO p. 156), though he recalled in the foreword to the first English translation: "I composed the Russian original exactly a quarter of a century ago in Berlin, some fifteen years after escaping from the Bolshevist regime, and just before the Nazi regime reached its full volume of welcome. The question whether or not my seeing both in terms of one dull beastly farce had any effect on this book, should concern the good reader as little as it does me." And he discouraged his mother in 1935 from searching for symbolism in the book, explaining, "[I]t's extremely logical and real, it is the simplest everyday reality and doesn't need any special explanation" (TRY p. 419). Boyd, however, writes:

It was no accident that Nabokov began *Invitation To A Beheading* while Goebbels as Minister of People's Enlightenment and Propaganda was striving to make all German culture Nazi "culture," or while Stalin's grip on the Union of Soviet Writers and on everything else in the Soviet Union was becoming still tighter.

But he qualifies this, writing: "[H]is novel is not a narrowly political one. He could keep his invented world lightly comic in a way he could not in the much more grimly political Bend Sinister, written one brutal decade later...(TRY p. 411)

Aspects of VN's story of a man imprisoned and finally executed for his free-thinking tendencies are clearly reminiscent of Kafka's The Trial despite the fact that, as of 1934, VN had not yet encountered Kafka's work. Still, his protagonist, Cincinnatus, who waits 19 days in persistent ignorance of his hour of execution, seems a fraternal twin to Kafka's Herr K. In later years VN optimistically, if impossibly, imagined he might have shared a street car with the German writer in the fall of 1921 or '22, though Kafka was not in Berlin until 1923 (TRY p. 202). In the mid-thirties Kafka was still virtually unknown outside of German circles and, if he was known by VN's community, the comparison which by now seems obvious apparently escaped the literate Russian émigrés who reviewed VN's work. But the argument that even if his colleagues had known of The Trial, VN himself supposedly could not have read it, is specious. Throughout his career he held tenaciously to the claim that he could not read any German beyond a street sign, menu, or perhaps a newspaper, but Boyd has discovered that VN had five years of German at Tenishev School in his teens, and in Strong Opinions VN himself admitted to having translated Heine at that time: "Later I read Goethe and Kafka en regard as I also did Homer and Horace. And of course since my early boyhood I have been tackling a multitude of German butterfly books with the aid of a dictionary" (Hoffman interview, 1971, p. 187).

Invitation to a Beheading was the first title to be picked up by Radio Liberty's CIA-sponsored publication project, Editions Victor, devoted to bringing émigré literature, censored as little as possible and distributed gratis, into the former Soviet Union; it received a positive response, and was followed soon after by The Defense, brought out by Editions de la Seine.

39 Invitation to a Beheading. Translated by Dmitri Nabokov in collaboration with the author. New York: Putnam's, (1959).

8vo.; grey streaked paper-covered boards; red cloth spine, heel bumped; dust-jacket, few inconsequential chips to top edge, minor rubbing on rear panel.

First edition of the first English translation; with a foreword written specially for this edition. VN's first Russian work to be translated in the States and the first collaborative translation by VN and his then 25-year-old son, Dmitri, of one of his own works. Juliar A16.2. A presentation copy, inscribed on the half-title in Russian and English: *Véra (to my darling) from V. Sept 1959 NYC.* The inscription is in blue ink, with a butterfly in pencil, decorated in blue ink and red pencil. With a second butterfly, *Wesen standen* (female), on the recto of the rear endpaper, in profile in pencil with red highlights, approaching a pencil-drawn flower. The copy VN used to examine the first German translation (Reinbek bei Hamburg: Rowohlt, 1970), with his pencil note on the half-title, *German trans checked*, and copious pencil "X's in the margins of over 125 pages—these are probably Véra's—and occasional words underlined or circled; on page 182 either VN or Véra translated in the margin "patent-leather" as *lackleder!*, and "frock coat" as *gerock!*; on several pages spelling is corrected and words are altered; about two-thirds through the underlining becomes heavier and more frequent.

VN summed up his need for English translations of his Russian works in the afterword to *Lolita*, which is excerpted on this dust-jacket: "None of my American friends have read my Russian books and thus every appraisal on the strength of my English ones is bound to be out of focus." In reviewing the project of translating his work years after its original conception, he claimed that "the only corrections which its transformation into English could profit by were routine ones, for the sake of that clarity which in English seems to require less elaborate electric fixtures than in Russian. My son proved to be a marvelously congenial translator, and it was settled between us that fidelity to one's author comes first, no matter how bizarre the result." He continued, establishing his credo: "*Vive le pédant*, and down with the simpletons who think that all is well if the 'spirit' is rendered (while the words go away by themselves on a naïve and vulgar spree—in the suburbs of Moscow for instance—and Shakespeare is again reduced to play the king's ghost)."

Dmitri had had a wide experience in translation before he embarked on this project, including "several years as a translator-editor of *The Current Digest Of The Soviet Press*, published by the Joint Committee on Slavic Studies, as a translator for several agencies of the United States Government and by collaboration with his father on a translation of Lermontov's *Hero Of Our Times*" (from the dust-jacket). VN spent one month composing the foreword to this edition and reviewing Dmitri's labor—realizing, apparently too late, that an even better title might have been "*Welcome To The Block* with its splendidly gruesome double entendre..." (to Walter Minton, January 20, 1959, SL p. 276). The translation impressed him enough to "urge Dmitri to drop his job and work full-time on the translation of his father's books...Dmitri accepted his father's principle of literality and knew that an undulating or knobbly Russian phrase should not be flattened into plain English..." (TAY p. 377). Despite VN's enthusiasm for his son's efforts, Véra admitted to one friend: "Poor Dmitri did not get enough credit from the papers...For reasons of copyright, this translation had to be described as done 'in collaboration with the author.' With the next one it will be different" (to Morris Bishop, December 7, 1959, SL, p. 303). This translation of *Invitation To A Beheading* marked the beginning for Dmitri of what would become a life-long, welcome task of translating his father's stories, novels, poetry, drama, essays, and letters, "in collaboration with the author" and on his own.

40 **Invitation to a Beheading.** Translated by Dmitri Nabokov in collaboration with the author. New York: Putnam's, (1959).

8vo.; marbled endpapers; top edge gilt; full red leather stamped "V. N." in gilt on front panel; slight bump to one edge.

First edition of the first English translation. In the publisher's presentation binding, with VN's initials stamped in gilt on the cover. Juliar A16.2.

Corrected

Charaxes verae Nabokov
Montreux, Vaud. 15.IV.68 ♂

Вотъ достойная годовщина
Нетлѣнная забота
В
1925 - 68

Corrected

for Véra

for Véra

VLADIMIR
NABOKOV

THE
GIFT

for Véra

for Véra

A NOVEL · WEIDENFELD & NICOLSON

To Vera

from V. Nabokov, V. Sirin, and Basilio Šiškov

April, 1962

Montreux

NO SCIENCE WITHOUT FANCY, NO ART WITHOUT FACTS: THE LEPIDOPTERY OF VLADIMIR NABOKOV

I The Paradox of Intellectual Promiscuity

No one ever accused Francis Bacon of modesty, but when England's Lord Chancellor proclaimed his "great instauration" of human understanding and vowed to take all knowledge as his province, the stated goal did not seem ludicrously beyond the time and competence of a great thinker in Shakespeare's age. But as knowledge exploded, and then fragmented into disciplines with increasingly rigid and self-policed boundaries, the restless scholar who tried to operate in more than one domain became an object of suspicion—either a boastful pretender across the board ("jack of all and master of none" in the old cliché), or a troublesome dilettante in an alien domain, attempting to impose the methods of his genuine expertise upon inappropriate subjects in a different world.

We tend towards benign toleration when great thinkers and artists pursue disparate activities as a harmless hobby, robbing little time from their fundamental achievements. Goethe (and Churchill, and many others) may have been lousy Sunday painters, but Faust and Werther suffered no neglect thereby. Einstein (or so I have heard from people with direct experience) was an indifferent violinist, but his avocation fiddled little time away from physics.

However, we grieve when we sense that a subsidiary interest stole precious items from a primary enterprise of great value. Dorothy Sayers's later theological writings may please aficionados of religion, but most of her devout fans would have preferred a few more detective novels featuring the truly inimitable Lord Peter Wimsey. Charles Ives helped many folks by selling insurance, and Isaac Newton must have figured out a thing or two by analyzing the prophetic texts of Daniel, Ezekiel and Revelation—but, all in all, humanity might have preferred more music or mathematics.

Therefore, when we recognize that a secondary passion took substantial time from a primary source of fame, we try to assuage our grief over lost novels, symphonies, or discoveries by convincing ourselves that a hero's subsidiary love must have informed or enriched his primary activity—in other words, that the loss in quantity must be recompensed by a gain in quality. But such arguments may be very difficult to formulate or sustain. In what sense did Paderewski become a better pianist by serving as Prime Minister of Poland (or a better politician by playing his countryman Chopin)? How did a former career in major league baseball improve (if we give a damn, in this case) Billy Sunday's evangelical style as a stump preacher. (He sometimes began sermons—I am not making this up—by sliding into the podium as an entering gesture.)

No modern genius has inspired more commentary in this mode than Vladimir Nabokov, whose "other" career as a taxonomist of butterflies has inspired as much prose in secondary criticism as Nabokov ever lavished upon Ada, Lolita, and all his other characters combined. In this case in particular—because Nabokov was no dilettante spending a few harmless Sunday hours in the woods with his butterfly net, but a serious scientist with a long list of publications and a substantial career in entomology—we crave some linkage between his two lives, some way to say to ourselves: "we may have lost several novels, but Nabokov spent his entomological time well, developing a vision and approach that illuminated, or even transformed, his literary work." (Of course, speaking parochially, professional taxonomists, including the author of this essay, might regret even more the loss of several monographs implied by Nabokov's novels!)

To allay any remaining suspicions among the literati, let me assure all readers about a consensus in my professional community: Nabokov was no amateur (in the pejorative sense of the term), but a fully qualified, clearly talented, duly employed professional taxonomist, with recognized "world-class" expertise in the biology and classification of a major group, the Latin American *Polyommatini*, popularly known to butterfly aficionados as "Blues."

No passion burned longer, or more deeply, in Nabokov's life than his love for the natural history and taxonomy of butterflies. He began in early childhood, encouraged by a traditional interest in natural history among the upper class intelligentsia of Russia (not to mention the attendant economic advantages of time, resources, and opportunity). Nabokov stated in a 1962 interview: "One of the first things I ever wrote in English was a paper on Lepidoptera I prepared at age 12. It wasn't published because a butterfly I described had been described by someone else" (Zimmer p. 216). Invoking a lovely entomological metaphor in a 1966 interview, Nabokov spoke of childhood fascination, continuous enthusiasm throughout life, and regret that political realities had precluded even more work on butterflies:

But I also intend to collect butterflies in Peru or Iran before I pupate... Had the Revolution not happened the way it happened, I would have enjoyed a landed gentleman's leisure, no doubt, but I also think that my entomological occupations would have been more engrossing and energetic and that I would have gone on long collecting trips to Asia. I would have had a private museum. (ibid.)

Nabokov published more than a dozen technical papers on the taxonomy and natural history of butterflies, mostly during his six years of full employment as Research Fellow (and unofficial curator) in Lepidoptery at the Museum of Comparative Zoology at Harvard University, where he occupied an office three floors above the laboratory that has been my principal scientific home for 30 years. (I arrived twenty years after Nabokov's departure and never had the pleasure of meeting him, although my knowledge of his former presence has always made the venerable institution, built by Louis Agassiz in 1859 and later tenanted by several of the foremost natural historians in America, seem even more special.)

Nabokov worked for Harvard, at a modest yearly salary of about $1000, between 1942 and 1948, when he accepted a teaching post in literature at Cornell University. He was a respected and recognized professional in his chosen field of entomological systematics. The reasons often given for attributing to Nabokov either an amateur, or even only a dilettante's status arise from simple ignorance of accepted definitions for professionalism in this field.

First, many leading experts in various groups of organisms have always been "amateurs" in the admirable and literal (as opposed to the opposite and pejorative) sense that their love for the subject has inspired their unparalleled knowledge, and that they do not receive adequate (or any) pay for their work. (Taxonomy is not as expensive, or as laboratory-driven, as many scientific fields. Careful and dedicated local observation from childhood, combined with diligence in reading and study, can supply all the needed tools for full expertise.)

Second, poorly remunerated and inadequately titled (but full time) employment has, unfortunately, always been *de rigueur* in this field. The fact that Nabokov worked for little pay, and with a vague title of Research Fellow, rather than a professorial (or even a curatorial) appointment, does not imply nonprofessional status. When I took my position at the same museum in 1968, several heads of collections, recognized as world's experts with copious publications, worked as "volunteers" for the symbolic "dollar a year" that gave them official status on the Harvard payroll.

Third, and most important, I do not argue that all duly employed taxonomists can claim enduring expertise and righteous status. Every field includes some clunkers and nitwits, even in high positions! I am not, myself, a professional entomologist (I work on snails among the *Mollusca*), and therefore cannot judge Nabokov's credentials on this crucial and final point. But leading taxonomic experts in the large and complex group of "Blues" among the butterflies testify to the excellence of his work, and grant him the ultimate accolade of honor within the profession by praising his "good eye" for recognizing the (often subtle) distinctions that mark species and other natural groups of organisms (see bibliography for two articles by leading butterfly taxonomists: Remington; and Johnson, Whitaker and Balint). In fact, as many scholars have stated, before Nabokov achieved a conventional form of literary success with the publication of *Lolita*, he could have been identified (by conventional criteria of money earned and time spent) as a professional lepidopterist and amateur author!

In conjunction with this collegial testimony, we must also note Nabokov's own continual (and beautifully stated) affirmation of his love and devotion to all aspects of a professional lepidopterist's life. On the joys of field work and collecting, he effuses in a letter to Edmund Wilson in 1942: "Try, Bunny, it is the noblest sport in the world" (quoted in Zimmer p. 30). Of the tasks traditionally deemed more dull and trying – the daily grind of the laboratory and microscope – he waxed with equal ardor in a letter to his sister in 1945, in the midst of his Harvard employment:

My laboratory occupies half of the fourth floor. Most of it is taken up by rows of cabinets, containing sliding cases of butterflies. I am custodian of these absolutely fabulous collections. We have butterflies from all over the world ... Along the windows extend tables holding my microscopes, test tubes, acids, papers, pins, etc. I have an assistant, whose main task is spreading specimens sent by collectors. I work on my personal research ... a study of the classification of American "blues" based on the structure of their genitalia (minuscule sculpturesque hooks, teeth, spurs, etc., visible only under the microscope), which I sketch in with the aid of various marvelous devices, variants of the magic lantern... My work enraptures but utterly exhausts me... To know that no one before you has seen an organ you are examining, to trace relationships that have occurred to no one before, to immerse yourself in the wondrous crystalline world of the microscope, where silence reigns, circumscribed by its own horizon, a blindingly white arena—all this is so enticing that I cannot describe it. (quoted in Zimmer p. 29)

Nabokov worked so long and so intensely in grueling and detailed observation of tiny bits of insect anatomy that his eyesight became permanently compromised—thus placing him in the company of several of history's most famous entomologists, especially Charles Bonnet in the 18th century and August Weismann in the 19th, who sacrificed their sight to years of eyestraining work. In a television interview of 1971, Nabokov stated:

Most of my work was devoted to the classification of certain small blue butterflies on the basis of their male genitalic structure. These studies required the constant use of a microscope, and since I devoted up to six hours daily to this kind of research my eyesight was impaired forever; but on the other hand, the years at the Harvard Museum remain the most delightful and thrilling in all my adult life. (ibid.)

Nonetheless, and as a touching, final testimony to his love and dedication to entomology, Nabokov stated in a 1975 interview that his enthusiasm would still pull him inexorably in ("like a moth to light" one is tempted to intone) if he ever allowed impulse to vanquish bodily reality:

Since my years at the Museum of Comparative Zoology in Harvard, I have not touched a microscope, knowing that if I did, I would drown again in its bright well. Thus I have not, and probably never shall, accomplish the greater part of the entrancing research work I had imagined in my young mirages. (quoted in Zimmer, p. 218)

Thus, in conclusion to this section, we cannot adopt the first solution to "the paradox of intellectual promiscuity" by arguing that Nabokov's lepidoptery only represents the harmless diversion of an amateur hobbyist, ultimately stealing no time that he might realistically have spent writing more novels. Nabokov loved his butterflies as much as his literature. He worked for years as a fully professional taxonomist, publishing more than a dozen papers that have stood the test of substantial time.

Can we therefore invoke the second solution by arguing that time lost to literature for the sake of lepidoptery nonetheless enhanced his novels, or at least distinguished his writing with a brand of uniqueness? I will eventually suggest a positive answer, but by an unconventional argument that exposes the entire inquiry as falsely parsed. I must first, however, show that the two most popular versions of this "second solution" cannot be defended, and that the paradox of intellectual promiscuity must itself be rejected and identified as an impediment to proper understanding of the relationships between art and science.

II Two False Solutions to a Nonproblem

In surveying commentaries written by literary scholars and critics about Nabokov's work on butterflies, I have been struck by their nearly universal adherence to either of two solutions for the following supposed conundrum: why did one of the greatest writers of our century spend so much time working and publishing in a markedly different domain of such limited interest to most of the literate public.

A) *The Argument for Equal Impact.* In this first solution, Nabokov's literary fans may bemoan their losses (just as any lover of music must lament the early deaths of Mozart and Schubert). Still, in seeking some explanation for legitimate grief, we may find solace in claiming that Nabokov's transcendent genius permitted him to make as uniquely innovative and distinctive a contribution to lepidoptery as to literature. However much we may wish that he had chosen a different distribution for his time, we can at least, with appropriate generosity, grant his equal impact and benefit upon natural history. Adherents to this solution have therefore tried to develop arguments for regarding Nabokov's lepidoptery as specially informed by his genius, and as possessing great transforming power for natural history.

But none of these claims can be granted even a whisper of plausibility by biologists who know the history of taxonomic practice and evolutionary theory. Nabokov, as documented above, was a fully professional and highly competent taxonomic specialist on an important group of butterflies – and for this fine work, he gains nothing but honor in my world. However, no natural historian has ever viewed Nabokov as an innovator, or as an inhabitant of what the humanities call the "vanguard" (not to mention the *avant-garde*) and scientists the "cutting edge." Nabokov may have been a major general of literature, but he can only be ranked as a truthworthy, highly trained career infantryman in natural history.

Nabokov was a conservative specialist on a particular group of organisms, not in any way a theorist or a purveyor of novel ideas or methods. He divided and meticulously described; he did not unify or generalize. (I will explain in the next section why a natural historian can make such a judgment without intending any condescension or lack of respect). Nonetheless, four arguments have been advanced again and again by literary commentators who seem driven by a desire to depict Nabokov as a revolutionary spirit in natural history as well.

1. *The myth of innovation.* Many critics have tried, almost with an air of desperation, to identify some aspect of Nabokov's methodology that might be labeled as innovative. But taxonomic professionals will easily recognize these claims as fallacious – for the putative novelty represents either a fairly common (if admirable) practice, or else an idiosyn-

crasy (a "bee in the bonnet") that Nabokov surely embraced with great ardor, but that cannot be regarded as a major issue of scientific importance.

As a primary example, many critics have stressed Nabokov's frequent complaints about scientists who fail to identify the original describers when citing the formal Latin name of a butterfly—either in listing species in popular field guides, or in identifying subspecies in technical publications. Zimmer, for example, writes: "A growing number of non- and semi-scientific publications nowadays omit the author. Nabokov called it 'a deplorable practice of commercial origin which impairs a number of recent zoological and botanical manuals in America'" (p. 10).

By the rules of nomenclature, each organism must have a binomial designation consisting of a capitalized genus name (*Homo*) and a lower case "trivial" name (*sapiens*), with the two together forming the species name (*Homo sapiens*). (Linnaean taxonomy is called "binomial" in reference to these two parts of a species name.) It is also customary, but not required, to add (not in italics) the name of the first describer of the species after the binomial designation—as in *Homo sapiens* Linnaeus. This custom certainly helps specialists by permitting easier tracing of the history of a species's name. But this practice is also extremely time-consuming (locating the original describer is often tedious and difficult; I don't know the first authors for several of the snail species most central to my own research). Moreover, when hundreds of names are to be listed (as in popular field guides), rigid adherence to this custom requires a great deal of space for rather limited benefit.

Therefore, popular publications (especially the manuals of Nabokov's ire above) generally omit the names of describers. In addition, and for the same reason, technical publications often compromise by including describers' names for species, but omitting them for subspecies (trinomial names for geographically defined subgroups within a species). Honorable people can argue either side of this issue; I tend to agree with Nabokov's critics in this case—but I cannot generate much personal passion over this relatively minor issue.

In another example, Boyd praises Nabokov's methods: "Nabokov's mode of presentation was ahead of his time. Instead of showing a photograph of a single specimen of a butterfly species or a diagram of the genitalia of a single specimen, he presented when necessary a range of specimens of certain subspecies in nine pages of crowded plates" (TAY p. 128). Here I side entirely with Nabokov and his proper recognition of natural history's primary subject matter: variation and diversity at all levels. But Nabokov was not being either unique or unusually progressive in illustrating multiple specimens (I rather suspect that his decision reflected his fussy and meticulous thoroughness more than any innovative theoretical vision about the nature of variation). This issue has provoked a long history of discussion and varying practice in taxonomy—and many other specialists have stood with Nabokov on the right side (as I would say) of this question.

2. *The myth of courage.* As an adjunct (or intensification) to claims for innovation, many literary critics have identified Nabokov as theoretically courageous (and forward looking) in his expressed doubts about Darwinian orthodoxies, particularly on the subject of adaptive value for patterns of mimicry in butterfly wings.

In this context, a remarkable passage from *Speak, Memory* has often been cited. Nabokov apparently wrote, but never published, an extensive scientific article in an attempt to refute natural selection as the cause of mimicry by denying the purely adaptive value of each component of resemblance (see Charles Lee Remington, "Lepidoptera studies," page 282). (Darwinians have assumed that mimicry—the evolution in one butterfly species of striking resemblance, usually in color patterns of the wings, to another unrelated form – arises for adaptive benefit, usually for permitting a "tasty" species to gain protection by simulating a noxious species that predators have learned to avoid). This paper has been lost, except for the following fragment that Nabokov included in *Speak, Memory*:

"Natural selection," in the Darwinian sense, could not explain the miraculous coincidence of imitative aspect and imitative behavior, nor could one appeal to the theory of "the struggle for life" when a protective device was carried to a point of mimetic subtlety, exuberance, and luxury far in excess of a predator's power of appreciation. I discovered in nature the nonutilitarian delights that I sought in art. Both were a form of magic, both were a game of intricate enchantment and deception.

An understandable prejudice of intellectual life leads us to view tilters at orthodoxy as courageous front-line innovators. Nonetheless, one may also attack a common view for opposite reasons of conservative allegiance to formerly favored ideas. On Nabokov's forcefully expressed doubts about Darwinian interpretations of mimicry, two observations identify his stance as more traditionally conservative than personally innovative or particularly courageous. First, when Nabokov wrote his technical papers in the 1940s, the modern Darwinian orthodoxy had not yet congealed, and a Nabokovian style of doubt remained quite common among evolutionary biologists, particularly among taxonomists immersed in the study of anatomical detail and geographic variation (see Robson and Richards for the classic statement; see Gould and Provine for documentation that a hardline Darwinian orthodoxy only coalesced later in the 1950s and '60s. Thus, Nabokov's views on mimicry represent a common attitude among biologists in his time, a perspective linked more to earlier consensuses about non-Darwinian evolution than to legitimate modern challenges. (I am, by the way and for my sins, well recognized, and often reviled, for my own doubts about Darwinian orthodoxies, so I do not make this judgment of

Nabokov while acting as *defensor fidei*).

Second—although we must always struggle to avoid the primary error of historiography (the anachronistic use of later conclusions to judge the cogency of an earlier claim) in assessing Nabokov's views on mimicry—it remains fair to note that Nabokov's convictions on this subject have not withstood the standard scientific test of time (*veritas filia temporis*, to cite Bacon once again). The closing words of a world's expert on the evolutionary biology of butterflies, and a firm admirer of Nabokov's science, may be cited here. My colleague Charles Lee Remington writes:

Impressive though the intellectual arguments are... it would be unreasonable to take them very seriously in science today. Mimicry and other aspects of adaptive coloration and shape involve such superb and elaborate resemblances that various biologists had questioned the Darwinian explanations during the early decades of this century. Subsequent publication of so many elegant experimental tests of mimicry and predator learning... and color-pattern genetics... has caused the collapse of the basic challenges, in my view as a specialist in the field. However, I do guess that Nabokov had such a strong metaphysical investment in his challenge to natural selection that he might have rejected the evolutionary conclusions for his own satisfaction. He was an excellent naturalist and could cite for himself very many examples of perfect resemblances, but he may have been too untrained in the complexities of modern population genetics. (p. 282)

Finally, I must also note that several other prime components of Nabokov's biological work would now be viewed as superseded rather than prescient, and would also be judged as a bit antiquated in their own time rather than innovative or even idiosyncratic. In particular, as a practical taxonomist, Nabokov advocated a definition of species based only on characters preserved in specimens of museum collections. Today (and, for the most part, in Nabokov's time as well), most evolutionary biologists would strongly insist that species be recognized as "real" and discrete populations in nature, not as units defined by identifiable traits in artificially limited data of human collections. Many species owe their distinction to genetic and behavioral features that maintain the cohesion of a population in nature, but may not be preserved in museum specimens. Nonetheless, Nabokov explicitly denied that such populations should be recognized as species—a view that almost all naturalists would now reject. Nabokov wrote in one of his technical papers: "For better or worse our present notions of species in Lepidoptera is based solely on the checkable structure of dead specimens, and if Forster's Furry cannot be distinguished from the Furry Blue except by its chromosome number, Forster's Furry must be scrapped" (cited in Zimmer p. 15).

3. *The myth of artistry.* Nabokov made many drawings of butterflies, both published, and as charming, often fanciful, illustrations in copies of his books presented to friends and relatives, especially to his wife Véra. These drawings are lovely, and often quite moving in their sharp outlines and naïve brightnesses—but, putting the matter diplomatically, the claim (sometimes made) that these drawings are either unusual in their accuracy or special in their beauty can only be seen as kindly hagiographical, especially in the light of a truly great tradition for wonderful and sensitive art among the best natural history illustrators, from Maria Merian to Edward Lear (who wrote limericks as a hobby, but worked as a skilled illustrator for a profession).

4. *The myth of literary quality.* Some critics, recognizing the merely conventional nature of Nabokov's excellence in taxonomy, have stated that, at least, he wrote his non-innovative descriptions in the most beautifully literate prose ever composed within the profession. Zaleski, for example, extols Nabokov for writing, in technical papers, "what is surely the most polished prose even applied to butterfly studies" (p. 36).

Again, such judgments can only be subjective—but I have spent a career reading technical papers in this mode, while applying at least a serious amateur's eye to literary style and quality. Nabokov's descriptive prose flows well enough, but I find nothing distinctive in his contributions to this highly restricted genre, where rules and conventions of spare and "objective" writing offer so little opportunity to spread one's literary wings.

B) *The Argument for Literary Illumination*

Once we debunk, for Nabokov's case, two false solutions to the paradox of intellectual promiscuity—the argument, refuted in section one, that his lepidoptery represented a harmless private passion, robbing no substantial time from his literary output; and the claim, rejected in the first part of this section, that his general genius at least made his lepidoptery as distinctive and as worthy as his literature—only one potential source for conventional solace remains: the proposition that, although time spent on lepidoptery almost surely decreased his literary output, the specific knowledge and the philosophical view of life that Nabokov gained from his scientific career directly forged (or at least strongly contributed to) his unique literary style and excellence.

We can cite several important precedents for such a claim. Jan Swammerdam, the greatest entomologist of the 17th century, devoted the last part of his life to evangelical Christianity, claiming that a fundamental entomological metaphor had directed his developing religious views: the life cycle of a butterfly as an emblem for the odyssey of a Christian soul, with the caterpillar (larva) representing our bodily life on earth, the pupa denoting the period of the soul's waiting after bodily death, and the butterfly marking the glorious resurrection.

In another example, one that would be viewed as more fruitful by most contemporary readers, Alfred Kinsey spent 20 years working as an entomologist on the taxonomy of the gall-wasp *Cynips* before turning to the surveys of human sexual behavior that would mark his notoriety as a pivotal figure in the social history of the 20th century. In a detailed preface to his first great treatise on *Sexual Behavior in the Human Male* (1948), Kinsey explained how a perspective gained from insect taxonomy upon the nature of populations – particularly the copious variation among individuals, and the impossibility of marking one form as normal and the others as deviant – had directly informed and inspired his research on sexual behavior. He wrote:

The techniques of this research have been taxonomic, in the sense in which modern biologists employ the term. It was born out of the senior author's long-time experience with a problem in insect taxonomy. The transfer from insect to human material is not illogical, for it has been a transfer of a method that may be applied to the study of any variable population.

We know that Nabokov made continual and copious reference to entomological subjects, particularly to butterflies, in all his literary productions – in passages ranging from the minutely explicit, to the vaguely cryptical, to the broadly general. Several scholars have tabulated and annotated this rich bounty (I have relied on Zimmer's most recent and most thorough account in writing this essay). Nabokov's critics could therefore scarcely avoid the potential hypothesis, especially given the precedents of Swammerdam and Kinsey, that Nabokov's lepidoptery shaped his literature in direct and crucial ways.

Literary scholars have often ventured such a claim, particularly by asserting that Nabokov used his knowledge of insects as a rich source for metaphors and symbols. In the strongest version, most, if not nearly all, citations of butterflies convey a level of deep symbolic meaning in Nabokov's prose. For example, Joann Karges wrote in her book on Nabokov's Lepidoptera: "Many of Nabokov's butterflies, particularly pale and white ones, carry the traditional ageless symbol of the anima, psyche, or soul . . . and suggest the evanescence of a spirit departed or departing from the body" (cited in Zimmer p. 8).

Two arguments, one a specific denial of this search for symbolism, and the other a more general statement about art and science, strongly refute this last hope for the usual form of literary solace in Nabokov's dedication to science – a claim that the extensive time thus spent strongly improved Nabokov's novels. For the first (quite conclusive and specific) argument, Nabokov himself vehemently insisted that he not only maintained no interest in butterflies as primary symbols, but that he would also regard such usage as a perversion and desecration of his true concerns. (Artists, and all of us of course, have been known to dissemble, but I see no reason to gainsay Nabokov's explicit and heartfelt comments on this subject.) For example, he stated in an interview: "That in some cases the butterfly symbolizes something (e.g. *Psyche*) lies utterly outside my area of interest" (quoted in Zimmer p. 8).

Over and over again, Nabokov debunks symbolic readings in the name of respect for factual accuracy as a primary criterion. For example, he criticizes Poe's symbolic invocation of the death's-head moth because Poe didn't describe the animal and, even worse, because he placed the species outside its true geographic range: "Not only did he [Poe] not visualize the death's-head moth, but he was also under the completely erroneous impression that it occurs in America" (quoted in Zimmer p. 186). Most tellingly, in a typical Nabokovian passage in *Ada*, he playfully excoriates Hieronymous Bosch for including a butterfly as a symbol in his *Garden of Earthly Delights*, but then depicting the wings in reverse by painting the gaudy top surface on an insect whose folded wings should be displaying the underside!

A tortoiseshell in the middle panel, placed there as if settled on a flower – mark the 'as if,' for here we have an example of exact knowledge of the two admirable girls, because they say that actually the *wrong* side of the bug is shown, it should have been the underside, if seen, as it is, in profile, but Bosch evidently found a wing or two in the corner cobweb of his casement and showed the prettier upper surface in depicting his incorrectly folded insect. I mean I don't give a hoot for the esoteric meaning, for the myth behind the moth, for the masterpiece-baiter who makes Bosch express some bosh of his time, I'm allergic to allegory.

Finally, when Nabokov does cite a butterfly in the midst of a metaphor, he attributes no symbolic meaning to the insect, but only describes an accurate fact to carry his more general image. For example, he writes in *Mary*: "Their letters managed to pass across the terrible Russia of that time—like a cabbage white butterfly flying over the trenches" (cited in Zimmer, p. 161).

Second, and more generally, if we wish to argue that Nabokov's lepidoptery gave direct substance, or set the style, of his literature, then we must face a counterclaim—for the best case of explicit linkage led Nabokov into serious error. (And I surely will not propagate the smug scientist's philistine canard that literary folks should stick to their lasts and leave us alone because they always screw up our world with their airy-fairy pretensions and insouciance about accuracy.) If I wanted to advance a case for direct linkage, I would have to emphasize a transfer from Nabokov's artistic vision to his science, not *vice versa*—unfortunately, in this instance, to the detriment of natural history. Nabokov frequently stated that his non-Darwinian interpretation of mimicry flowed directly from his literary attitude—as he tried to find in nature "the nonutilitarian delights that I sought in art" (see page 94 for a fuller citation of this passage). And, as argued previously, this claim represents the most serious general error in Nabokov's scientific writing.

III The Solution of Accuracy

In standard scientific practice, when tests of a favored hypothesis have failed, and one is beating one's head against a proverbial wall, the best strategy for reclaiming a fruitful path must lie in the empirical record, particularly in scrutinizing basic data for hints of a pattern that might lead to a different hypothesis. In Nabokov's case, both his explicit statements and his striking consistency of literary usage build such a record and point clearly to an alternative solution. The theme has not been missed by previous critics, for one can hardly fail to acknowledge something that Nabokov emphasized so forcefully. But I feel that most published commentary on Nabokov's lepidoptery has failed to grasp the centrality of this argument as a primary theme for understanding Nabokov's own concept of the relationship between his literary and scientific work – primarily, I suppose, because we have been befogged by a set of stereotypes about conflict and difference between these two great domains of human understanding.

Conventional solutions fail because they have focussed on too specific a level – that is, to the search for how one domain, usually science in this case, impacted the other. But the basic source of relationship may be hiding at a deeper level (deeper, that is, in a geometric sense, not in any claim about morality or greater importance). Perhaps the major linkage lies in some distinctive, *underlying* approach that Nabokov applied *equally* to both science and literature – a procedure that conferred the same special features upon his efforts in both domains. In this case, we should not posit a primary and directional impact of one domain upon the other. Rather, we should investigate the hypothesis that Nabokov's art and science both benefited, in like measure, from his application of a method, or a mode of mental functioning that exemplifies the basic character of his particular genius.

All natural historians know that "replication with difference" builds the best test case for a generality – for how can we prove a coordinating hypothesis unless we can apply it to multiple cases, and how can we be confident in our conclusion unless these cases be sufficiently different in subject matter to demonstrate that any underlying commonality must lie in a single mental approach applied to disparate material? Among great 20th-century thinkers, I know no better case than Nabokov's for testing the hypothesis that an underlying unity of mental style (at a level clearly meriting the accolade of genius) can explain one man's success in extensive and fully professional work in two disciplines conventionally viewed as maximally different, if not truly opposed. If we can validate this model for attributing interdisciplinary success to a coordinating and underlying mental uniqueness, rather than invoking the conventional argument about overt influence of one field upon another, then Nabokov's story may teach us something important about the unity of creativity and the falsity (or at least the contingency) of our traditional separation, usually in mutual recrimination, of art from science.

Above all else—and why we should not take him at his word?—Nabokov vociferously insisted that he cherished meticulous accuracy in detail as the defining feature of all his productions (as illustrated in the passage quoted on pages 99–100 from *Ada*). All commentators have noted these Nabokovian claims (for one could hardly fail to mention something stated so frequently and forcefully by one's principal subject). Previous critics have also recognized that a commitment to detailed accuracy not only defines Nabokov's maximally rich and meticulously careful prose, but might also be greatly valued for professional work in the description of butterfly species. Unfortunately, however, most commentary then follows a lamentable stereotype about science (particularly for such "low status" fields as descriptive natural history), and assumes that Nabokov's commitment to accuracy must have imposed opposite qualities upon his work in these two professions—thus, and again lamentably, reinforcing the conventional distinction of art and science as utterly different and generally opposed. Such detail, we are told, enriches Nabokov's literature, but also brands his science as pedestrian, unimaginative and "merely" descriptive (as in the cliché about folks who never see forests because they only focus on distinctive features of individual trees). The stereotype of the taxonomist as a narrow-minded, bench-bound pedant then reconfirms this judgment. Zaleski, for example, sums up his article on Nabokov's lepidoptery by writing:

In both books and butterflies, Nabokov sought ecstasy, and something beyond. He found it in the worship of detail, in the loving articulation of organic flesh and organized metaphor . . . He was perfectly suited as a master novelist and a laboratory drudge. (p. 38)

Zaleski reports that Nabokov importuned his Cornell students with a primary motto: "Caress the details, the divine details." "In high art and pure science," he stated, "detail is everything" (ibid.). Indeed, Nabokov often praised the gorgeous detail of meticulous taxonomic language as inherently literary in itself, speaking of "the precision of poetry in taxonomic description" (quoted in Zimmer, p. 176). He also, of course, extolled precision in anatomical description for its scientific virtue. He wrote a letter to Pyke Johnson in 1959, commenting upon a proposed jacket design for his *Poems* (cited in Remington p. 275):

I like the two colored butterflies on the jacket but they have the bodies of ants, and no stylization can excuse a simple mistake. To stylize adequately one must have complete knowledge of the thing. I would be the laughing stock of my entomological colleagues if they happened to see these impossible hybrids.

In reading through all Nabokov's butterfly references (in his literary works) as preparation for writing this essay, I was struck most of all by his passion for accuracy in every detail of anatomy, behavior or location. Even his poetical or metaphorical descriptions capture a common visual impression – as when he writes in "The Aurelian," a story from 1930, about "an oleander hawk [moth] . . . its wings vibrating so rapidly that nothing but a ghostly nimbus was visible about its streamlined body." Even his occasional fantasies and in-jokes, accessible only to a few initiates (or readers of such study guides as

Zimmer's) build upon a strictly factual substrate. For example, Nabokov thought he had discovered a new species of butterfly during his Russian boyhood. He wrote a description in English and sent it to a British entomologist for publication. But the English scientist discovered that Nabokov's species had already been named in 1862 by a German amateur collector named Kretschmar, in an obscure publication. So Nabokov bided his time and finally chose a humorous form of revenge in his novel *Laughter in the Dark*: "Many years later, by a pretty fluke (I know I should not point out these plums to people), I got even with the first discoverer of my moth by giving his own name to a blind man in a novel" (quoted in Zimmer page 141). Literary critics sometimes chided Nabokov for his obsessive attention to detail. Nabokov, in true form, described these attacks with a witty (and somewhat cryptic) taxonomic reference—speaking in *Strong Opinions* of detractors "accusing me of being more interested in the subspecies and the subgenus than in the genus and the family" (quoted in Zimmer page 175). (Subspecies and subgenera represent categories for fine subdivision of species and genera. The rules of nomenclature recognize these categories as available for convenience, but not required in practice. That is, species need not be divided into subspecies, nor genera into subgenera. But genera and families represent basic and more inclusive divisions that must be assigned to all creatures. That is, each species must belong to a genus, and each genus to a family.)

Nabokov generalized his defense of meticulous detail beyond natural history and literature to all intellectual concerns. In a 1969 interview, he scornfully dismissed critics who branded such insistence upon (and provision of) detail as a form of pedantry: "I do not understand how one can label the knowledge of natural objects or the vocabulary of nature as pedantry" (my translation from Nabokov's French, as cited in Zimmer page 7). In annotating his personal copy of the French translation of *Ada*, Nabokov listed the three unbreakable rules for a good translator: intimate knowledge of the language from which one translates, experience as a writer of the language into which one translates, and the third great dictate of detail: "that one knows, in both languages, the words designating concrete objects (natural and cultural, the flower and the clothing)" (my translation from Nabokov's French original, cited in Zimmer page 5).

Zimmer epitomizes the central feature of Nabokov's butterfly citations: "They are all real butterflies, including the invented ones which are mimics of real ones. And they usually are not just butterflies in general, but precisely the ones that would occur at that particular spot, behaving exactly the way they really would. Thus they underscore, or rather help constitute, the veracity of a descriptive passage" (page 8). In an insightful statement, he generalizes this biological usage to an overarching Nabokovian principle with both aesthetic and moral components:

Both the writer of fiction and the naturalist drew on a profound delight in precise comparative observation. For Nabokov, a work of nature was like a work of art. Or rather it *was* a profound work of art, by the greatest of all living artists, evolution, and as much a joy to the mind and a challenge to the intellect as a Shakespeare sonnet. Hence it deserved to be studied like it, with never ending attention to detail and patience. (page 7)

But perhaps the best summary of Nabokov's convictions about the ultimate value of accurate detail can be found in "A Discovery," a short poem written in 1943:

> Dark pictures, thrones, the stones that pilgrims kiss
> Poems that take a thousand years to die
> But ape the immortality of this
> Red label on a little butterfly.

(Again, some taxonomic exegesis must be provided to wrest general understanding from the somewhat élitist—scarcely surprising given his social background—and not always user-friendly Nabokov. Museum curators traditionally affix red labels only to "holotype" specimens—that is to individuals chosen as official recipients of the name given to a new species. The necessity for such a rule arises from a common situation in taxonomic research. A later scientist may discover that the original namer of a species defined the group too broadly by including specimens from more than one genuine species. Which specimens shall then keep the original name, and which shall be separated out to receive a separate designation for the newly-recognized species? By official rules, the species of the designated holotype specimen keeps the original name, and members of the newly-recognized species must receive a new name. Thus, Nabokov tells us that no product of human cultural construction can match the immortality of the permanent name-bearer for a genuine species in nature. The species may become extinct of course, but the name continues forever to designate a genuine natural population that once inhabited the earth. The holotype specimen therefore becomes our best example of an immortal physical object.)

Nabokov's two apparently disparate careers therefore find their common ground on the most distinctive feature of his unusual intellect and uncanny skill—the almost obsessive attention to meticulous and accurate detail that served both his literary productions and his taxonomic descriptions so well, and that defined his uncompromising commitment to factuality as both a principle of morality and a guarantor and primary guide to aesthetic quality. Science and literature therefore gain their union on the most palpable territory of concrete things, and on the value we attribute to accuracy, even in smallest details, as a guide and an anchor for our lives, our loves, and our senses of worth.

This attitude expresses a general belief and practice in science (at least as an ideal, admittedly not always achieved due to human frailty). Of all scientific subfields, none raises the importance of intricate detail to such a plateau of importance as Nabokov's chosen profession of taxonomic description for small and complex organisms. To function as a competent professional in the systematics of Lepidoptera, Nabokov really had no choice but to embrace such attention to detail, and to develop such respect for nature's endless variety.

But this attitude to detail and accuracy carries no ineluctable status in literature – so Nabokov's unaltered skills and temperament, now applied to his second profession, conferred distinction, if not uniqueness, upon him. The universal and defining excellence of a professional taxonomist built a substrate for the uncommon, and (in Nabokov's case) transcendent, excellence of a writer. After all, the sheer glory of voluminous detail does not ignite everyone's muse in literature. Some folks can't stand to read every meandering and choppy mental detail of one day in the life of Leopold Bloom, but others consider *Ulysses* the greatest novel of the 20th century. I ally myself with the second group. I also love *Parsifal* – and the writing of Vladimir Nabokov. I have always been a taxonomist at heart. Nothing matches the holiness and fascination of accurate and intricate detail. How can you appreciate a castle if you don't cherish all the building blocks, and don't understand the blood, toil, sweat and tears underlying its construction?[1]

I could not agree more with Nabokov's emphasis upon the aesthetic and moral – not only the practical and factual – value of accuracy and authenticity in intricate detail. This sensation, this love, may not stir all people so ardently (for *Homo sapiens*, as all taxonomists understand so well, is nothing if not a highly variable entity). But such a basic aesthetic, if not

1. Incidentally, Nabokov represented an intractable mystery to me until I learned that he grew up trilingual in Russian, English, and French – a common situation among the Russian upper classes in his day. Even as a teenager reading *Lolita*, I couldn't understand how anyone who learned English as a second tongue could become such a master of linguistic detail. Indeed, one cannot. Conrad narrated wonderful stories, but could never play with his adopted language as Nabokov did with one of his native tongues.

consensual, surely animates a high percentage of humanity, and must evoke something very deep in our social and evolutionary heritage. May I mention just one true anecdote to represent this general argument. The head of the National Air and Space Museum in Washington, DC once hosted a group of blind visitors to discuss how exhibits might be made more accessible to their community. In this museum the greatest airplanes of our history—including the Wright Brothers' biplane from Kitty Hawk and Lindbergh's Spirit of St. Louis— hang from the ceiling, entirely outside the perception of blind visitors. The director apologized, and explained that no other space could be found for such large objects, but then asked his visitors whether a scale model of the Spirit of St. Louis, made available for touch, would be helpful. The blind visitors caucused and returned with their wonderful answer: yes, they responded, we would appreciate such a model, but it must be placed directly under the unperceptible original. If the aesthetic and moral value of genuine objects can stir us so profoundly that we insist upon their presence even when we can have no palpable evidence, but only the assurance that we stand in the aura of reality, then factual authenticity cannot be gainsaid as a fundamental desideratum of the human soul.

This difficult and toughminded theme must be emphasized in literature (as the élitist and uncompromising Nabokov understood so well), particularly to younger students of the present generation, because an ancient, and basically antiintellectual, current in the creative arts has now begun to flow more strongly than ever before in recent memory—the tempting Siren song of a claim that the spirit of human creativity stands in direct opposition to the rigor in education and observation that breeds both our love for factual detail and our gain of sufficient knowledge and understanding to utilize this record of human achievement and natural wonder.

No more harmful nonsense exists than this supposition that deepest insight into great questions about the meaning of life or the structure of reality emerges most readily from a free, undisciplined, and uncluttered (read, rather, ignorant and uneducated) mind soaring above mere earthly knowledge and concern. The primary reason for emphasizing the supreme aesthetic and moral value of detailed factual accuracy, as Nabokov understood so well, lies in our need to combat this alluring brand of philistinism if we wish to maintain artistic excellence as both a craft and an inspiration. (Anyone who thinks that success in revolutionary innovation can arise *sui generis*, without apprenticeship for basic skills and education for understanding, should visit the first (chronological) room of the Turner annex at the Tate Gallery in London—to see the early products of Turner's extensive education in tools of classical perspective and representation, the necessary skills that he had to master before moving far beyond into a world of personal innovation.)

This Nabokovian argument for a strictly *positive* correlation (as opposed to the usual philistine claim for negative opposition) between extensive training and potential for creative innovation may be more familiar to scientists than to creative artists. But this crucial key to professional achievement must be actively promoted within science as well. Among less thoughtful scientists, we often encounter a different version of the phoney argument for dissociation of attention to detail and capacity for creativity—the fallacy embedded in Zaleski's statement (cited on page 103) that Nabokov's obsessive love of detail made him a "laboratory drudge," even while opening prospects of greatness in literature.

The false (and unstated) view of mind that must lie behind this assertion—and that most supporters of the argument would reject if their unconscious allegiance were made explicit—assumes a fixed and limited amount of mental "stuff" for each intellect. Thus, if we assign too much of our total allotment to the mastery of detail, we will have nothing left for general theory and integrative wonder. But such a silly model of mental functioning can only arise from a false metaphorical comparison of human creativity with irrelevant systems based on fixed and filled containers—pennies in a piggy bank or cookies in a jar.

Many of the most brilliant and revolutionary theoreticians in the history of science have also been meticulous compilers of detailed evidence. Darwin developed his theory of natural selection in 1838, but prevailed because, when he finally published in 1859, he had also amassed the first credible factual compendium (overwhelming in thoroughness and diversity) for the evolutionary basis of life's history. (All previous evolutionary systems, including Lamarck's, had been based on speculation, however cogent and complex the theoretical basis.) Many key discoveries emerged and prevailed because great theoreticians respected empirical details ignored by others. In the most familiar example, Kepler established the ellipticity of planetary orbits when he realized that Tycho Brahe's data yielded tiny discrepancies from circularity that most astronomers would have disregarded as "close enough"— whereas Kepler knew that he could trust the accuracy of Tycho's observations.

I do not deny that some scientists see trees but not forests, thereby functioning as trustworthy experts of meticulous detail, but showing little interest or skill in handling more general, theoretical questions. I also do not deny that Nabokov's work on butterfly systematics falls under this rubric. But I strenuously reject the argument that Nabokov's attention to descriptive particulars, or his cherishing of intricate factuality, precluded strength in theory on principle. I do not understand Nabokov's psyche or his ontogeny well enough to speculate about his conservative approach to theoretical questions, or his disinclination to grapple with general issues in evolutionary biology. We can only, I suspect, intone some clichés about the world's breadth (including the domain of science), and about the legitimate places contained therein for people with widely divergent sets of skills.

I therefore strongly reject any attempt to characterize Nabokov as a laboratory drudge for his love of detail and his lack of attention to theoretical issues. The science of taxonomy has always honored, without condescension, professionals who develop Nabokov's dedication to the details of a particular group, and who establish the skills and "good eye" to forge order from nature's mire of confusing particulars. Yes, to be frank, if Nabokov had pursued only butterfly taxonomy as a complete career, he would now be highly respected in very limited professional circles, but not at all renowned in the world at large. But do we not honor the dedicated professional who achieves maximal excellence in an admittedly restricted domain of notoriety or power? After all, if Macbeth had been content to remain Thane of Cawdor–a perfectly respectable job–think of the lives and grief that would thus have been spared. But, of course, we would then have to lament a lost play. So let us celebrate Nabokov's excellence in natural history , and let us also rejoice that he could use the same mental skills and inclinations to follow another form of bliss.

IV An Epilog on Science and Literature

Most generously minded intellectuals (that is, I trust, most of us) favor a dialogue between professionals in science and the arts. But we also assume that these two subjects stand as polar opposites in the domain of learning, and that diplomatic contact for understanding between adversaries forms the major rationale for such a dialogue. At best, we hope to dissipate stereotypes and to become friends (or at least neutrals), able to put aside our genuine differences for temporary bonding in the practical service of a few broader issues demanding joint action by all educated folk.

A set of stereotypes still rules perceptions of "otherness" in these two domains–images based on little more than ignorance and parochial fear, but powerful nonetheless. Scientists are soulless dial-twirlers; artists are arrogant, illogical self-absorbed blowhards. Dialogue remains a good idea, but the two fields, and the personalities attracted to them, are truly and deeply different.

I do not wish to forge a false union in an artificial love feast. The two domains differ, truly and distinctly, in their chosen subject matter and established modes of validation. The magisterium (teaching authority) of science extends over the factual status of the natural world, and to the development of theories proposed to explain why these facts, and not others, characterize our universe. The magisteria of the arts and humanities treat ethical and aesthetic questions about morality, style and beauty. Since the facts of nature cannot, in logic or principle, yield ethical or aesthetic conclusions, the domains must remain formally distinct on these criteria.

But many of us who labor in both domains (if only as an amateur in one) strongly feel that an overarching mental unity builds a deeper similarity than disparate subject matter can divide. Human creativity seems to work much as a coordinated and complex piece, whatever the different emphases demanded by disparate subjects—and we will miss the underlying commonality if we only stress the distinctions of external subjects and ignore the unities of internal procedure. If we do not recognize the common concerns and characteristics of all creative human activity, we will fail to grasp several important aspects of intellectual excellence—including the necessary interplay of imagination and observation (theory and empirics) as an intellectual theme, and the confluence of beauty and factuality as a psychological theme—because one field or the other traditionally downplays one side of a requisite duality.

Moreover, as argued previously (see page 101), we must use the method of "replication with difference" if we wish to study and understand the human quintessence behind our varying activities. I cannot imagine a better test case for extracting the universals of human creativity than the study of deep similarities in intellectual procedure between the arts and sciences.

No one grasped the extent of this underlying unity better than Vladimir Nabokov, who worked with different excellences as a complete professional in both domains. Nabokov often insisted that his literary and entomological pursuits shared a common mental and psychological ground. In *Ada*, while invoking a common anagram for "insect," one of Nabokov's characters beautifully expresses the oneness of creative impulse and the pervasive beauty of chosen subject matter: "'If I could write,' mused Demon, 'I would describe, in too many words no doubt, how passionately, how incandescently, how incestuously – *c'est le mot* – art and science meet in an insect.'"

Returning to his central theme of aesthetic beauty in both the external existence and our internal knowledge of scientific detail, Nabokov wrote in 1959: "I cannot separate the aesthetic pleasure of seeing a butterfly and the scientific pleasure of knowing what it is" (quoted in Zimmer page 33). When Nabokov spoke of "the precision of poetry in taxonomic description" – no doubt with conscious intent to dissipate a paradox that leads most people to regard art and science as inexorably distinct and opposed – he used his literary skills in the service of generosity (a high, if underappreciated, virtue underlying all attempts to unify warring camps). He thus sought to explicate the common ground of his two professional worlds, and to illustrate the inevitably paired components of any integrated view that could merit the label of our oldest and fondest dream of fulfillment – the biblical ideal of "wisdom." Thus, in a 1966 interview, Nabokov broke the boundaries of art and science by stating that the most precious desideratum of each domain must also characterize any excellence in the other – for, after all, truth is beauty, and beauty

[113]

truth. I could not devise a more fitting title for this essay, and I can imagine no better ending for this text:

The tactile delights of precise delineation, the silent paradise of the *camera lucida*, and the precision of poetry in taxonomic description represent the artistic side of the thrill which accumulation of new knowledge, absolutely useless to the layman, gives its first begetter . . . There is no science without fancy, and no art without facts.

Stephen Jay Gould
Museum of Comparative Zoology
Harvard University
Cambridge, MA

for Véra

ℙ𝕍

Adorata adorata

from P

Jan. 5, 1970

Montreux

Papers on Lepidoptera

1952

8 August

The Lepidopterists' News

One   6 (1-3)   279^35

1952

THE FEMALE OF *LYCAEIDES ARGYROGNOMON SUBLIVENS* ✱

by V. Nabokov

Last summer (1951) I decided to visit Telluride, San Miguel County, Colorado, in order to search for the unknown female of what I had described as *Lycaeides argyrognomon sublivens* in 1949 (*Bull. Mus. Comp. Zool.*, vol. 101: p. 513) on the strength of nine males in the Museum of Comparative Zoology, Harvard, which had been taken in the vicinity of Telluride half a century ago. *L. sublivens* is an isolated southern representative (the only known one south of northwestern Wyoming, southeast of Idaho, and east of California) of the species (the holarctic *argyrognomon* Bergstr.= *idas auct.*) to which *anna* Edw., *scudderi* Edw., *aster* Edw. and six other nearctic subspecies belong. I bungled my family's vacation but got what I wanted.

Owing to rains and floods, especially noticeable in Kansas, most of the drive from New York State to Colorado was entomologically uneventful. When reached at last, Telluride turned out to be a damp, unfrequented but very spectacular cul-de-sac (which a prodigious rainbow straddled every evening) at the end of two converging roads, one from Placerville, the other from Dolores, both atrocious. There is one motel, the optimistic and excellent Valley View Court where I stayed, at 9,000 feet altitude, from the 3rd to the 29th of July, walking up daily to at least 12,000 feet along various more or less steep trails in search of *sublivens*. Once or twice Mr. Homer Reid of Telluride took *us* me up in his jeep. Every morning the sky would be of an impeccable blue at 6 a.m. when I set out. The first innocent cloudlet would scud across at 7:30 a.m. Bigger fellows with darker bellies would start tampering with the sun around 9 a.m., just as I emerged from the shadow of the cliffs and trees onto good hunting grounds. Everything would be cold and gloomy half an hour later. At around 10 a.m. there would come the daily electric storm, in several installments, accompanied by the most irritatingly close lightning I have ever encountered anywhere in the Rockies, not excepting Longs Peak, which is saying a good deal, and followed by cloudy and rainy weather through the rest of the day.

After ten days of this, and despite diligent subsequent exploration, only one sparse colony of *sublivens* was found. On that one spot a few males were emerging on the 15th. Three days later I had the pleasure of discovering the unusual-looking female. Between the 15th and the 28th, a dozen hours of windy but passable collecting weather in all (not counting the hours and hours uselessly spent in mist and rain) yielded only 54 specimens, of which 16 were females. Had I been younger and weighed less, I might have perhaps got another 50, but hardly much more than that, and, possibly, the higher ridges I vainly investigated between 12,000 and 14,000 feet at the end of July, in the *magdalena-snowi-centaureae* zone, might have produced *sublivens* later in the season.

The colony I found was restricted to one very steep slope reaching from about 10,500 to a ridge at 11,000 feet and towering over Tomboy Road between "Social Tunnel" and "Bullion Mine". The slope was densely covered with a fine growth of lupines in flower (*Lupinus parviflorus* Nuttall, which did not occur elsewhere along the trail) and green gentians (the tall turrets of which were assiduously patronized by the Broad-Tailed Hummingbird and the White-

✱ Now known as *Plebejus* (*Lycaeides*) *idas sublivens* or *Lycaeides sublivens* Nab.; it has too dubbed "Nabokov's Blue" by F. Martin Brown (1955)

NO. 41

41 **Lepidopterological Papers** 1941–1953.

8vo.; 16 articles, 12 in self-wrappers bound together with several type-script leaves; tan cloth, morocco spine label stamped in gilt.

A unique compilation assembled by VN, comprised of 12 of his lepidopterological papers, excised or off-printed from various entomological journals, all recorded by Juliar; specially bound together with two clippings and a related typescript. A presentation copy, inscribed on the front endpaper: *For Véra/Montreux/Aug. 31, 1964*, with a diminutive butterfly sketched in blue ink and pencil.

VN selected these dozen papers from among his published writings on butterflies – 20 in all: the 18 identified by Juliar plus two collector's notes – and bound them for Véra in book form, paginating the leaves continuously and preparing a typescript table of contents leaf. The implication seems clear: he intended to publish a collection of his best lepidopterological writings (he has omitted five publications noted by Juliar). With numerous textual emendations throughout, adding clarifying notes and corrections. The typescript title page reads "Vladimir Nabokov/Lepidopterological Papers/1941–1953," and is followed by the typescript table of contents leaf. Included are four black and white photographs of butterfly specimens, one butterfly per shot (the holotype and paratype of *Lysandra cormion* Nabokov), and one photo with five butterflies which VN identified in an autograph chart. He noted the year of publication in red pencil at the top of several articles, presumably for his own reference, and added additional bibliographic information to others. That he determined that a book-length publication would not come to fruition in his lifetime is suggested by his inclusion of three of these articles – numbers 11, 12 and 14 below – in *Strong Opinions*, his selection of essays, interviews, and letters to editors published in 1973.

The articles included, most written under the auspices of his eight-year research fellowship at Harvard University's Museum of Comparative Zoology, where he was commissioned to organize their butterfly collection, are listed below in bibliographic order, along with their bibliographic citations. This varies slightly from the order VN mapped out in his book. All of these will be incorporated in *Nabokov's Butterflies: Unpublished and Uncollected Writings* (edited and annotated by Brian Boyd and Robert Michael Pyle. Boston: Beacon Press, 1999).

[1] "On Some Asiatic Species of *Carterocephalus*." Reprinted from *Journal of the New York Entomological Society*, Vol. XLIX, September, 1941, pages 221–223. Juliar AA3.1.

[2] "*Lysandra Cormion*, A New European Butterfly." Reprinted from *Journal Of The New York Entomological Society*, Vol. XLIX, September, 1941, pages 265–267. Juliar AA4.1. With two autograph notes cross-referencing other VN articles, and a note referencing the four plates bound-in on two leaves immediately preceding the offprint: *See figures: p. 5 Holotype, upper and under side; p. 7 paratype,...*

[3] "Some New or Little Known Nearctic *Neonympha*." Reprinted from *Psyche*, Vol. XLIX, Nos. 3–4. (1942), pp. [61]–80. Juliar AA5.1. With one spelling emendation, a cross-reference, and a note to *See figures p. 17.*

[4] "The Nearctic Forms of *Lycaeides* Hüb. (Lycaenidae, Lepidoptera)." Museum of Comparative Zoölogy. Reprinted from *Psyche*, Vol. 1, Nos. 3–4, [1943], pp. [87]–99. Juliar AA7.1. Docketed by VN, *Corrected*, with the publication information (*(1943) publ. March 6, 1944*), with four emendations to the text. A major publication; VN wrote to Edmund Wilson:

A summary of part of my scientific work on the Blues (the *Lycaeides* genus – "Silver studded Blues" in English) in which I correlate the nearctic and palaearctic representatives, is due to appear in a week or two. The labour involved has been immense; the number of my index cards exceeds a thousand references – for half a dozen (very polytpic species; I have dissected and drawn the genitalia of 360 specimens and unraveled taxonomic adventures that read like a novel. This has been a wonderful bit of training in the use of our (if I may say so) wise, precise, plastic, beautiful English language. (November 28, 1943, NWL p. 116)

[5] "Notes on the Morphology of the Genus *Lycaeides* (Lycaenidae, Lepidoptera)." Reprinted from *Psyche*, Vol. LI, Nos. 3–4 (1944), pp. [105]–138. Juliar AA8.1. Docketed by VN on the first leaf, *Corrected*, with the note *published Feb. 1945*. With four emendations to the text. VN wrote to Wilson of this article on October 11, 1944:

I have spent a month in arranging Part I of my butterfly work for publication and have had a good deal of trouble with the drawings. It goes to the printers to-day and the trees are green and rusty brown, stepwise, like gobelins. Enfin – c'est fait. It is going to remain a wonderful and indispensable thing for some 25 years, after which another fellow will show how wrong I was in this and that. Herein lies the difference between science and art. (NWL p. 143)

[6] "Notes on Neotropical *Plebejinae* (Lycaenidae, Lepidoptera)."

Reprinted from *Psyche*, Vol. 52, Nos. 1–2, pp. [1]–61. Juliar AA9.1, variant A. Docketed by VN, *Corrected*, with the publication date (October 26, 1945) and with notes and emendations to five pages derived from later research. By the time of this compilation, VN was able to answer his own fifteen-year-old query. In the printed text, he wrote: "Traces of a thin membrane (? Rudiments of sagum)"; in the margin he wrote: *yes*, and added his scientific findings. Before the end of the article, he added in the margins three species he had since discovered, and in other spots cross-references his more recent studies. On one page he changed a designation from "Pseudothecla n.g." to *Nabokovia Hemming*, offering a 1961 periodical citation. When he corrected or emended a species he would append the suffix "nab." to its existing designation, according to convention.

[7] "A Third Species of *Echinargus* Nabokov (Lycaenidae, Lepidoptera)." Museum of Comparative Zoölogy. Reprinted from *Psyche*, Vol. 52, Nos. 3–4. One leaf only, labeled by VN with a 1945 publication date. Juliar AA10.1.

[8] "A New Species of *Cyclargus* Nabokov (Lycaenidae, Lepidoptera)." Cornell University, Ithaca, N.Y. Reprinted from *The Entomologist*, Vol. LXXXI, December, 1948, pp. [275]–280. Printed by Adlard & Son, Limited, Bartholomew Press, Dorking. Juliar AA13.1.

[9] "The Nearctic Members of the genus *Lycaeides* Hüb. (Lycaenidae, Lepidoptera)." With nine plates. *Bulletin of the Museum of Comparative Zoölogy at Harvard College*, Vol. 101, No. 4, pp. [479]–541 plus nine plates. Cambridge, MA: Printed for the Museum, February, 1949. Juliar AA14.1. Signed in full by VN on the title page, with his initialed note on the cover, *corrected V.N.* and four minor emendations. VN's most significant lepidopteral study.

[10] *The Lepidopterists' News*, Vol. IV, Nos. 6–7, 1950, pp. 75–76, single leaf sliced in half horizontally. Juliar AA15.1. The page – labeled in his hand, *Omit* – prints his "Remarks on F. Martin Brown's 'Measurements and Lepidoptera,'" which continues to the verso, where Brown's "In Reply to Prof. Nabokov" is also printed. The page to which the clipping is affixed is also labeled *omit*.

[11] "The Female of *Lycaeides Agyrognomon Sublivens*." Excised from *The Lepidopterists' News*, Vol. 6, Nos. 1–3, [8 August] 1952, pp. 35–36. Juliar AA16.1. One of the shortest, most copiously emended articles included, with additions, corrections and notes to both pages. Republished in *Strong Opinions*.

[12] "On Some Inaccuracies in Klots' *Field Guide*." Reprinted from

The Lepidopterists' News, Vol. 6, Nos. 1–3. [August 8] 1952, p. 41. Juliar AA17.1. With a few formatting alterations and minor changes. VN's review of Klots's guide is excised from a newspaper and affixed to a leaf later in this collection. Included in *Strong Opinions.*

[13] "Butterfly Collecting in Wyoming, 1952." Excised from *The Lepidopterists' News*, Vol. 7, No. 2, [26 July] 1953, pp. 49–52. Juliar AA18.1. With a few emendations and formatting changes to the text, with the bibliographic citation added at the end.

[14] Typescript, 3 leaves, double spaced, lightly emended. A book review by VN on *Audubon's Butterflies, Moths And Other Studies* by Alice Ford (*New York Times Book Review* December 28, 1952). Juliar C527. Republished in *Strong Opinions.*

[15] Two leaves excised from the *Proc. Brit. Ent. Nat. Hist. Soc. Journal*, uncharacteristically undated by VN, with a passage marked in which he is mentioned. The paragraph sketches a communication sent to the journal from R. Rappaz, an entomologist who ran a café in Sion, and who questioned an article from a previous journal discussing hybrids. The editor writes:

Whether there are, as Rappaz thinks, no intermediates between the lowland and alpine forms of M. aurinia is still open to proof, and in this connection I quote from a personal letter which Vladimir Nabokov, who lives in Switzerland, wrote to me on 22nd August, 1965: "Just below Leukerbad, on its west side slope, in a tiny marsh at 1,350 m., in June 1963, near a steep meadow full of St. Bruno's lilies and mnemosyne males, I found a small colony of perfect intergrades between Euph. Aurinia and glaciegenita Verity (= 'merope')."

VN marked the margin of the paragraph in pencil, noting the quote from his own letter in red. With a newspaper clipping loosely inserted, dated *NY Time Mar 21 '75*: "Butterflies to Be First Insects on U. S. Endangered List."

42 Notes on the Morphology of the Genus *Lycaeides* (Lycaeinidae, Lepidoptera). Reprinted from *Psyche*, Vol. LI, Nos. 3–4, pp. 104–138. Cambridge, MA: Psyche, Journal of Entomology, (Sept.–Dec. 1944).

Slim 8vo.; printed wrappers, stapled.

Juliar C477. Inscribed on the cover in Russian: *Véra's copy.* On March 26, 1944, VN wrote to Edmund Wilson about this paper, then still in progress:

It has produced a tremendous stir in the butterfly-man world since it completely upsets the system of old conceptions. I am now busy preparing for publication my main work on this group, and as hundreds of drawings must be made, this takes a good deal of time. It will be a monograph of some 250 pages. The taxonomic part reads like a *roman d'aventures* because it involves terrific feuds between entomologist and all kinds of interesting psychological matters. In 1938 there were five (5) people in the whole world who knew anything of the particular group I am discussing: one of them is dead by now and another, an Alsatian, has vanished. So that's that. (NWL p. 131)

He replied: "Your butterfly paper is too technical for me to get out of it all that I am sure is there" (NWL p. 138).

43 The Real Life of Sebastian Knight. Norfolk, CT: New Directions, (1941).

8vo.; red burlap, white labels on spine and front cover printed in large print; a lovely copy.

First edition, issue A of VN's first English-language novel, bound in red burlap; 1500 copies, divided almost evenly between the two issues (749 in this binding, 751 in smooth red cloth). Advance copies – at least all that we have encountered – were bound in burlap. Variant labels, using different sizes of type, were made for the spine and front cover. It is likely that both bindings were issued with a dust-jacket, but evidence is inconclusive: Véra claimed that the first issue did not have a jacket; the publisher, James Laughlin, found the single-issue jacket scenario unlikely, and suspected both issues were jacketed, though no corroborating records survive. Juliar concludes: "If Mrs. Nabokov is correct and James Laughlin is not, then the only explanation for issues with dust jackets is that issue a books have been artificially married to issue b dust jackets. I am assuming this has not happened." Juliar A21.1. We concur: copies in the issue A binding regularly surface in trade with the jacket. The jacket exists in two states, with variant spellings of "Nabokov" – VN had an example of each in his library. As early as 1933 VN began to consider dropping his pseudonym: the first edition of *Camera Obscura* stated the copyright in English on the verso of the title page: "Copyright by V. Nabokoff-Sirin." Winifred Roy's English translation of *Camera Obscura* for Hutchinson was published under the same name, and VN's own translation in 1938, *Laughter in the Dark*, was by "Vladimir Nabokoff." It seems likely that by 1941 the confusion about which spelling was more desirable had reached an apex, resulting in two states of the dust-jacket.

A presentation copy, inscribed with one of several diminutives VN used for Véra, in pencil on the front endpaper: *for my Verinka/VN/ 1941*. With a lovely butterfly in profile, gently colored in red and blues and pencil grey.

VN composed *The Real Life of Sebastian Knight*, his first novel written in English, in 1939 in Paris, which had been the center of the emigration for over a decade when they moved there from Berlin in 1937. Their one-room apartment was scarcely big enough for the three of them, and VN used a bidet in the bathroom as a desk to write this novel (Appel interview, 1966, SO p. 89). Its hero is an exiled English-speaking Russian aristocrat on the trail of biographical information on his dead, estranged half-brother whose life he is writing. Lucie Léon Noël, VN's close friend and the wife of Paul Léon—who in 1941 still had fresh memories of editing *Finnegans Wake* with James Joyce—proofed his English: "He was most anxious that this first novel in English should sound neither 'foreign' nor read as though it had been translated into English. We both sat at the large mahogany desk and worked for several hours each time" (quoted in TRY p. 503). He brought the completed manuscript with him to the United States where, for two years, he could not find a publisher.

In January 1941 he was contacted by James Laughlin, "the wealthy young scion of a steel family" whose new publishing house, New Directions, was devoted to "works of high literary and low commercial value" (TAY p. 33). Edmund Wilson, who had met VN shortly after his arrival in the States and quickly became his *de facto* literary agent, had referred his work to Laughlin. VN's initial response to Laughlin's appeal for manuscripts was an attempt to define what he called his "very singular predicament": "In modern Russian literature I occupy the particular position of a novator, of a writer whose work seems to stand totally apart from that of his contemporaries. At the same time, owing to my books being banned in the Soviet Union, they can circulate only among the limited group of émigré intellectuals (chiefly in Paris)." He offered, among other things, *Sebastian Knight*, stating simply: "I wrote it in English and rather like it" (January 24, 1941, SL pp. 34–35).

VN accepted a meager $150 advance from Laughlin, who also wanted to option his next three books. Despite minor quibbling and a misinterpretation of the book as a chess problem, Wilson wrote to VN after reading it in proof that it was "absolutely enchanting. It's amazing that you should write such fine English prose and not sound like any other English writer, but be able to do your own kind of thing so subtly and completely...The whole book is brilliant and beautifully done...It is all on a high *poetic* level, and you have succeeded in being a first-rate poet in English. It has delighted and stimulated me more than any new book I have read since I don't know what" (October 20, 1941, NWL pp. 49–50). Though *Sebastian Knight* did not sell well, it did receive a small amount of favorable criticism. Laughlin next commissioned several translations from VN—which ultimately took the form of a collection of English renderings of Pushkin, Lermontov, and Tyutchev, and a separate critical study of Gogol. To say relations had grown strained between the two by the time Laughlin's last VN work, *Nine Stories*, came out in 1947, is to put it mildly. Wilson wrote to VN on January 30, 1947, "I'm completely finished with Laughlin—wrote him long ago, when he asked me to do some favor, telling him what I thought of his practices. I regard it as a calamity that he is bringing out a book of your stories. Do try to have Holt take it over" (NWL p. 184). VN, fed up in his own right, was ready to move on; he took Wilson's advice and wrote to Allen Tate: "I am very much bored with Laughlin of the New Directions. Do you think Holt might be interested in buying from him all my contracts *in toto*?" (January 28, 1947, SL p. 73).

Boyd details the "purely Russian factors" that engendered this "English" novel in a comparison between the composition of this and *The Gift*:

...the real research Nabokov had carried out for Fyodor's *Life Of Chernyshevsky* and the invented frustrations of Fyodor's life of his father; Nabokov's affair with Irina Guadanini and his determination to keep that an unknown part of his own biography. Most of all the novel relies on Nabokov's effort in *The Gift* to construct at length and in detail the life of a writer. Now he redeployed similar themes, but without *The Gift*'s compulsion to be compendious and with the parodic lightness he had mastered in *The Event* and *The Waltz Invention*. Never before had he packed such a complex structure into such a small space with such seeming ease. (TRY p. 496)

44 The Real Life of Sebastian Knight. London: Weidenfeld and Nicolson, (1960).

8vo.; black cloth; blue dust-jacket, light rubbing to spine and top edge.

Second English edition; the first English edition was produced by Editions Poetry London in December 1945 or March 1946, and was substantially more popular than the New Directions edition. Juliar A21.4.

A presentation copy, inscribed on the front endpaper: *to Véra/Sept. 1960/L.A.* Signed with an artfully swooping *V* composed in pink and grey, with a pretty pink and blue Brushfoot butterfly, whose wing shape, pattern, and color strongly resemble the brilliant tropical *Terinos* group (Johnson). It is alighting on a pink and blue flower, whose stem flows into the inscription.

In 1959 New Directions, caught up in the centrifugal force of VN's popularity, reissued *Sebastian Knight*, eighteen years after their first edition; Editions Poetry London, who had brought out an English edition of *Nikolai Gogol* in 1947 (for VN's annotated copy, see next entry), quickly followed suit.

45 Nikolai Gogol. Norfolk, CT: New Directions, (1944).

12mo.; front endpapers lightly rubbed; tan cloth, top edge slightly darkened.

Together with:

Nikolai Gogol. London: Editions Poetry London, (1947).

8vo.; tan cloth.

First edition and first English edition of VN's five critical studies of Gogol, which include some of his own translations – primarily of *Dead Souls* and *The Inspector General*; with his four-page commentary and six-page chronology at the end. Each copy is heavily emended; the annotations in the English edition supercede those in the American. The New Directions copy is issue A with the spine stamping in brown and five titles listed on the half-title; the fifth volume of the "Makers of Modern Literature Series," preceded by studies of Joyce (by Harry Levin), Woolf (by David Daiches), Forster (by Lionel Trilling), and Lorca (by Donald Honig). Juliar A22.1. VN's copiously annotated copy: labeled in pencil on the front endpaper: *the only correct text is my revised PL edition 1972* and *corrections superceded by those in the PL edition 1972*; with two earlier notes crossed out: *The only corrected copy/ V.N./ 1947* and *to be revised again/ 1948*; and a note on the cover: *The only corrected copy*. Opposite the half-title he listed four pages of *insertions,* crossing out two of them, and a dozen *corrections or deletions,* crossing out two of these also, and circling two in red pencil, others in blue ink. A few examples: "dialogue" to *speeches*; "behind stage" to *back stage*; "The Inspector General" to *Government Inspector*; and "cloak" to *carrick*. He added a single editorial note, in a large, emphatic hand, indicating the global change of *sky*-ending names to *ski*, and *ia* to *ya*. He put his hand to nearly every page in this volume, making additions and deletions, correcting spelling errors and making other textual emendations. The most significant annotations include footnotes to pages 3 and 144, and an insertion to page 79. The spine is labeled: *Corrected copy,* with his Cyrillic initials, and two index cards relating to pages 70 and 79 are loosely inserted, bearing VN's notes.

The first English edition is in the first of two bindings; the second is in green cloth. With the publisher's "Not for sale" label tipped to the front endpaper. Juliar A22.2a. With VN's copious emendations, added in anticipation of the 1973 edition (A22.5). His autograph revisions appear throughout in pencil and ink, interspersed in a manner suggesting at least two read-throughs, and include substantial deletions (nearly 20 lines), spelling and translation adjustments, word changes, footnotes, and more. On the front endpaper VN listed fourteen pages in pencil and ink, with emendations of particular significance. He also noted in pencil: *also misprints & transliterations corrected.*

The high volume of corrections might be explained by a statement VN made to Edmund Wilson just on May 8, 1944: "I did not send you the Gogol proofs because I got bored by the book and sent them back to Laughlin" (NWL p. 135).

In a 1967 interview for *The Paris Review* VN claimed of Gogol that he "was careful *not* to learn anything from him. As a teacher, he is dubious and dangerous. At his worst, as in his Ukrainian stuff, he is a worthless writer; at his best, he is incomparable and inimitable" (Gold interview, SO p. 103). It is the "incomparable and inimitable" best of Gogol that VN selected for review in this ground-breaking critical study that vastly expanded Gogol's English-language readership with over 150 pages of new translations and commentary. Boyd discounts the common assumption that VN "devoted a book to Gogol because he had a greater affinity for him than for other Russian writers. In fact, as his lectures reveal, he cared more for Pushkin, Tolstoy, and Chekhov: his affinity is not so much for the mottled conglomerate of the actual Gogol as for the polished proto-Nabokov he can extract from this recalcitrant ore" (TAY p. 55).

Laughlin commissioned this work in mid-May 1942, along with translations of Pushkin, Tyutchev, and Lermontov which he issued in 1944 as *Three Poets.* By July VN was working eight to ten hours a day on the translations, yet fell behind schedule: "What causes this irritating delay is the fact that I have to translate every scrap of quotation myself: most of the Gogol material (letters, articles etc.) is not translated at all, and the rest is so abominably botched that I cannot use it. I have lost a week already translating passages I need in the 'Inspector General' as I can do nothing with Constance Garnett's dry shit" (to James Laughlin, July 16, 1942, SL p. 41). He would repeatedly note throughout his career that translation and composition required different parts of the brain, and that switching between the two was exhausting. By August he willingly admitted to Wilson: "The book is progressing slowly, mainly because I get more and more dissatisfied with my English. When I have finished it, I shall take a three months' vacation with my ruddy robust Russian muse" (August 9, 1942, NWL p. 69). A year after Laughlin's commission, VN sent him the manuscript – having unsuccessfully attempted to break his contract – then titled, perhaps jocularly, "Gogol through the Looking-Glass":

This little book has cost me more trouble than any other I have composed. The reason is clear: I had first to create Gogol (translate him) and then discuss him (translate my Russian ideas about him). The recurrent jerk of switching from one rhythm of work to the other has quite exhausted me. The book has taken me exactly one year to write. I never would have accepted your suggestion to do it had I known how many gallons of brain-blood it would absorb; nor would you have made the suggestion had you known how long you would have to wait . . .

There are probably some slight slips of the pen here and there. I would like to see the Englishman who would write a book on Shakespeare in Russian. (May 26, 1943, SL p. 45)

He told Wilson: "It is a peach, an overripe peach with the velvet peeling off on one buttock and a purple bruise on the other – but still a peach" (June 11, 1943, NWL p. 102).

Boyd notes that "as a study of Gogol, it is deliberately incomplete," including only "what Nabokov values within the best" (TAY p. 55). Laughlin, too, commented on its "incompleteness" on other levels, a charge that caused VN significant irritation. His demands, which VN acceded to after a fashion, were brought to light in the final chapter in which he dramatizes one of Laughlin's criticisms: "I mean the student ought to be told more about Gogol's books. I mean the plots. He would want to know what those books are about" (TAY p. 65). The final version came out on August 15 and, despite high praise on the whole, suffered an attack from Wilson for "poses, perversities, and vanities which sound as if [VN] had brought them away from the St. Petersburg of the early nineteen-hundreds . . . and piously preserved them in exile . . . His puns are particularly awful" (TAY p. 78). VN himself recalled a quarter-century after the publication of his study that "verbal inventiveness is not really a bond between authors, it is merely a garland. [Gogol] would have been appalled by my novels and denounced as vicious the innocent, and rather superficial, little sketch of his life that I produced twenty-five years ago" (Talmey interview, SO p. 156).

46 **Nikolai Gogol.** Norfolk, Connecticut: New Directions, (1944).

8vo.; taupe cloth; light general wear.

First edition, issue A; Juliar A22.1. Extensively annotated by VN in pencil, with six emendations in ink, on approximately 60 pages, to words, transliterations, diacritical marks, typefaces, etc., apparently in preparation for the 1959 New Directions paperback. The most substantive and interesting alterations are his suggestion of *lunatic* for "Bedlamite" (p. 1); *entrails* for "liver" (p. 2); *sapless* for "lifeless" (p. 19); and the insertion of the note: *the freck[led] guy is the regular guy* (p. 67).

47 **Three Russian Poets.** Selections from Pushkin, Lermontov and Tyutchev. In new translations by Vladimir Nabokov. Norfolk, CT: New Directions, The Poets of the Year Series, (1944).

Slim 8vo.; grey printed paper-covered boards; grey printed dust-jacket, two nicks.

First edition, variant A in grey printed boards; variant B is a tan stapled pamphlet. Collects 18 Russian poems translated into English, with biographical notes on each poet. Juliar A23.1, 1991 update. A presentation copy, inscribed to Véra in Russian on the front endpaper, with the backwardly-written inscription backdated nearly a decade: *gnilrad ym ot. V. ii–1936*.

On January 24, 1941, VN sent James Laughlin at New Directions a pithy run-down of his career to date, and offered several publishable pieces be had on hand including his English translation of *Despair* and his first novel in English, *The Real Life of Sebastian Knight*. Apparently in response to Laughlin's query, his next missive includes a suggestion for a collection of Russian poetry in translation: "The most representative kind of collection would be 10 Khodasevich, 10 Pasternak and 20 The Rest...My own impression is that, inspite [*sic*] of political distress, the best poetry produced in Europe (–and the worst fiction) during these last twenty years has been in the Russian language, so that a volume of Russian poetry would be a very good thing" (February 10, 1941,

SL p. 36). Ultimately the volume VN undertook for Laughlin included five Pushkin (two poems and three scenes from verse drama, one with a brief introduction by Edmund Wilson), three Lermontov, and 13 Tyutchev, a significant showing in light of his developing sense of what translation should and could be. Seventeen years later Véra would write the editor of one solicitous magazine: "As to [VN's] own translations from Pushkin, Lermontov and Tyutchev, he does not want to reprint them. His approach to the problems of translating has changed since he published his *Three Russian Poets*. He does not believe in verse translations any more. He thinks that a translation's merit is determined by its literalness alone, and that, since a verse translation is inevitably a compromise, it cannot claim to be a 'translation', but is, at best, an imitation or (at its worst) a mutilation of the original" (to Peter Russell, March 12, 1958, SL pp. 251–52). This was written just after VN had completed his eight-year labor translating Pushkin's *Eugene Onegin*, an effort accompanied by his three volumes of commentary which, after publication, he would spend another decade strenuously revising and republishing, enduring ceaseless delays.

48 **Three Russian Poets.** Selections from Pushkin, Lermontov and Tyutchev. In new translations by Vladimir Nabokov. Norfolk, CT: New Directions, The Poets of the Year Series, (1944).

Slim 8vo.; grey paper-covered boards; light wear to extremities; grey dust-jacket, lightly rubbed, soiled and frayed, with two negligible closed tears and a crease to the cover.

First edition, variant A. Juliar A23.1, 1991 update. VN's teaching copy, evidently used for one of his Russian literature courses: he numbered the poems in pencil and made a number of marginal notes, though these were subsequently erased for mimeographing–his note at the head of the "Biographical Notes" section (p. 37) reads: *Not to be mimeogr.* Presumably he obliterated his marginal notes in order to provide a cleaner copy for his students.

49 **Pushkin-Lermontov-Tyutchev: Poems.** (Drawings by Donia Nachshen.) London: Lindsay Drummond Limited, 1947.

12mo.; red cloth with images of the three poets stamped in gilt; light wear to extremities; brown dust-jacket, light edgewear, two small chips and a minor tape repair to the rear.

First English edition; expanded from the New Directions edition, published in February of 1945, adding three Pushkin poems and seven by Lermontov. Volume 8 of the publisher's Russian Literary Library. Juliar A23.2, incorrectly stating the contents as those of the first edition (A23.1). A presentation copy, inscribed to Véra in Russian on the front endpaper: *To my darling. V. i–iv–1947*. With a four-quatrain poem transcribed by VN on page [57], and the note card from which he transcribed it clipped to the leaf.

50 **Bend Sinister.** New York: Henry Holt, (1947).

8vo.; black cloth, lightly rubbed and frayed; dust-jacket, light wear to extremities; small closed tear on front panel; rear panel rubbed.

First edition of the "long and terrifying" second novel VN wrote in English, the first written in the United States (to Elena Sikorski, April 14, 1946, SL p. 67). The only edition of this title with section breaks marked with a printer's device rather than chapter divisions. Juliar A24.1 A presentation copy, inscribed to Véra in Russian: *To my darling, my beloved/ V. 26.iv.1947.*

Bend Sinister, a creative indictment of totalitarianism, is VN's most overtly anti-fascist and anti-communist novel. It recounts the life of a philosopher blackmailed by an oppressive political regime into prostituting his talents. He envisioned it as early as 1942 under the title "The Person from Porlock"; later as "Game to Gunm"; still later as "Solus Rex," or possibly "Vortex." Just after completing it, he wrote that "[i]t's general atmosphere resembles *Invitation to a Beheading* but is even more catastrophic and jolly" (to Elizabeth Marinel Allan and Marussya Marinel, May 22, 1946, SL p. 68). Much later, in a retrospective analysis, he saw *Invitation to a Beheading* and *Bend Sinister* as "the two bookends of grotesque design between which my other volumes tightly huddle" (*Anniversary Notes*, p. 4).

To explain the novel to an editor at Doubleday, VN wrote in March 1944:

I propose to portray in this book certain subtle achievements of the mind in modern times against a dull-red background of nightmare oppression and persecution. The scholar, the poet, the scientist and the child – these are the victims and witnesses of a world that goes wrong in spite of its being graced with scholars, poets, scientists and children.

He adds, "I am putting this rather bluntly, I am afraid, as it is difficult to give a synopsis of something, the rhythm and atmosphere of which are more essential than a physical outline" (March 22, 1944, SL p. 48). In addition to the unique "rhythm and atmosphere," VN introduced the narrative innovation of a protagonist who gradually becomes aware of his own fictional status, of the existence of the author—"a device never yet attempted in literature" (ibid.). It took VN four years to complete the manuscript, and Doubleday, four months to decide that "novels about 'dictators' have no appeal at present, that the public wants 'escapist' books and that therefore my novel would come out at the 'wrong' moment" (to Edmund Wilson, [between the 13th and 30th of] September 1946, NWL p. 173), and to offer a $1000 advance.

In the meantime VN had showed it to Allen Tate at Henry Holt, "as one private individual to another...with the clear understanding that I was *not* submitting it to his firm" (ibid.). Tate sent him, in response, a barrage of letters and telegrams expressing his interest, and finally offered a $2000 advance. Ultimately brought out by Holt, *Bend Sinister* was surprisingly under-promoted and, therefore, barely sold, despite positive reviews. Tate told Wilson he was "tremendously excited" about it (Wilson to VN, January 30, 1947, NWL p. 182), though Wilson himself found that this was, like other VN's attempts to incorporate politics into his fiction, unsuccessful (he had not yet read *The Gift* or *Invitation to a Beheading*), and decided not to review it as he had few positive remarks. Hal Borland wrote in the *New York Times* that it was "a moving and powerful novel about the plight of a civilized man caught in a tyrant state. There is a terrible inevitability about its movement and a warm humanity about its main character which are not often found in what is essentially a thesis novel" (June 15, 1947). Years later, Boyd called it VN's "private contribution to the war effort: an attempt to show that Nazi Germany and Soviet Russia represented fundamentally the same brutish vulgarity inimical to everything most vulnerable and most valuable to human life" (TAY p. 40).

51 **Bend Sinister.** New York: Henry Holt, (1947).

8vo.; top edge gilt; satin bookmark; three-quarter navy blue morocco, stamped in gilt, lower panel lightly rubbed.

First edition. Juliar A24.1. A specially bound publisher's presentation copy; inscribed to Véra in Russian within the wings of a very unstructured ink butterfly, in 1948, on the binder's front endpaper: *To Véren[ka?] from V. 194[7?]*.

52 Bend Sinister. London: Weidenfeld and Nicolson, (1960).

8vo.; black cloth, spine stamped in silver; bumped.

First English edition, published thirteen years after the American edition. Juliar A24.2. VN's partially corrected copy, with his note on the front endpaper: *See other copy with all corrected corrections* with a single pencil line through the whole page (we have not located that "other copy"), a list of five page numbers and corresponding spelling emendations to be made in this copy, and his underlining and marginal X's on eleven other pages.

53 Bend Sinister. New York: Time Incorporated, (1964).

8vo.; stiff illustrated wrappers.

First book club edition, a "subscription edition," expanded with VN's introduction and the editor's preface; 75,000 copies, in stiff wrappers; Juliar notes: "Sometimes includes bookmark with quotation from author's introduction. Later printings of this edition have a 'Time-Life Books' device occupying three lines on copyright-page and 'XX' (second printing) or 'XXX' (third printing) in colophon. Publisher records show a part of a 'mail order series' discontinued in Aug68. The series was revived in Mar80 and *Bend Sinister* was reissued 1May81 in wrappers and cloth." Juliar A24.4 and 1991 update.

According to VN's note on the first leaf, this copy was *received Sept. 15, 1964 at Montreux*. He began to mark it *Corr* in marker on the rear panel, but some ink rubbed off and what remains is faint. It is, in fact, a corrected copy: he listed on the half-title *noticed misprints* on six pages. The first four of these refer to printer's mistakes; the last two, to minor errors in the introduction.

54 Nine Stories. *Direction*, Number Two. [New York: New Directions, 1947].

Slim 8vo.; page 19 detached and loosely inserted; pages 22–34 excised; wrappers, edgeworn with a few stains.

First edition of VN's first collection of stories in English; his last project for New Directions; a cloth issue of "perhaps a dozen," was also produced. Of these nine short stories five were composed in English, one he translated from the original French ("Mademoiselle O.," his study of his nanny, which became chapter five of *Speak, Memory*), and four were translated from the Russian, under VN's guidance, by either Peter

Pertzov or Hilda Ward. A fragile production, printed on acidic paper and bound in uncoated paper wrappers. Both Juliar and Dieter Zimmer, VN's first bibliographer, have inexplicably recorded the order of the contents erroneously. Juliar A25.1. "The Assistant Producer" in this collection prints the last two paragraphs, present in its first appearance in *The Atlantic Monthly* but omitted in *Nabokov's Dozen* and all subsequent editions, "owing perhaps to Nabokov's oversight" (Barabtarlo p. 105).

VN's working copy, used in compiling the contents for *Nabokov's Dozen* in 1959; all nine stories, as well as the four whose titles Véra penciled in at the table of contents (along with various publication notes for several of the stories), appeared in that later, sturdier collection, despite the fact that the pages for "Mademoiselle O." were excised here and its title was crossed out. Several pencil ticks and minor emendations by VN or Véra are sprinkled throughout the remaining texts.

Gennady Barbartarlo, in a survey of VN's English short stories, concludes that VN "used the short stories of the 1940s as a proving ground on which to test many designs and discoveries that he had made first trial of in his last Russian fiction of 1937–40 and that later went into his English novels" (p. 104). After his emigration to the States and the publication of his first memoir, *Conclusive Evidence*, he wrote eight stories in English ("or ten, depending on definition"). These stories—and the fourteen essays that combined to form *Conclusive Evidence* after their periodical publication—established his popular reputation and, though as magazine publications they did not merit public critical remark, two of them were included in *Best American Stories* for 1944 and 1946.

55 **Nine Stories.** *Direction*, Number Two. [New York: New Directions, 1947].

Slim 8vo.; faint water spots to preliminaries; two pages dog-eared; wrappers, well-worn, soiled with chips to edges and spine, two tears to cover.

First edition. Juliar A25.1. A presentation copy, inscribed to Anna Feigin on the half-title: *To my dear Anuta/ with love/ from the author/ xii.1947*, with a tiny butterfly.

56 **"To Prince S.M. Kachurin [Kachurin, tvoi sovet ia prinial]."** In *The New Review [Novyi zhurnal]*, Number 15, pp. 81–83. New York: The New Review, 1947.

8vo.; printed grey wrappers, spine partially unglued and torn.

First appearance of this poem, published under his Russian guise, "V. Sirin," presumably to attract the audience that formerly knew him under that name. Juliar C502. With the title of the poem scrawled across the front cover in VN's hand.

57 A Second Book of Russian Verse. Translated into English by various hands, and edited by C. M. Bowra. London: Macmillan, 1948.

8vo.; blue cloth; dust-jacket, lightly frayed, two small tears.

First edition of this anthology, with two translations by VN that had previously appeared in a *New Directions* annual (1941). Not in Juliar. With four emendations by VN to his own contributions, translations of poems by Khodasevich: "What Is the Use of Time and Rhyme" and "Stanzas" (pp. 91–92); and translations, comments, ticks, and question marks on four other pages, annotating translations of Pushkin, Gumilev (he adds to one verse), Akhmatova, Esenin, and Sayanov. Some of his marginal notes are listed on the rear pastedown, and the dust-jacket is labeled: *Hodasevich = Nabokov*. Khodasevich was arguably the leading poet of the Russian emigration, and VN's friend, for whom he never lost his esteem; the only essay from his Berlin exile that he translated for inclusion in *Strong Opinions* is "On Hodasevich."

58 The Italian Principia – Part II. A First Italian Reading Book. New York: Harper & Brothers, 1885.

8vo.; all edges stained red; brown cloth, worn, extremities frayed.

A gift copy of this grammar, inscribed on the front endpaper in pencil: *for Véra/from VN*, with a quirky pencil butterfly. With copious pencil notations to nine pages in Véra's hand. With a contemporary ownership signature in pencil in three places, two of which are docketed "Cornell University," dating this book to the end of the Nabokovs' sojourn at Cornell, when Véra began to acquire a working knowledge of Italian in order to check an Italian edition of VN's English and Russian poems.

CHAPTER

13

1

In 1919, by way of the Crimea and Greece, a flock of Nabokovs—three families in fact—fled from Russia to Western Europe. It was arranged that my brother and I would go to the University of Cambridge, on a scholarship awarded more in atonement for political tribulations than in acknowledgement of intellectual merit. The rest of my family expected to stay for a while in London. Living expenses were to be paid by a handful of jewels that a farsighted old chambermaid in our St. Petersburg home had swept off a dresser into my mother's suitcase when packing it for our hurried departure in 1917. We had left them home for what we thought would be a brief wait, a prudent perching pause on the southern ledge of Russia; but the fury of the new regime had refused to blow over. In Greece, during two spring months, braving the constant resentment of intolerant shepherd dogs, I trudged butterflies. On the liner *Pannonia* which was bound (twenty years too soon,

as far as I was concerned) for New York, but let us off at Marseilles, I learned to foxtrot. France rattled by in the coal-black night. The pale Channel was still oscillating inside us, when the Dover-London train quietly came to a stop. Repetitive pictures of grey pears on the grimy walls of Victoria Station advertised the bath soap English governesses had used upon me in my childhood.

My father had visited London before—the last time in February, 1916, when, with five other prominent representatives of the Russian press, he had been invited by the British Government to take a look at England's war effort (which, it was hinted, did not meet with sufficient appreciation on the part of Russia's public opinion). They had been shown the Fleet. Dinners and speeches had followed in noble succession. The timely capture of Erzerum by the Russians and the pending introduction of conscription in England ("Will you march too or wait till March 2?" as the punning posters put it) had provided the speakers with easy topics. There had been an official banquet presided over by Sir Edward Grey, and a funny interview with George V whom the *enfant terrible* Chukovski, a writer of the group, insisted on asking if he liked the works of Oscar Wilde—"dze ooarks of Ooald." The king, who was baffled by his interrogator's accent and who, anyway, had never been a voracious reader, neatly countered by inquiring how his guests liked the London fog (later, Chukovski used to cite this triumphantly as an example of British cant—tabooing a writer because of his morals).

A recent visit to the Public Library in New York has revealed that the above incident does not appear in my father's book *Iz*

187

Rough map
of the Nabokov lands
in the St Petersburg
Province.

South

LUGA

S.P. Warsaw Railway

Warsaw highway

E

W

chemin du Pont

house

Rozhestveno estate

Batovo estate

house

house

Ozedezh R.

Rozhestveno village

Vira estate

Siverskaya

road to railway station

St Petersburg

Gryazno and Daymischche villages

Scale:
1 verst (=1.067 км)

V.N.
1965

North

NO. 64B

SPEAK, MEMORY

The best part of a writer's biography is not the
record of his adventures but the story of his style . . .

(Talmey interview, SO p. 155)

The first star to appear in VN's autobiographical constellation was
"Mademoiselle O.," published in the Parisian journal *Mesures*, April
15, 1936; it became, in its English translation, chapter 5 of *Speak,
Memory*. From January 1948 to February 1951 VN published fourteen
reminiscences in various American journals—primarily *The New
Yorker*—with the intention of ultimately collecting them. The pieces
cover the years from August 1903, his "awakening of consciousness" at
the age of four (*Speak, Memory* p. 21), to May 1940, with his family's
emigration to the States and a parallel dawning in his son Dmitri.

If *Speak, Memory* is indeed the "story of his style," then the correspondence surrounding the publication of its discrete chapters is a
well-preserved "record of his adventures" in establishing that style in
America. He wrote to Katharine White at *The New Yorker* of her editorial interference with what would become chapter three, "Portrait of My
Uncle":

I shall be very grateful to you if you help me to weed out bad grammar but I
do not think I would like my longish sentences clipped too close, or those
drawbridges lowered which I have taken such pains to lift. In other words,
I would like to discriminate between awkward construction (which is bad)
and a certain special—how shall I put it—sinuosity, which is my own and
which only at first glance may seem awkward or obscure. Why not have the
reader re-read a sentence now and then? It won't hurt him. (November 10,
1947, SL p. 77)

He exhibited remarkable restraint, considering that in the letter he
sent Wilson about the matter he wrote that the editing "upset me so
much that I almost decided to stop trying to earn my living that way.
This is strictly *entre nous* as I would not like to hurt Mrs. White's feelings. She did her best" (August 29, 1947, NWL p. 192). When he sent
"Colette" to her he wrote: "If you accept the story, *please* let us not have
any unnecessary changes. Everything is crystal-clear in the story and
my syntax is becoming a grammarian's delight" (quoted in TAY p. 127).
His tact and good humor were not rewarded. When he got back "Portrait
of My Mother," Boyd reports, "his new manuscript was defaced with

editorial ink as the *New Yorker* demonstrated its compulsion to query phrase after phrase," which VN responded to with dozens of rebuttals (TAY p. 137). In addition to playing the over-zealous watchdog of his style and grammar, *The New Yorker* rejected one essay—"Student Days"—for content, claiming it was too politically charged; it became "Lodgings in Trinity Lane" (*Harper's Magazine*, January 1951).

While planning the compilation of these essays VN considered many titles, ringing with personal significance and literary, chess, and lepidopterological allusions. A few examples are "The House Was There"; "Clues"; "The Rainbow Edge"; "Speak, Mnemosyne!" (his favorite, ultimately rejected); "The Prismatic Edge"; "The Moulted Feather"; "Nabokov's Opening"; and "Emblemata" (to Sheila Hodges at Gollancz, March 22, 1951, SL pp. 118–19). He ultimately decided on *Conclusive Evidence*—"conclusive evidence," he later wrote, "of my having existed" (foreword, *Speak, Memory: An Autobiography Revisited*, 1967) despite the admission that none of his friends (especially Wilson) liked it.

As VN began his search for a publisher for *Conclusive Evidence* he sent promotional letters to prospective editors. To Kenneth McCormick at Doubleday he wrote as early as 1946 that it would be "a new kind of autobiography, or rather a new hybrid between that and a novel... It will be a sequence of short essay-like bits, which suddenly gathering momentum will form into something very weird and dynamic: innocent looking ingredients of a quite unexpected brew" (September 22, 1946, SL p. 69). Writing over two years later to John Fischer at Harper and Brothers, which ultimately undertook the book's publication, he was able to offer a more concrete overview:

It is an inquiry into the elements that have gone to form my personality as a writer. Starting with several phases of childhood in northern Russia, it will wind its way through the years of Russian revolution and civil war, thence to England (Cambridge University), to Germany and France, and finally to America (1940). All I have written up to now has been published in *The New Yorker* and should give the reader a fair idea of the method used. However... the flow of the book I contemplate is more ample and sustained than the sharp pieces carved out of it for magazine publication might suggest. (December 14, 1948, SL p. 88)

By the time *Conclusive Evidence* was published, he had been teaching literature at Cornell University for three years and had published six books in the States, as well as short fiction, poetry, and reviews in leading periodicals. But this was, in his own estimation, the work that inevitably brought him "a lot of fame but little money" (to Elena Sikorski, September 6, 1951, SL p. 122). It was very well-received both serially and in book form and the first English edition, retitled *Speak, Memory* (but printing identical text), came out that same year.

In the summer of 1953, "between butterfly-hunting and writing *Lolita* and *Pnin*," VN decided to translate the autobiography into a Russian "version and recomposition" (to Katharine White, August 11, 1954, SL p. 149), lest another less able contender make an attempt, with Véra's help. Though his books were officially banned in the Soviet Union, he had a reasonably large audience among émigrés still in Europe and in the States, as well. He wrote to White that after surviving the "atrocious metamorphosis" from Russian to American writer, "I swore I would never go back from my wizened Hyde form to my ample Jekyll one – but there I was, after fifteen years of absence, wallowing again in the bitter luxury of my Russian verbal might ..." (ibid.). Boyd offers an assessment of that version – *Other Shores* [*Drugie berega*], which appeared in New York, in Russian, in 1954: "there was much to insert, much he could not omit ... The new material he added blurred the outlines of certain chapters – a blurring that would remain when he retranslated *Drugie berega* for the revised *Speak, Memory* in the mid-1960s" (TAY pp. 257–58).

VN found that recalling what had been "Russian memories in the first place" in his first language sharpened his memory, and called attention to the deficiencies of *Conclusive Evidence*. He began a revised English-language edition in 1965 which came out in 1967 under the title *Speak, Memory: An Autobiography Revisited*, in which he incorporated recent corrections and "introduced basic changes and copious additions," adding, in the foreword: "What I still have not been able to rework through want of specific documentation, I have now preferred to delete for the sake of over-all truth. On the other hand, a number of facts relating to ancestors and other personages have come to light and have been incorporated in this final version of *Speak, Memory*." The enthusiasm with which this book was received was jump-started by Alfred Appel's two-part study in the *Partisan Review*. By the time of its publication he had already begun to assemble material for a future installment, *Speak on, Memory* or *Speak, America*, reviewing the twenty years spent in States, but the project never came to fruition; dozens of preliminary note cards documenting potential anecdotes to incorporate survive in the Berg Collection at the New York Public Library.

59 Conclusive Evidence. A Memoir. New York: Harper & Brothers, (1951).

8vo.; blue and black cloth; dust-jacket, edgeworn with three tape repairs.

First edition. Juliar A26.1. The dedication copy, inscribed to Véra on the dedication page, in Russian: *My darling 23.i.1951*, with VN's list of three misprints corrected: "classroom" to s*choolroom*; "1919" to *1918*; "rustled" to *soughed, still leafless*. With a large, colorful, detailed Brushfoot, from an African genus, on the front endpaper, named *Eugenia onegini* for Pushkin's classic, which he would spend a decade translating and publishing (1964) and another ten years revising (1975). Johnson notes that the African genus *Panacea* "is an exotic often purchased by collectors," offering as evidence not just the wing shape and large size, but also "precisely this tinted silvery green iridescent color on the uppersurfaces." Though these traits characterize several species of *Panacea*, Johnson suggests *procilla* as the real-life model for this drawing: "only *procilla* has the vivid eyespots along the margin of the hindwing...If indeed this was the butterfly Nabokov was thinking of, he may have added the eyespots to the forewing as his idea of what a grand '*Panacea*' would look like."

   With an additional inscription to Véra beneath the butterfly: *To my darling*. Boyd cites "a little-known interview" during which VN "explained that he chose *Conclusive Evidence* for the two *v* sounds together at the center of the title, as a secret link looping together Vladimir and Véra. Like its title, the whole autobiography was designed as a tribute to his wife. When she emerges late in the story as the 'you' to whom the book has been addressed, it becomes apparent that the love affairs of childhood and youth that Nabokov has described with mounting intensity will find their apotheosis in her. But he will *not* describe their relationship directly" (TAY p. 629).

   Clipped to the title page is a typescript leaf, printing the "[d]iscarded introduction to *Conclusive Evidence*," and the explanation, "the title was tentatively *The House Was There.*" Signed in full in pencil and dated 1951, it merits quoting in full:

The house was there. Right there. I never imagined the place would have changed so completely [since nineteen seventeen]. How dreadful−I don't recognize a thing. No use walking any farther. Sorry, Hopkinson, to have made you come such a long way. I had been looking forward to a perfect orgy of nostalgia and recognition! That man over there seems to be growing suspicious. Speak to him. *Turistï. Amerikantsï.* [Tourists. Americans.] Oh, wait a minute. Tell him I am a ghost. You surely know the Russian for "ghost"? *Mechta. Prizrak. Metafizicheskiy kapitalist.* [A dream. A ghost. A metaphysical capitalist.] Run, Hopkinson!.

This poetic introduction—so unlike the explanatory forewords he would write for many subsequent works—projects a return to Russia that VN never undertook. The "house" was Vyra, the Nabokovs' country retreat 50 miles outside St. Petersburg, vividly described in *Conclusive Evidence* and in several of the early Russian novels, notably *Mary*; its location is depicted on the map of the family lands printed (from VN's sketch) on the endpapers of the 1967 revision. The estate was converted into an orphanage and school after the Nabokovs fled to the Crimea to evade the most immediate threat: VN and his brother Sergei would likely have been drafted into the Red Army had they stayed. During World War II the Germans commandeered it for their headquarters, and after they abandoned it in 1944 it was burned to the ground. "Today where Vyra stood there is nothing but a scraggly clump of trees" (TRY p. 46).

Eudora Welty is among those whose praise of *Conclusive Evidence* is quoted on the dust-jacket, along with that of S.N. Behrman and Anne Parrish. She proclaims the memoir "a charming record of the personality of a vanished era and a vanished day." The implications of loss inform the tone of many of VN's works, and this memoir justifies the statement made by John Updike in his obituary for VN in 1977: "Few who have lost so much have complained so little." The dust-jacket summary similarly laments that the milieu of which VN writes as "the kind of iridescent society which the world is never likely to know again...*Conclusive Evidence* tells the story of the author's opulent childhood and youth in Czarist Russia, his escape abroad when Bolshevism enslaved the country, his college years in England, and his life on the Continent in the twenties and thirties. The book has nothing in common with the usual memoirs of exiled noblemen. It is the work of an artist, who has discovered a new, and delightful, method of auto-biography."

60 Speak, Memory. A Memoir. London: Victor Gollancz, 1951.

8vo.; blue-green cloth; cream dust-jacket reproducing an image of St. Petersburg; rubbed with a few small chips and some tape repair to the spine.

First English edition of *Conclusive Evidence*; first issue (blue-green cloth stamped in black; later copies were bound in blue cloth stamped in gilt). Juliar A26.2. The dedication copy, inscribed to Véra in Russian on the front endpaper: *Nice little creatures.* [Shapiro notes that this is in Russian, in Roman transliteration]. *V. xii–1951.* With Véra's copious annotations on page 7, as well as her notes, question marks, ticks and underlining on four other pages. She also corrected *The True Life Of Sebastian Knight* on the dust-jacket flap to *The Real Life of Sebastian Knight.* In his 1967 foreword to the revised edition, VN explains the sudden title change from *Conclusive Evidence*: "Unfortunately, the phrase suggested a mystery story, and I planned to entitle the British edition *Speak, Mnemosyne* but was told that 'little old ladies would not want to ask for a book whose title they could not pronounce.' I also toyed with *The Anthemion* which is the name of a honeysuckle ornament, consisting of elaborate interlacements and expanding clusters, but nobody liked it; so we finally settled for *Speak, Memory...*" This final title aptly reflects VN's compositional process and recalls, according to Boyd, walks around the family estate he took in his childhood with his mother, who would exhort him to "remember."

61 Speak, Memory. A Memoir. London: Victor Gollancz, 1951.

8vo.; blue-green cloth.

First English edition, first issue. Juliar A26.2. A heavily annotated copy, used by VN in considering the Russian translation of his memoir into *Other Shores* [*Drugie berega*] in 1954: He added spot translations of words, phrases, and lines into Russian in pencil and ink on over two dozen pages. In addition, he added hundreds of entomological doodles throughout. There are pencil butterflies, moths, and caterpillars on most of the pages, with a concentration of tiny "leps" appearing in large numbers on pages in the beginning, and large, more detailed butterflies populating the final pages, one or two per page, with two lovely pencil butterflies alighting on a flower on the final text page. Pages in two of the later sections are numbered at the top in red pencil, and are annotated with dates and times. Véra labeled the front endpaper: *Author's copy/Return to:/Professor V. Nabokov/Goldwin Smith Hall/Cornell University/Ithaca, N.Y./USA.*

62 Other Shores [Drugie berega]. New York: Chekhov Publishing House, 1954.

8vo.; grey cloth, printed wrappers bound-in.

First edition of the first Russian translation, with his foreword specially written for this edition, composed "in summer 1953 in Arizona, Oregon, and other places in the West and Midwest." This "revised and Russianized version of his memoir" first appeared in 1954 in *Opyty*, New York, No. 3, Chapters 1–3 and in *Novyi zhurnal*, New York, Nos. 37–38, Chapters 4–9. Juliar A26.3.

The dedication copy, specially bound, preserving the wrappers, and inscribed to Véra on the title page: *with love from V. 5.i.1955/Ithaca*. With three large, colorful, distinctive butterflies. The first, *Papilio vérae*, is on the first blank; it's labeled *very rare*. The ink outline bled through the page, and VN filled in the blank spaces on the verso to create another butterfly. He cut the bottom corner of the page and labeled it *turn*, to reveal a third butterfly, *Morpho vérae*, on the title page, labeled *very, very rare*. One of several tiny specimens is on the dedication page (where VN wrote a prepublication note in Russian: *My dear, beloved. 22 XI 1954*) and five are on the front wrapper: one on each of the sides and the bottom, and two at the top: a smaller one in profile facing a larger one, in full view, named for VN and his wife: *Vladimiria vérae*. Johnson addresses all the butterflies in this copy, large and small; working from the inside out:

Nabokov uses *Morpho*, which is the genus of big blue iridescent butterflies so famous from the New World tropics, but has taken the liberty to draw a species with very odd forewings for that group. The forewings of *Morpho* usually, if not completely blue, have blue framed within black ground color. Nabokov draws the opposite—black markings over blue, in a configuration more like some of the exotic Milkweed butterflies where the black would overlay a colorful beige-orange.

He goes on to suggest other possible parallels, but concludes that the forewing is likely more fanciful than representative, while "the hindwing would fit well as any of the all blue *Morpho* species." The butterfly opposite *Morpho vérae*—the one created by ink bleeding through the first blank—is an exotically colored Swallowtail butterfly clearly showing the shape and spikelike tails of the *Eurytides* group: "It appears that Nabokov imaginatively adopted the general wing pattern of the *orabilis*-like group of *Eurytides* but made the blackish outer areas of the wings wider and grander, and the bases of the wings, which are ordinarily white, his rainbow of pinkish-hued blue." The minute butterflies on the cover represent "butterflies that Nabokov might have caught on a typical collecting day near his boyhood home in Russia: *Vladimiria véra* looks like a small Copper butterfly"; the one resting on the fore-edge is "*Vanessa*-like"; the "dull colored little butterfly at the bottom of the cover is, most likely, a Ringlet." The "lep" drawn on the left-hand side of the cover is unfortunately partially obscured by the binding, making identification impossible.

Boyd details the revisions VN incorporated into this translation:

[I]n preparing his book for an émigré audience to whom V. D. Nabokov and Vladimir Sirin were major figures and every memory of Russia a treasure, there was much to insert, much he could not omit. Since in its Russian form, the book could afford to be even more nostalgic than in English, its Russian title, *Drugie berega* [*Other Shores*], lifts a phrase from a famous Pushkin lyric in which the poet revisits a scene from his past ("again I have visited...")...Chapter 3 of *Conclusive Evidence*, "Portrait of My Uncle," had been a lighthearted romp through Nabokov's ancestors before settling on what were to him much more important: his own ineradicable memories of one near twig on the family tree, his Uncle Vasily. In the Russian version, Nabokov not only incorporated more about Vasily but skewed the chapter by dwelling at considerable length on the idyllic, quintessentially Russian landscape around the Oredezh. (TAY pp. 257–58)

63 Other Shores [Drugie berega]. New York: Chekhov Publishing House, 1954.

8vo.; .5 cm tear to one leaf; printed wrappers; spine sunned.

First edition of the first Russian translation. Juliar A26.3. With frequent marginal pencil lines throughout; notes on ten pages, including the cryptic *M.A.M.Y.Y.A.S.* on page 47; *Ross* on page 163; a couple of Russian notes, no more than a few words each; an erased translation on page 129; and a sentence translated into English on page 123 (*We have all seen the face of the world-famous grandmaster at the moment of losing his queen by an absurd oversight to the local amateur and pediatrician*) which Shapiro notes is "a translation of the penultimate sentence, but with a slight change: in the Russian original, this 'local amateur' chess-player is identified as Boris Isidorovich Shakh (note the word-play: in Russian, *shakh* – German-borrowed *schach* – means 'check,' a chess term), whereas in the English rendition here he is identified merely by profession, pediatrician (cf. *Speak, Memory*, 133 lns. 3–4: 'the local amateur and pediatrician, Dr. Schach')." His note at the top of page 164, the beginning of chapter 9, indicates the most significant change to this edition: *Insert 20 cards (Father's Biography)*.

64 Speak, Memory. A Memoir. New York: Grosset & Dunlap, the Universal Library, [1960].

8vo.; many pages and signatures detached; tape repair; wrappers, well-worn.

First paperback edition in English, reproduced from the first edition of *Conclusive Evidence.* Juliar A26.4. VN's rigorously annotated copy, aggressively rewritten for the 1967 revision. With over two hundred lines of text crossed out—several full paragraphs and scattered lines throughout—as well as individual words and phrases on nearly every page; this is the text that did not make it into the 1967 edition. Chapter Three, "Portrait of My Uncle," was especially reworked. In addition, VN crossed out pages, emended and moved anecdotes, and added marginal instructions to substitute text from various note cards now housed in the Berg Collection at the New York Public Library (frequently the note card text matches the printed, crossed out text almost verbatim). With nearly 100 marginal pencil and colored butterflies, moths, and caterpillars of various shapes and sizes; one is labeled: *January 4, 1966/Montreux/the best so far* (p. 166). The most spectacular feature of this annotated edition is VN's full color sketch map of the family lands in and around St. Petersburg on the rear endpaper, that served as the model for the printed endpapers for the 1967 Putnam's edition and has remained a feature of all subsequent editions.

65 Speak, Memory: An Autobiography Revisited. New York: Putnam's, (1966) [1967].

8vo.; black cloth; white dust-jacket, light wear.

Second revised edition, first revised English-language edition; VN's final memoir, significantly altered from its first incarnation in 1951 as *Conclusive Evidence*; with 18 photographs and a new foreword detailing the history of the text's evolution. VN was planning a future installment, to review his twenty years spent in America, but died before he could complete the project. The endpapers are printed with "a sketch map of the Nabokov lands in the St. Petersburg region" and a butterfly, both from VN's drawings. Juliar A26.5. VN wrote in the foreword: "This re-Englishing of a Russian re-version of what had been an English re-telling of Russian memories in the first place, proved to be a diabolical task, but some consolation was given me by the thought that such multiple metamorphosis, familiar to butterflies, had not been tried by any human before."

The dedication copy, inscribed to Véra in Russian on the front paste-down: *To you, my darling, this Mnemosyne grown prettier. V. Nov. 2, 1966.* VN adorned the printed black and white butterfly on that page with red and blue pencil, and made autograph emendations – mostly cosmetic changes, correcting misspellings and verb tenses – on nine pages; the most substantive alteration makes his "stylish" town house less stylish, by deleting that adjective. He labeled the dust-jacket spine *Vé* in pencil, and the cover, *Véra/corrected.* With a black and white postcard clipped to p. 117, of "Russian and Japanese ambassadors" in 1905, including his father, VDN.

VN detailed the primary changes incorporated into this new edition in the foreword:

...While writing the first version in America I was handicapped by an almost complete lack of data in regard to family history, and, consequently, by the impossibility of checking my memory when I felt it might be at fault. My father's biography has been amplified now, and revised. Numerous other revisions and additions have been made, especially in the earlier chapters...Because of the psychological difficulty of replaying a theme elaborated in my *Dar* [the English translation of which was published in 1963], I omitted one entire chapter [eleven: "First Poem"]. On the other hand, I revised many passages and tried to do something about the amnesic defects of the original...For the present, final, edition of *Speak, Memory* I have not only introduced basic changes and copious additions into the initial English text, but have availed myself of the corrections I made while turning it into Russian.

...What I still have not been able to rework through want of specific documentation, I have now preferred to delete for the sake of over-all truth. On the other hand, a number of facts relating to ancestors and other personages have come to light and have been incorporated in this final version of Speak, Memory.

66 Speak, Memory: An Autobiography Revisited. New York: Putnam's, (1966) [1967].

8vo.; black cloth, spine bumped; dust-jacket; edgeworn with a few small chips.

Second revised edition, first revised English-language edition. Juliar A26.5. VN's working copy – he docketed the dust-jacket in marker, *Corrected* and in pencil, *Author's copy* – with emendations on 16 pages, nearly all included on his list on the half-title. He labeled the dust-jacket spine with a *V.* to distinguish it from Véra's copy which is similarly labeled "Vé." This is the most heavily corrected copy extant: several of the emendations which appear here—including word changes, insertions, a date change, and several spelling corrections—were not made in Véra's copy. On the half-title he noted which changes were made on the Penguin galleys.

67 **Speak, Memory: An Autobiography Revisited.** New York: Putnam's, (1966) [1967].

8vo.; top edge gilt; satin bookmark; full red morocco, front panel stamped "V. N." in gilt.

Second revised edition, first revised English-language edition. Juliar A26.5. In the publisher's presentation binding. Docketed by VN on the first leaf: *Not corrected.*

68 **Speak, Memory: An Autobiography Revisited.** New York: Putnam's, (1966) [1967].

8vo.; black cloth; dust-jacket, edgeworn with a 4-cm closed tear to the front panel and a few smaller tears to the rear.

Second revised edition, first revised English-language edition. Juliar A26.5. A working copy annotated by VN with word counts at the top of each page in the first chapter, textual corrections, emphases, and instructions for excerpting portions throughout on nearly twenty pages, belying his note on the dust-jacket: *Uncorrected, 1966* (with the blue marker note, *Author's Copy,* vigorously scratched out in blue ink). He noted on the half-title: *More ancestry inserted in Ch. Three, p. 54* in ink (with a corresponding note on the dust-jacket: *At p. 54 insert Genealogical Note on Niclaus von Korff*), but crossed it out in pencil and added a new note: *See Strong Opinions p. 188 insert in p. 54 here.* A second ink note remains: *Additions in paragraph one of ch. Seven, p. 142,* as well as a final pencil note, *anxietas tibiarum p. 266.*

69 **Speak, Memory: An Autobiography Revisited.** London: Weidenfeld and Nicolson, (1967).

8vo.; blue cloth; light wear to extremities.

First English edition of the revised memoir. Juliar A26.6. With VN's list of alterations *to be added in later editions* filling the half-title. These changes, affecting nine pages, range from spelling and misprint corrections to adjustments of genealogy, word changes, and emendations of picture captions. He circled seven of these nine page numbers, and noted: *corrected in Penguin galleys*. He listed an additional seven pages, but subsequently crossed them out in blue marker, turning the deletion into a three color landscape drawing. The illustration bled through onto the title page, and he embellished this bleed into another landscape. The textual corrections are in red and black pencil as well as blue ink, suggesting repeated readings. They were not incorporated into the 1968 American paperback edition, but were made in the English paperback edition which appeared the following year. With a typed letter signed, "Barley Alison," to "Mrs. Nabokov," January 27, 1967, on one leaf of Weidenfeld & Nicolson letterhead, regarding advance copies, loosely inserted.

ВЛАДИМИР НАБОКОВ

Другие берега
MORPHO VERAE

very, very rare

with love from

V.

5-I-1955

ИЗДАТЕЛЬСТВО ИМЕНИ ЧЕХОВА

Нью-Йорк • 1954

Eugenia onegini

моя душенька

NABOKOV AS MEMOIRIST

Vladimir Nabokov was born in St. Petersburg, in the large corner townhouse of Finnish granite that belonged to his wealthy, liberal family, in the spring of 1899, very close to and perhaps capable of being calculated as on the same day as Shakespeare, the twenty-third of April. The approximation comes from the discrepancy between the Julian calendar, then in use in Tsarist Russia, and the Gregorian to which the rest of the world adhered. Some thirty-six years later, in exile, as he was to be for all of his adult life following the revolution of 1917 and the subsequent civil war, he began to reclaim his homeland and early years by recalling them in writing.

The sum of these recollections covering the first forty-odd years of the author's life eventually appeared as a book, in its first version titled *Conclusive Evidence* and in its final version as *Speak, Memory: An Autobiography Revisited*. Nabokov wrote that he hoped one day to write a sequel perhaps to be called *Speak on, Memory*, but never did.

Like Tolstoy's *Childhood*, which was written at the age of twenty-three or twenty-four and which overnight made him a literary figure, *Speak, Memory* is divided into relatively short chapters, fifteen in all. These were not written in chronological order nor did they appear that way in various publications. The first to make its debut was Chapter Five (the complete list of chapters and the order in which they were published and presumably written – Nabokov is always scrupulous in matters of bibliography – is in the 1967 Foreword to *Speak, Memory*) written in French in 1936 and published in *Mesures* by Jean Paulhan, the French editor for whom Dominique Aury, his mistress and Scheherezade, wrote the extraordinary love letter, *L'Histoire d'O*. It was translated, revised, and published in 1943 in *The Atlantic Monthly*. The long run of chapters that appeared in *The New Yorker* began in 1948 – Edmund Wilson having introduced Nabokov to the magazine – with what was to become Chapter Three, titled "Portrait of My Uncle," and the final chapter, Thirteen, appeared in 1951, in *Harper's Magazine*. Both Tolstoy's and Nabokov's recollections – Tolstoy's being fiction closely based on fact – are distinguished by indelible portraits and masterly description as potent as any photograph.

Vividly recalling the past was something that Nabokov avows he did with great pleasure throughout his life. What is remarkable is that, impoverished, in exile, a nondescript professor (in the words of Maurice Girodias who first brought out *Lolita*, in Paris), Nabokov was successful in wresting his country from its murderers and tyrants, in the end a conqueror. He did this in imperishable language, incredibly not his own, but in which he wrote more fully and imaginatively than all but a handful of native speakers. Though he learned in the Anglophile society he grew up in to read and write English at the age of six, and though his mother read to him in English at bedtime and he prayed English prayers, it was by no means his primary tongue. Conrad, with whom Nabokov hated to be compared, also wrote in acquired English in a style, as Virginia Woolf noted, "a little somnolent sometimes in repose" though glorious despite its stiffness for "its reserve, its pride, its vast and implacable integrity."

Nabokov is another matter. His style, never more clearly in evidence than in the memoir, is splendid, playful, rich in metaphor, easily – despite adornment of arcane words – digestible, civilized, haughty, seductive, serene. Poetic in the strongest sense of the word, it is filled with surprises and always a joy. To the above list of its attributes should be added "witty." Nabokov was a clown, a bit ponderous, to be sure, but genuine nevertheless. "One of the great clowns of all time," he once called himself. Of the staid, bourgeois Swiss town to which he and his wife, Véra, retreated for their last years, he claimed, "I introduced kidding into Montreux."

Short words are more powerful than longer ones. Syllables are a kind of burden. It has been observed that this is particularly true in English where the native words tend towards shortness and the foreign words are long. Nabokov paid little attention to this. He more or less reveled in long, complex words. In addition Nabokov displayed his command of the entire language by traveling to its least known corners. The "ophyron of a brow," "susurrous lip," "hypnagogic," "praedormitary," "xanthis," are but a handful of many exotic specimens in the sentences of *Speak, Memory*. Very few indigenous writers would voyage into such regions.

Pushkin, one of Nabokov's gods whose *Eugene Onegin* he translated in a four-volume annotated edition, believed that precision and brevity were the prime qualities of prose, but Nabokov subscribed only to the first of these. His vocabulary, which he himself once described as occasionally being a Rolls Royce sent to do a job when a Jeep would have done perfectly well, is a kind of annexation of English. Familiar photographs show Nabokov with a butterfly net in his hand, intent on the only form of hunting he recognized. As in lepidoptery, so in writing – he is ever alert to the perfect, rare specimen, never before seen in these parts. Sometimes the word for what is true is not as evocative as another word, not as pleasing, but Nabokov in his punctiliousness, seems always to find a way that is both handsome and exact. It is always the aesthetic as well as absolutely correct achievement.

One of the effects of the marvelous language, or perhaps increased by it, is a certain haughtiness of tone, lofty parentheses, tossed-off "of courses," words like "amusing," "charming," enchanting," "truly remarkable" – the adjectives of a society woman. Nabokov is a writer of the upper realms. His illustrious family, privileged birth, the country estate, the staff of fifty, tutors, governesses, maids, cooks, gardeners, chauffeurs, stewards, coachmen – despite the fact that they, and it, all

vanished on the stroke of an historic midnight – these are his
sources, his headwaters, so to speak, and the broad and majes-
tic river that the writer became was fed by them. Like any aristocrat he is outspoken in his scorn for the vulgar, the preten-
tious or fraudulent, as well as for certain things and people he
does not approve of for whatever reason, Freud being notable
among these last ("the Viennese quack"). A list of Nabokov's
dislikes can easily be viewed as an honor roll: Cervantes,
Molière, Faulkner, Henry James, Dostoevsky ("The writer
Dostoevski, author of *The Double*, etc."). He is equally dis-
dainful of ideology, symbols, and what is usually thought of as
morals. Though somewhat like Evelyn Waugh or Gore Vidal in
his jagged prejudices, he possesses a grandeur that they do not.
He is seigneurial but mild, unsentimental but not cold in his
view of life. The caterpillar groping in vain for a hold, the
unnamed little black dog (with very white teeth) dashing out at
terrific speed to race after them and saving its bark until the last
second, the kind-hearted tutor, the first girlfriend (and his
heartbreaking sentences of farewell, echoed perhaps in the
farewell to the girl who was Lolita in his great hymn to the
ideal), the green leaf, the coachman, they are all given their
place. There is a feeling of generosity and understanding, both
as a matter of heritage and of admirable qualities ingrained in
the individual.

Nabokov in his early days had thought of becoming a
painter, and nothing could be more intensely visual than his
descriptions with their detail and exact shades of color
selected, as it were, before one's eyes, their sensitivity to light
and shadow, their overwhelming brilliance. "Caress the
details, the divine details!" In passage after passage all that
has vanished comes alive, his mother being driven in a sled
through the snowy streets of St. Petersburg, her seal furs, "the
voluminous spread of bearskin that covered her up to the
waist," the muff as the icy speed increased "raised to her face

— that graceful, winter-ride gesture of a St. Petersburg lady," his father being tossed in the air as a traditional gesture of thanks by grateful peasants "in his wind-rippled white summer suit...gloriously sprawling in midair, his limbs in a curiously casual attitude, his handsome, imperturbable features turned to the sky," this seen at the moment of his father's apogee through the dining room window. It is as memorable and affecting as the more Spartan and workmanlike descriptions of Hemingway, admired for their visual and sensual power. But there is more than realism; there is the flowering into unexpected metaphor and more, into the sort of dreamer's world one finds in Gogol where instead of following the path the writer veers, wanders off into completely surprising but tender scenes. In *Dead Souls* the gentlemen's black coats at an evening party flitting here and there somehow become flies circling a sparkling sugar-loaf on a hot summer day. There is the old housekeeper breaking the loaf into pieces with a hammer, the children all around her, the dazzling sunshine, the squadrons of flies flying in not only for the food but to display themselves, rubbing their hind legs, scratching themselves under their wings, stretching, until we are no longer at the governor's party but somewhere else entirely from where we return as from a curious journey. Nabokov admired Gogol and wrote a critical biography of him with some ambivalence, calling him, "[a]t his worst...a worthless writer; at his best...incomparable and inimitable." The Gogol-like moments in *Speak, Memory* are probably not so much emulation as inspired parallel leaps.

The recollections in *Speak, Memory* begin in 1903 with Nabokov, four years old, walking between his uniformed father and his mother, each holding one of his hands, down an alley of small trees in the dappled sunlight at Vyra, the estate fifty miles south of St. Petersburg, "the harmonious world of a perfect childhood." Some thirty-seven years later the narrative ends, pausing in Cambridge where Nabokov went to college, then continuing on into dreary exile in Berlin and Paris. A huge amount has happened. He and his family have lost everything and fled from Russia, his father is later assassinated by virulent right-wing monarchists in Berlin, he marries, has a child, writes novels, poems, and chess problems in the narrow émigré world of post-World War I Berlin, arriving finally in the U. S. in May 1940. The years have been harsh, disastrous, but there is a classic serenity in Nabokov's recounting of them. Not a line of self-pity. He is above that. He is in the long process of acquiring genius.

The Gift, Lolita, Pale Fire, and perhaps *Ada* are Nabokov's most important novels. None surpasses *Speak, Memory* in richness. When Nabokov is writing in the first person he seems most comfortable. There is no intrusion of the writer in comments or asides, no solemn creak of floorboards; he is already present. In *Speak, Memory*, when the first person is most direct, Nabokov is at his full height. One sees the gifted, philosophic, unflinching man. It is extremely moving as well as consolation of the deepest kind. The many portraits are as fine as the day they were written. They confer a measure of immortality upon their subjects, unforgotten teachers, favorite uncles, sour Nobel Prize winners (Bunin, portrayed in a page and a half). The greatest love is given to Nabokov's parents, and to his wife and child, but a broader and more profound love falls on all he has seen and known. The attentive reader may entertain him or herself with possibly misleading hints of the source of Nabokov's works. There is a foretremor of *Lolita* in the account of one of Nabokov's forebears, Elizabeth von Stägemann with whose twelve-year-old daughter, Hedwig Marie, the much older writer, Heinrich von Kleist, fell passionately in love.

I don't recall when I first read *Speak, Memory*, mostly likely as *Conclusive Evidence*. I have reread it any number of times. There are no longer unfamiliar facts in it, but there are paragraphs and pages that manage to burst into flame in unexpected, fresh places, and faces that had grown dim but reappear alive and bright. Nabokov said the book had aspects of a novel and it is this rare quality which makes one regard it, along with another book that is both autobiographic and novelistic, Isak Dinesen's *Out of Africa*, as an example of what might be done.

Recognition, in Nabokov's case, came late. The tracing of his rise to eminence would be difficult to imagine – only someone like Nabokov himself might have been able to make it into believable fiction. Throughout his life he paid little attention to food and drink, saw few movies, had no television, was uninterested in music. He was consumed by two things, literature and butterflies. "You will die in dreadful pain and complete isolation," Bunin told him. It proved untrue. Nabokov lived in privacy but could summon the world. He died a great man.

James Salter

XXXIV

A votary of fame and freedom,
in the excitement of his stormy thoughts,
Vladimir might have written odes,
only that Olga did not read them.
Have ... larmoyant poets ...
to read their works before the eyes of loved ones
... in the world, there are no higher reward...
And, verily, blest is the modest lover
reading his daydreams ...
of songs and love, ...
a pleasantly languorous ...
Blest ...

XXXV

But I the products of my ...
and of harmonious ... designs
read but to an old nurse,
companion of my youth;
or after a dull dinner,
stray in to see my neighbor having caught
him by a ... unexpectedly
I choke him in a corner with a tragedy,
or else (but that's apart from jesting),
by yearnings and by rhymes ...
roaming along my lake,
I scare a flock of wild ducks; they, on heeding
the chant of sweet-toned strophes,
fly off the banks.

XXXV

1 But I the products of my reveries
   or of harmonious fancies
4 read only to an old nurse,
   companion of my youth;
   or after a dull dinner,
   the neighbor who has strayed my way,
   catching abruptly by a coat-skirt,
8 I choke him in a corner with a tragedy,
   or else (but that's apart from jokes),
   by yearnings and by rhymes oppressed,
   roaming along my lake,
12 I scare a flock of wild ducks:
   on hearing the chant of sweet-toned strophes,
   they fly off from the banks.

XXXVI

. . . .

XXXVII

But what about Onegin? By the way, brothers!
I beg your patience:
his daily occupations in detail
I shall describe to you.
Onegin anchoretically lived;
he rose in summer between six and seven
and, lightly clad, proceeded to the river
that ran below the hill,
the songster of Gulnara, imitating,
across this Hellespont he swam,
then drank his coffee,
through some worthless review,
and dressed

199

Verochka verochka

for you my DAR, my darling

from V.

Montreux
Xmas
1975

NO. 78

70 Tales [Povesti]. By Nikolai Gogol. New York: Chekhov Publishing House, 1952.

8vo.; printed grey wrappers; some corners bent; edgeworn.

First edition; the only publication, to date, of VN's seven-page introduction to this edition of Gogol's *Tales*. Though his name does not appear on the cover or title page, his introduction is signed "Vladimir Nabokov-Sirin." With the publisher's advertisements and original packing slip – suggesting he received two copies – loosely inserted. Juliar B18.1. Docketed by VN on the cover: *Gogol/with a foreword by VN/1952/Stories.*

71 The Gift [Dar]. New York: Chekhov Publishing House, 1952.

8vo.; abrasions to nine pages; grey cloth, cream printed wrappers, lightly browned, bound-in.

First edition of VN's Russian masterwork, published in New York under the name "Sirin"; incompletely serialized in *Sovremennye zapiski* fifteen years earlier (April 1937–October 1938), without the controversial *The Life of Chernyshevsky* chapter, with the editors' explanatory note: "Chapter 4, consisting entirely of 'the Life of Chernyshevski,' written by the novel's hero, has been omitted with the consent of the author." *Dar* was also excerpted in *Poslednie novosti* (March 1937–April 1938). Juliar A17.1. It is dedicated in memory of VN's mother, who had died May 2, 1939.

VN's copiously annotated copy, specially (if economically) bound in grey pebbled cloth, stamped in black and labeled by hand, inscribed to Véra in Russian, on the first blank, in blue ink: *To my dear darling. V.* English: *Cambridge, Mass 16.v.1952* ([three words]). Russian: *My love!* in blue pencil, *9 Maynard Place* and in grey pencil in Véra's hand, *u May Sarton* [Russian for "at the house of May Sarton" (Boyd)], *Cambridge, Mass.* (Sarton had rented them her place.) On the half-title VN listed by page number, in pencil, several dozen corrections – mostly typographical and printer's errors, to spelling and punctuation. Many of these marginal ticks are crossed out and a few are erased. The only note on the half-title in English reads: *corrections checked on Aug. 23, 1975, for Ardis edition.* The corrections have been made in ink, pencil, and colored pencil, suggesting multiple readings. With four leaves loosely inserted – three are on Montreux Palace letterhead, one is blank

−all sides covered with Dmitri's autograph notes in Russian. With minor abrasions to multiple leaves due to the removal of post-its from the fragile, acidic paper; a few dozen post-its still remain.

VN had more trouble with the publication of *The Gift* than with any of his other Russian novels. In order to finalize an agreement with *Sovremennye zapiski* in 1937 he had resigned himself to publishing a truncated version. The Chekhov Publishing House came to his rescue in 1951, prepared to publish *The Gift* in a complete, unbowdlerized edition. Established by the Ford Foundation in affiliation with its East European Fund, the Chekhov House pursued the goal of publishing the works of "Russian émigré authors like Bunin, Aldanov, and Nabokov-Sirin, or by Soviet authors like Bulgakov and Akhmatova, who had become 'internal émigrés'" (TAY p. 204). VN wasted no time in approaching them, knowing that, with the support of the Ford Foundation and the intention to produce relatively cheap editions−paperbacks designed along the lines of those brought out by the Berlin émigré publishing houses of the '20s and '30s−Chekhov House could afford fairly sizable advances. He sent them his manuscript before the firm was officially up and running.

Even before he began *The Gift* VN knew it would be controversial. The "story of a great writer in the making" (to James Laughlin, November 27, 1941, SL p. 39), *The Gift* would contain more autobiographical material than any of his other novels. At the center is Fyodor, a Russian émigré literary aspirant in Berlin in the late '20s, whose marriage was as ordained as VN's own: like VN and Véra, Fyodor and Zina seem to have been shadowing each other for years before finally meeting. Fyodor's deceased father is embodied in a reverent depiction of VDN that "astounded Elena Nabokov by its accuracy and penetration. Nabokov makes his hero's admiration for his father and his desire to commemorate him central to the book..." (TRY p. 68).

But it was not the autobiographical content that shocked publishers; nor was it the innovative form (VN includes samples of Fyodor's literary attempts throughout the novel). It was the 100 pages of Fyodor's monumental biography of Nikolay Chernyshevsky, a literary leader in 1860s Russia and the founder of socialist realism. Writing in a style completely new for him−precise and well-trained but imaginative non-fiction−VN lampooned a Russian giant, though Fyodor's own reverence for Chernyshevsky was genuine. Boyd writes that the Chernyshevsky chapter "would reveal in Fyodor a spirit as daring as his father's and distinguish him utterly from Sirin, whose prose works had all been pure fiction. It would allow Nabokov to pay tribute to the Russian literary tradition and to exorcise its grim shadow of censorship from right and from left; it would provide a chance to expose the philosophical flaws of utilitarian materialism and to advance an alternative metaphysic; its gleeful debunking and its tragic note would offset the celebratory tones of Fyodor's account of his father and his own lucky life" (TRY p. 399).

The Gift was Nabokov's tribute to the whole Russian literary heritage, which he saw as oscillating between tribulation and triumph. In the center, the genius of writers like Pushkin, Gogol, Tolstoy, and Chekhov, ready to speak the truth as they saw it; to their right, a government that did not want the truth spoken at all; to their left, those who, rightly opposing an autocratic government, tried to press-gang writers' free imaginations into a disciplined army of liberation. Nabokov had to tackle Chernyshevsky and his contemptible opponents in the tsarist secret police and the Pushkin whose genius remained so immeasurably beyond Chernyshevsky's clumsy grasp. (TRY p. 466)

The Gift was, without a doubt, the most labor-intensive of VN's novels. He wrote to Khodasevich that it was "monstrously difficult," explaining that he had of course to do Fyodor's research for him before composing the Chernyshevsky biography. He tackled that chapter first, establishing a compositional precedent of writing the most difficult sections of a novel before the balance, a practice he followed for both *Pale Fire* and *Ada*. After reading all of Chernyshevsky's works he could track down—a feat in itself, he wrote to Khodasevich, as by the 1930s "every one of his books [was] of course utterly dead"—as well as "all the masses of books written on the gent" (and, he wrote, "digesting all this my own way, so that now I have heartburn"), VN was ready to back up his own evaluation of Chernyshevsky: "He had less talent than a lot of people, but more courage than many ... He was thoroughly tormented" (TRY pp. 406–07).

The fact that he had put so much more time into writing *The Gift* than any previous work made his inability to publish an unmolested edition all the more frustrating. Of the six novels written over the course of the preceding five years (none of which took more than a year, most of which took much less), none had been subjected to censorship in Berlin. A reading of parts of *The Gift* in April of 1935 at the home of Iosif Hessen—editor of *Pravo* and a friend of VDN—got a positive response, as did a public reading of two excerpts in Paris in January of 1937. (It was at that reading that VN first met Irina Guadanini, with whom he had a love affair in Véra's absence—she was still in Berlin.) Though in the novel Fyodor's publishers reject *The Life of Chernyshevsky*, VN hadn't guessed that his own publishers would themselves hold back that chapter of *The Gift*. He later rightly described *Sovremennye zapiski's* decision to omit chapter four as "a pretty example...of life finding itself obliged to imitate the very art it condemns" (quoted in TRY p. 457). At the time of their refusal, VN was not, however, as pithy; his tirade against the editors, who had already published the first chapter, presents the publishing climate of émigré Paris, and VN's own plight:

I'll tell you straight out, I can accept no compromises or joint efforts and have no intention of striking out or altering a single line. Your turning down the novel hurts all the more because I have always harbored a special feeling for [*Sovremennye zapiski*]. The fact that from time to time it has printed both creative work and articles developing views with which the editors plainly could not be in agreement has been a singular phenomenon in the history of our journals and a declaration of freedom of thought...that was a telling indictment of the situation of the press in present-day Russia. Why do you talk of "society's reaction" to my piece?...society's reaction to a literary work can only be a consequence of its artistic function, and not an a priori judgment...(quoted in TRY p. 442)

In addition to his ostentatious disregard for a Russian literary legend —and this constituted the majority of the complaint against him—VN's vindictive mockery of a contemporary critic caused discomfort among his editors. Georgy Adamovich, who so virulently disparaged VN's work in print at every opportunity, was clearly the model for Fyodor's own nemesis, Christopher Mortus. VN answered this charge: "I was guided not by an urge to laugh at this or that person (although there would be no crime in that—we are not in class or in church), but solely by a desire to show a certain order of literary ideas, typical at a given time—which is what the whole novel is about (its main heroine is literature). If in this case a style of criticism I feature corresponds to the style of particular figures and fops, that is natural and unavoidable" (quoted in TRY p. 480).

By the time *The Gift* was finally published in Russian in full, the Soviet Union (and, indeed, the world) had witnessed more ghastly totalitarian examples than even the émigré communities of the '30s could have envisioned. Boyd sums up a sound evaluation of *The Gift* in this context:

As Gleb Struve [author of the best known critical survey of émigré literature] commented in his role as historian of émigré literature, Nabokov for all his avowed apoliticism reflected the torments of the highly politicized decade of the 1930s more than other émigré writers. Though Fyodor disavowed any aims other than purely artistic ones in the *Life Of Chernyshevsky*, Nabokov did not. He had written the Chernyshevsky biography in reaction to the Soviet Union's enforced implementation of socialist realism as the state aesthetic, and he declared flatly that his critique of Chernyshevsky marked "the defeat of Marxism and materialism." (TRY p. 489)

72 **The Gift.** Translated from the Russian by Michael Scammell with the collaboration of the author. New York: Putnam's, (1963).

8vo.; black cloth; dust-jacket; minor wear to head of spine.

First edition of the first English translation; with a foreword written specially for this edition. Two segments of *The Gift* had been excerpted in *The New Yorker:* "Triangle in a Circle" (March 23, 1963); and "The Lyre" (April 13, 1963). Juliar A17.2. VN devoted considerable time to revising Dmitri's translation of the first chapter, preparing all of the poetry himself, and did not skimp in his review of Scammell's version of the balance of the text.

The dedication copy, inscribed *For Véra* in pencil on the half-title. With a butterfly, *Parnassius orpheus* Godunov (male), drawn and decorated in pencil, with a few red highlights. VN's hand was so heavy as he outlined the butterfly that some lead was transferred to the following leaf, the list of his works. He added a reference to page 124, where the writer-protagonist Fyodor writes of his father's discovery of the mating habits within this genus, adding: "And as a frontispiece to my present work I think I would like to display precisely this butterfly..."

The translation of *The Gift* into English was one of VN's earliest goals after his emigration to the States in 1940. In '42 he wrote to James Laughlin at New Directions to elicit interest in the project: "*The Gift* was published serially in the 'Annales Contemporaines' (the great Russian review that appeared in Paris during 20 years, since 1920), but the war, or rather the complete destruction of Russian intellectual life in Paris by the German invasion, has made its appearance in book form impossible – naturally" (July 16, 1942, SL p. 41). Endeavoring to interest the Viking Press in the project a decade after the failed attempt with New Directions, he related the novel's history to Pascal Covici:

This book deals with the development of a writer of genius. It contains his early poetry, the material he assembles for his second book (which he does not write), his first great book which is the biography of a famous Russian critic of the sixties (this biography, for some reason, created something of a furore in the Russian émigré circles, though it was never published until the recent edition by the Ford Foundation [Chekhov House]), and a happy love story involving my young man and his half-Jewish fiancée. (SL pp. 133–34)

But another ten years elapsed before VN saw his prized Russian novel made available to his English-speaking readership, by Putnam's. That year he discussed the project in a BBC interview, explaining it in terms of both its autobiographical strains as well as its evocation of his dual-literary citizenship:

...I am very much concerned with things Russian and I have just finished revising a good translation of my novel, *The Gift*, which I wrote about thirty years ago. It is the longest, I think the best, and the most nostalgic of my Russian novels. It portrays the adventures, literary and romantic, of a young Russian expatriate in Berlin, in the twenties; but he's not myself. I am very careful to keep my characters beyond the limits of my own identity. Only the background of the novel can be said to contain some biographical touches. And there is another thing about it that pleases me: probably my favorite Russian poem is one that I happened to give to my main character in that novel. (Duval-Smith interview, 1962, SO p. 14)

The Gift illustrates, perhaps more clearly than any of VN's Russian works later translated into English, the cohesion of his two bodies of literature by gracefully integrating the literary, personal, and political themes that dominate his canon. He wrote to his New York agent in 1938 of the unpublished chapter four, his hero's "chief book" on which he had labored four years, that it "lifts my novel to a wider plane, lending it an epic note and, so to say, spreading my hero's individual butter over the bread of a whole epoch. In this work...the defeat of Marxism and materialism is not only made evident, but it is rounded out by my hero's artistic triumph" (to Altagracia de Jannelli, July 14, 1938, SL p. 27).

His preservation of the meter and rhyme scheme of *Eugene Onegin* in the translation of his final paragraph – the verse is embedded in prose format – was one of his greatest coups in the project. His translation of Pushkin's classic, which he spent nearly a decade preparing for publication, and another decade revising, enduring interminable delays both times, is a monument to his belief in the need for fine translations into English of the best of Russian literature. Boyd sums up the critical response *The Gift* received, when finally published 25 years after its Russian original: "Advertised as 'the greatest Russian novel to appear in the last fifty years,' its appearance confirmed the depth and range of Nabokov's talent. A *New York Herald Tribune* review was not atypical: 'As if we all didn't know, there is a giant among us...'" (TAY p. 473).

73 **The Gift.** Translated from the Russian by Michael Scammell with the collaboration of the author. New York: Putnam's, (1963).

8vo.; black cloth; orange topstain; light wear to extremities; dust-jacket, well-worn, substantial internal and external tape repair.

First edition of the first English translation. Juliar A17.2. VN's corrected copy, labeled three times on the dust-jacket (in ink, pencil, and fading marker) *corrected*, with his note on the half-title and pencil list on the front endpaper of eight misprints, with two more added by Véra, with corrections and markings on these pages, as well as several additional emendations. With three leaves clipped to the front endpaper: a half-sheet of blank paper with six lines of pencil notes copying text from page 324; a typescript sheet, with autograph emendations in either VN's or Véra's hand, both sides covered, with a side-by-side comparison of changes to be made to the hardcover and paperback editions, listed by page number; and a leaf of tracing paper with VN's color sketch of Putnam's dust-jacket cover. Many of the typescript emendations are crossed out, checked off, or bear autograph notes next to them, and consist primarily of changes to spelling, the occasional addition, deletion, or substitution of words, or simple marginal ticks. VN was at odds with dust-jacket art and artists throughout his career, and his correspondence testifies to the seriousness with which he addressed the issue, frequently offering detailed designs of his own. This tracing paper design does not fit exactly over the printed dust-jacket; presumably it was not traced after the Putnam jackets were printed, but drawn before as a model. The Berg Collection at the New York Public Library houses a similar example in their Nabokov archive for *Speak, Memory: An Autobiography Revisited*; this lends credibility to the suggestion that VN himself designed the emblematic Putnam jackets, beyond his verbal sketch of the design in a letter to his publisher.

74 **The Gift.** Translated from the Russian by Michael Scammell with the collaboration of the author. New York: Putnam's, (1963).

8vo.; satin ribbon; top edge gilt; full brown morocco, stamped "V.N." in gilt on the front cover.

First edition of the first English translation. This appears to be a unique printing of the book, in the publisher's presentation binding: done-up on thicker paper than the regular edition, it bulks 5mm larger, and is trimmed 5mm shorter than any other copy we have examined. Juliar A17.2. This presentation copy was docketed by VN on the binder's front endpaper, *Corrected*, and bears his emendations to seven pages on which he has added or altered words and corrected the spelling of Greek references.

75 **The Gift.** Translated from the Russian by Michael Scammell with the collaboration of the author. London: Weidenfeld and Nicolson, (1963).

8vo.; black cloth; dust-jacket, three small closed tears, one discrete tape repair.

First English edition, from a new setting of type that incorporates only three of the changes VN made to his copy of the Putnam edition and introduces multiple new printing errors. Juliar A17.3. The earlier of two dedication copies, inscribed in pencil, on the front endpaper: *For Véra from the captor, Montreux 23.x.1963.* With an elaborate imagined butterfly, *Vanessa atalurticae* Nab., that Johnson calls a "'hybrid' between two Brushfoots, *Vanessa atalanta* and *Vanessa urticae*." With three autograph corrections made on two pages, both listed by VN. Of the ten corrections VN listed in his copy of the Putnam edition, only three were incorporated here. Of those apparently overlooked, only three were made again in this copy. The mistakes appearing in this edition on pages 47, 254, and 295, all slated for emendation in VN's Putnam copy, are not indicated in this copy.

76 **The Gift.** Translated from the Russian by Michael Scammell with the collaboration of the author. London: Weidenfeld and Nicolson, (1963).

8vo.; black cloth, front cover slightly bowed; white dust-jacket.

First English edition. Juliar A17.3. The later of two dedication copies, inscribed to Véra in Russian on the front endpaper on their 43rd wedding anniversary: *Here is the tenderest of butterflies worthy of the anniversary. V. 1925–68*–the dates indicate the span of their marriage. With a large, elaborate pencil butterfly, meticulously colored in blue with red, orange, purple, and yellow highlights, named *Charaxes verae Nabokov* (female)/ *Montreux, Vaud 15.iv.68.* VN wrote *for Véra* five times in red ink in various positions on the dust-jacket, labeled the spine with his Cyrillic initials and *Vé.* According to Johnson, "the genus *Charaxes* is the well-known African and Indo-Australian genus of spectacularly colored butterflies of the Brushfoot family. All exotic collections have *Charaxes* and they are very popular among collectors as 'wow-bugs.'" Here Nabokov has combined aspects of at least three different groups of this genus, taking arched tails from one, the blue colors of another and the yellow margins from a third. "In nature," Johnson comments, "the broad blue basal colors and the yellow marginal colors occur in different groups of *Charaxes*, not together. Nabokov's magnificent *Charaxes verae* apparently illustrates how Nabokov would have imagined these bold colors aligned side by side."

A corrected copy, so-docketed in pencil on the cover and front endpaper. Véra noted one change on the dedication page and VN made 26 minor emendations to wording, spelling, and spacing throughout (for example, "eighteenth" to *seventeenth*; "dinner" to *lunch*; "octavos" to *twelve-line poems*; "for" to *during*). A comparison with the emendations made in the Putnam edition reveals that two suggested changes were here ignored and three were made by hand along with an additional 20 changes noted for later editions.

77 **The Gift.** London: Weidenfeld & Nicolson, (1963).

8vo.; black cloth; covers lightly bowed.

First English edition; Juliar A17.3. The front endpaper is filled with VN's and Vé's list of 31 *Misprints and Mistranslations*, all of which have been indicated in the text at the appropriate location along with additional errors, primarily designated by marginal ticks, and minor spelling changes, along with some interesting word substitutions— *crude* for "disingenuous," for example. All of the changes VN made in the two dedication copies of this edition (see two previous entries) are included here, as are many more. A loosely inserted index card bears more of VN's notes on the text, corresponding to a series of X's and check-marks found throughout he book, concerning the temporal structure of the novel and the sequence of events, identifying specific dates and years in which the narrative develops.

78 **The Gift [Dar].** Ann Arbor, MI: Ardis, (1975).

8vo.; pinhole in page 55; blue cloth.

Second Russian edition, incorporating approximately 50 corrections to the first edition of the complete text as published in 1952 by New York's Chekhov Publishing House; first binding variant (the second was in white wrappers); 1000 copies. Juliar A17.7. A presentation copy, inscribed to Véra on the first blank: *For you my DAR, my darling/from V./Montreux/Xmas/1975*. With a detailed tropical Brushfoot in profile, drawn in blue ink and colored in red, blues, purple, orange, and brown, named *Verochka verochka*. With fourteen marginal lines and ticks in pencil, two of them noted by either VN or Véra on the title page.

Ardis Press, the "largest publisher of Russian works outside the Soviet Union" (TAY p. 516), was founded in 1969 by Carl Proffer who was one of the "key figures in the first phase of Nabokov scholarship" – the others were VN's Cornell student, Alfred Appel, editor of *The Annotated Lolita* (McGraw-Hill, 1970), and Andrew Field, writer of the critical study *Vladimir Nabokov: His Life in Art* (Boston: Little, Brown, 1967; a decade later he would produce the deeply flawed biography *Nabokov: His Life in Part*, Boston and Toronto: Little, Brown, 1977). Proffer's scholarship was "breezy, unpretentious, and avowedly provisional, but . . . [h]e and his wife, Ellendea, would become the publishers of all Nabokov's works in Russian, Nabokov's lifeline to the growing number of his readers in the Soviet Union, and rare but welcome visitors . . . " (TAY p. 516). Boyd offers a concise summary of the literary and political climate that made the success of a house like Ardis possible:

Between the 1920s and the 1960s there had been a sharp division between émigré and Soviet literature. Now émigré literature was moribund, with Bunin, Khodasevich, and Tsvetaeva long dead and Nabokov writing in English. In the 1960s and especially in the 1970s the division within Russian literature between Soviet and émigré began to break down as many Soviet writers escaped censorship at home by publishing in the West and often followed their works abroad . . . (TAY p. 647)

McGraw-Hill had issued the Russian language edition of *King, Queen, Knave* when VN signed on with them in 1969, but the edition sold poorly and they were wary of future Russian undertakings. They agreed to co-publish Russian editions of *Mary* and *Glory* with Ardis, who could more readily tap a Russian-language readership. The endeavor encouraged further effort on the part of the Proffers: "By the fall of [1974] the Proffers were preparing to republish more Russian Nabokoviana on their own, and by mid-1975 they had decided to reprint his complete Russian works" (TAY p. 647).

79 Poems 1929–1951 [Stikhotvoreniia 1929–1951]. Paris:
Rifma, 1952.

12mo.; first leaf unopened; printed grey wrappers; spine lightly
sunned; few minor nicks.

First edition of this Russian collection, published under his émigré
pseudonym, "Sirin." With the stated errors: the title of the fifth poem
("L'Inconnue de la Seine") is missing from the table of contents on p. 45,
where the last word of the first line of the fifteenth poem is "Dlilis," but
should be "Dlilas." Juliar quotes from the author's note: "The poems
selected for this edition were composed in Germany, France, and America between 1929 and 1951. The first of them concludes the period of my
youthful art. The poems presented here were published in émigré journals and newspapers, and nine of them appeared under pseudonyms: 'V.
Sirin' (the first seven) and 'Vasilii Shishkov' (the following two)." Juliar
A27.1, 1991 update. Docketed on the cover in an unrecognizable hand in
pencil, "Poems." VN added the missing title in autograph at the table of
contents, and numbered the poems. A loosely inserted index card contains three lines of Russian in Véra's hand.

NO. 80A

VLADIMIR NABOKOV
LOLITA
Volume One
THE OLYMPIA PRESS
my copy
VLADIMIR NABOKOV
LOLITA
Volume Two
THE OLYMPIA PRESS
Author's copy

NO. 80B

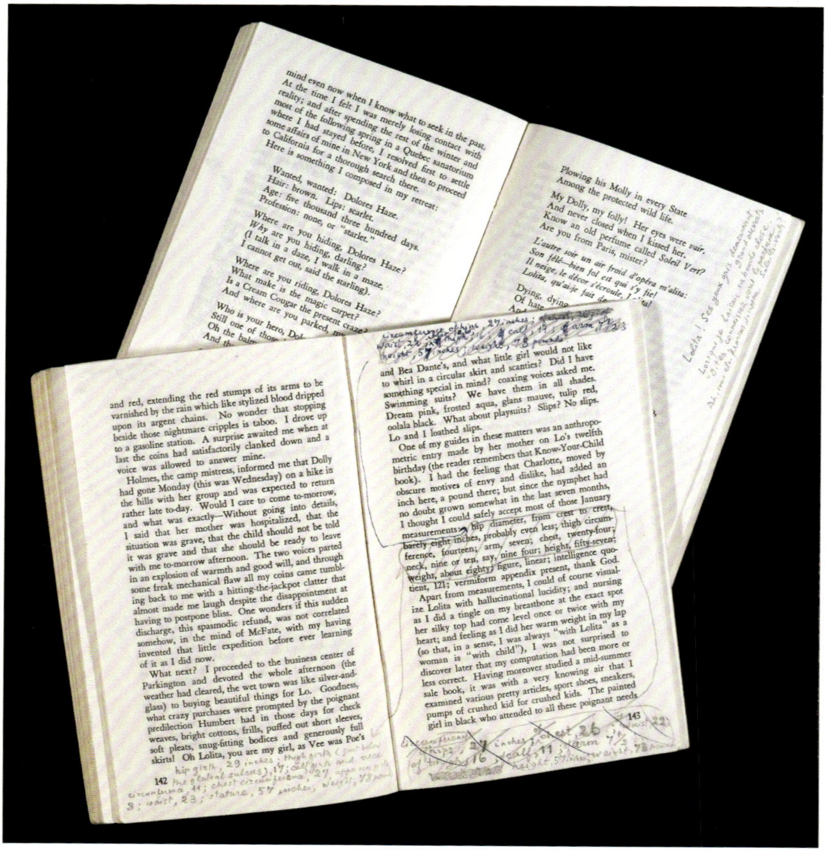

author's copy

LOLITA

ロリータ

LOLITA

ロリータ上

(LOLITA in Japanese)

ロリータ
上

NO. 87

LOLITA

...a number of words are not in Webster, but will be in its later editions.

(SL p. 251)

By 1951 VN's reputation, despite a resumé including lectureships at prominent universities and several critical works and translations well, if quietly, received, rested in America almost wholly on his periodical publications – eight stories and over a dozen autobiographical essays collected that year in *Conclusive Evidence*. *Lolita*, however, he knew would have to debut in book form. He wrote to Katharine White in 1953 that "the enormous, mysterious, heartbreaking novel that, after five years of monstrous misgivings and diabolical labors, I have more or less completed . . . has had no precedent in literature. In none of its parts will it be suitable for the *New Yorker*" (September 29, SL p. 140).

At least five American publishers rejected the book: Viking, Simon & Schuster, New Directions, Farrar Straus, and Doubleday. *The Partisan Review* agreed to print a portion of it, but only on the condition that VN would sign the work; he refused, having decided that "its subject is such that V., as a college teacher, cannot very well publish it under his real name. Especially, since the book is written in the first person, and the 'general' reader has the unfortunate inclination to identify the invented 'I' of the story with its author." He added, parenthetically, "This is, perhaps, particularly true of the American 'general' reader."

Madame Doussia Ergaz, VN's *de facto* agent in Paris since the early thirties (when she translated *Camera Obscura* into French), suggested Maurice Girodias and his Olympia Press, of whose salacious, pseudonymously published "obscene novelettes" ("*Lolita* and Mr. Girodias," SO p. 271) VN was vehemently unaware. Still, on July 18, 1955 he wrote to his new publisher: "You and I know that *Lolita* is a serious book with a serious purpose. I hope the public will accept it as such. A *succès de scandale* would distress me" (SL p. 175). The weeks after publication were distinctly anticlimactic: *Lolita* received virtually no attention until after it was banned in France under pressure from the British Home Office (though the United States Customs Office, still somewhat prudish, did not react). A victorious legal battle which lifted the ban brought the book new consideration and when Graham Greene included it in a year-end list of the three best novels of 1955, a public debate ensued between Greene in the *London Times* and John Gordon in the *Sunday Express*, with Greene winning many over to his side. Greene used his influence to shepherd the first English edition into print, writing to VN that "in England one may go to prison, but there couldn't be a better cause!" (January 1957, SL p. 198).

All the while VN defended his work to friends and publishers. He wrote to Morris Bishop:

I know that *Lolita* is my best book so far. I calmly lean on my conviction that it is a serious work of art, and that no court could prove it to be 'lewd and libertine'. All categories grade, of course, into one another: a comedy of manners written by a fine poet may have its 'lewd' side; but 'Lolita' is a tragedy. 'Pornography' is not an image plucked out of context; pornography is an attitude and an intention. The tragic and the obscene exclude each other. (March 6, 1956, SL p. 184)

Meanwhile, a plan was being concocted to bring *Lolita* into the States. Jason Epstein had long wanted it for Doubleday, and hoped to play upon the desire of the house's president, Douglas Black, to find the right book over which to re-fight the court battle the firm had recently lost over Wilson's *The Memoirs of Hecate County*. In an attempt to gain ground, Epstein arranged for an excerpt (about a third of the novel) to appear in Doubleday's *Anchor Review*, with critical praise from F. W. Dupee of the *Partisan Review*. The review, featuring "On a Book Entitled *Lolita*"—VN's specially written explanation of the genesis of the novel and his defense of it on the grounds of "aesthetic bliss"—came out in June 1957. Throughout the summer and into the fall VN endured delays and denials, by Doubleday, Simon & Schuster, and even by Putnam's. He settled on the small independent publisher Ivan Obolensky, but when his offer, too, fell through, Putnam's made good on an earlier, unfulfilled proposal, and went into production.

Walter Minton, Putnam's president, had introduced himself on August 30, 1957:

Being a rather backward example of that rather backward species, the American publisher, it was only recently that I began to hear about a book called *Lolita*. Since then we have heard much and read much. Briefly, I am wondering if the book is available for publication and if, as I have heard, the Olympia Press controls all English rights, we have your blessing to negotiate with them. I realize that there are distinct obligations to Doubleday and I would not wish to intrude on already established relationships. (SL, pp. 224–25)

When the first American edition came out, VN's first overwhelming financial success would soon follow. Minton sent a congratulatory telegram on August 18, nearly a year to the day after his initial contact:

EVERYBODY TALKING OF LOLITA ON PUBLICATION DAY YESTER-DAYS REVIEWS MAGNIFICENT AND NEW YORK TIMES BLAST THIS MORNING [panning the novel] PROVIDED NECESSARY FUEL TO FLAME 300 REORDERS THIS MORNING AND BOOK STORES REPORT EXCEL-LENT DEMAND CONGRATULATIONS ON PUBLICATION DAY. (SL p. 257)

80 **Lolita.** Paris: The Olympia Press, (1955).

2 vols., 12mo.; green wrappers; light edgewear.

First edition; probably 5000 copies. Juliar A28.1.1; second issue, with the "new price" sticker on the rear panel of the second volume. VN's heavily emended copy, annotated in preparation for the first American edition brought out by Putnam's in 1958. On the cover of volume one, docketed by VN, *My copy*, he has appended the note: *Add Anchor My Preface*, referring to his essay, "On a Book Entitled *Lolita*" which had appeared in the 1957 issue of the *Anchor Review* and was subsequently included in Putnam's edition as a postscript. He put his hand on nearly every page of the first volume, and only slightly fewer of the second, correcting spelling, punctuation, and format, listing several page numbers and corresponding changes on the covers, though these are only representative of his manifold revisions.

In volume one—the cover list of many of the corrections within has been smudged to illegibility—he wrote three versions of a passage on pages 142–43, in which Humbert physically describes Lolita. He crossed out two of the new possibilities; the third was ultimately used in Putnam's edition. *Hip girth, 29 inches; thigh girth (just below the gluteal sulcus), 17; calf girth and neck circumference, 11; chest cir-cumference, 27, upper arm girth, 8; waist, 23; stature, 57 inches; weight, 78 pounds.* He tinkered with the text, inserting, deleting, or altering language on dozens of pages, and questioned foreign-language pas-sages. He also crossed out "The Olympia Press" at every opportunity, reflecting his relief that he would at last dissociate the novel from Girodias, who had repeatedly failed to honor his contract and contin-ued to issue unauthorized reprints even after its expiration. Among the corrections listed on the cover of volume two is VN's note: *check*

Gaston's French against Kahane's p. 85 and p. 112 (Gaston Grodin, a homosexual pedophile in part two of *Lolita*; and Eric Kahane, *Lolita*'s French translator and Girodias's half-brother); page 155 bears VN's translation into French of one stanza of Humbert's love poem. Though vehemently opposed to poetic "mistranslations" of others' works, preferring to transliterate rather than preserve sound and rhyme, VN here turned his own quatrain into lyrical, rhyming French which reflects the sense, though not the precise meaning, of its English model.

A collation of this annotated first edition against his emended copy of Putnam's edition reveals that only one later change escaped VN's notice here: at this stage, he retained the spelling "Fantazia" (p. 70) for one of Lolita's classmates, whose name he would eventually emend to "Fantasia." A manuscript written after the first American edition suggests that he would alter, too, one line of Humbert's love poem to Lolita, substituting "Lolita" for "Dolores" in one stanza. (See item #105, *Poems*, London: Weidenfeld and Nicolson, 1961, for this unpublished emendation.) Excepting these two omissions, the annotations in this copy reflect VN's approved final text.

The gratitude VN felt towards Girodias for taking on *Lolita* waned as he began to confront his publisher's "aura of negligence, evasiveness, procrastination, and falsity" ("*Lolita* and Mr. Girodias," SO p. 272). He waited almost a month for a copy of the novel after its publication; waited weeks and months for overdue royalties; countenanced subsequent printings, published without his approval with a prefatory essay by Girodias; and waited *ad infinitum* for replies to his various complaints, chief among these that Girodias stood firmly in the way of American publication. In 1957 when more than one U. S. publisher was fishing for the rights, Girodias put them off with absurd demands and plans for unfair distribution of profits. VN quickly understood that Girodias had not been "the right person to undertake the thing," and what began as low grade aggravation ultimately blossomed into full-blown, publicly waged hostility that followed them into the next decade. Girodias published an error-riddled account of their dealings in the April 1961 issue of *Playboy* ("Pornologist on Olympus"). VN's rejoinder in the July issue prompted a more acerbic piece by Girodias, this time in the *Evergreen Review* ("Lolita, Nabokov, and I," No. 37, September 1965; reprinted in *The Olympia Reader*, NY: Grove Press, 1965, as "A Sad, Ungraceful History of Lolita"). VN had the last word in a final, detailed history, "*Lolita* and Mr. Girodias" (*Evergreen Review*, February 1967; reprinted in *Strong Opinions*, 1973).

81 "On a Book Entitled *Lolita*." Translated into French by
   Eric H. Kahane. **L'Affaire Lolita: Défense de l'Ecrivain.**
   Edited by Maurice Girodias. Paris: Olympia Press, April
   1957, pp. 43–50.

8vo.; yellow wrappers, rear panel lightly soiled.

First edition of Girodias's promotional paperback; 5000 press-numbered copies (this is copy #873). This includes the first appearance in
any language of VN's essay, originally written in English for the June
1957 *Anchor Review*, but published here in Kahane's French translation two months earlier with permission from Doubleday; it became the
afterword to the first American edition and, Boyd notes, "all foreign
editions except perhaps pirated ones." This also includes the first
French translation of *Lolita*—Kahane's version of the first six chapters,
as well as a biographical note; a note from the publisher; Dupee's preface; an article by Girodias with related legal documents, including a
lengthy discussion of the legal issues by Daniel Becourt; and three
appendices. Juliar B20.1.

A presentation copy, inscribed to Véra in Russian, in pencil, on his
birthday, April 23, 1957, with a simple, hand-drawn pencil butterfly:
Your copy, my darling. 23 Avril 1957. VN's annotations to Kahane's
translation of his essay include the underlining of several phrases on
page 47, copious question marks in the margin of that page and marginal ticks and lines to the following three pages suggesting an imper-
fect translation. He wrote *fresque!* in the margin, calling attention to
that typographical error in the text.

By the beginning of 1957 nearly twenty of Girodias's books were
either banned or under consideration for censorship of some kind. He
pinned his hopes for their release on a legal victory for *Lolita*. On
February 12, 1957, VN responded: "I very much regret that I lack the
funds to attack the ban independently, as you suggest. I simply do not
make enough money with my books to permit such action, much as I
would like to undertake it. Apart from this, I wish to give you every
assistance in your campaign." Toward that goal and despite his distaste
for Girodias, he gave permission to use "On a Book Entitled *Lolita*" and
secured permission for Dupee's essay, adding that "Doubleday were at
first opposed to allowing Dupee's article to be used and they consider it
a favor that they have finally agreed to have you use it. Of course, we
assume that both pieces will be used in a French translation only. I have
no objections to your using in your pamphlet parts of the French translation of *Lolita* provided Gallimard agrees to this" (SL p. 200).

82 **Lolita: An Excerpt.** In the *Anchor Review* Number Two of a Series. Including "A Preface to *Lolita*" by F. W. Dupee; Excerpts from "*Lolita*"; "On a Book Entitled *Lolita*." Garden City: Doubleday Anchor Books, 1957.

12mo.; hinges weakened at front cover and pages 132–33; yellow printed wrappers; single tape mark at head of spine.

First appearance of any part of *Lolita* in the United States; first English-language appearance of "On a Book Entitled *Lolita*"; also includes: foreword; pt. I, 2–4, 10, 15–18, 22; Pt. II, 1–2 partial, 4, 6, 11, 18, 23, 29, 35. Juliar C553. A presentation copy, inscribed in Russian and English: *For Véra My darling, May 6 1957/ V.* With a small, meticulously colored butterfly.

Jason Epstein at Doubleday was one of *Lolita*'s most fervent champions. Knowing that the house's president, Douglas Black, wanted a fresh chance to promote a controversial title after losing his court defense of Wilson's *Memoirs of Hecate County*—a loss of $60,000 and an important principle—Epstein targeted *Lolita*, proposing this excerpt-style publication as the foundation for a future defense. (Years later Epstein wrote that "there was considerable enthusiasm among the Doubleday editors for *Lolita*, though we were all apprehensive about possible legal consequences. As I recall, Ken McCormick, the editor-in-chief at the time, would have agreed to publish it if Douglas Black, the president of the company, authorized it. But Black was so strongly opposed that he refused even to read the manuscript" (to Sally Dennison, February 23, 1982, quoted in SL p. 191).) Epstein, the *Review*'s editor Melvin Lasky, and Fred Dupee of the *Partisan Review*, selected about a third of the novel for publication, along with Dupee's "weightily academic appraisal of the novel" (TAY p. 314) as an introductory essay and VN's defense, "On a Book Entitled *Lolita*" (TAY p. 300), an essay that Boyd characterizes as "witty and profound...nimble, elusive, deceptive" (TAY p. 300) in its discussion of the inspiration, composition, and style of *Lolita* in the realm of "aesthetic bliss" and, as such, beyond any allegations of obscenity.

VN had left the selection of text up to Epstein, approving his choices in advance: "It might be difficult for me to help there since in my mind I see the book as a whole" (October 1, 1956, SL p. 191). VN's response to the publication was favorable; he wrote Epstein: "Véra and I are both delighted with *Lolita* at Anchor. Despite your self-disparaging remarks, the cover is splendid and most enticing. Your arrangement and selection of the *Lolita* excerpts is above all praise. I also find that the rest of the material in the review is excellent (except Auden's piece)" (April 22, 1957, SL p. 217).

83 **Lolita.** Translated by Tom Bright. Copenhagen: Hans Reitzels Forlag, 1957.

8vo.; largely unopened; black illustrated wrappers, lightly rubbed with some edgewear.

First edition of the first Danish translation. This was the first translation into any language of *Lolita;* it was made, as were many of the early translations, from the Olympia Press edition. Juliar D28.1. Field records the tale, as told by VN's friend Alfred Parry, that upon his receipt of this volume "Nabokov had waved it in his hand and told his friend: '*Pomyanite moe slovo, vot otkuda nachnyotsya moe voskhozhdenie* [Mark my word. Here is where my ascension begins!]'." A presentation copy, inscribed on the half-title *For Véra*. With a penciled butterfly in reds, yellows, and greys, named *Polygonia thaïsoides* Nab. "Polygonia is a group of Brushfoot butterflies commonly called Anglewings," Johnson explains. "The well-known species occur across North America and Eurasia. Among them, the European species are more often marked with the kind of fine, reticulate, markings Nabokov represents in this imagined species. The pointed, nearly ragged, wing edges are typical of the group but no known species comes close to the refined detail of the markings Nabokov renders here, especially the blocks of whitish that cross the hindwing." With another of VN's lepidopteral creations, excised from an unidentified source and taped to the bottom of the page, that "might first jump out to a lepidopterist as a poorly rendered member of the *Colias* Sulphur butterflies that Nabokov so aptly rendered elsewhere. However," Johnson notes, "the drawings may not be an error at all—perhaps instead one of the maplike patterned Metalmarks, small and robust, some of which do show a darkened border and central spot on each wing."

84 **Lolita.** Stockholm: Wahlström & Widstrand, (1957).

Large 8vo.; unopened except first leaf; illustrated wrappers, well-worn edges with no chips or tears.

First edition of the first Swedish translation. Juliar reports: "Translated by Nils Kjellstrom. Withdrawn from sale on Nabokov's request because the translation was defective. Another edition was also withdrawn, for the same reason, and all copies were supposedly burnt." Juliar D28.3 A presentation copy, inscribed *for Véra* on the half-title in pencil. With a lovely, intricately decorated butterfly. VN's pressure was hard enough to leave the butterfly in relief on the title page.

VN did not know Swedish, and was troubled by rumors that this translation "high-lighted the passages of erotic tension and omitted as much as possible of the rest of the novel" (TAY p. 316). He arranged to have the entire edition—which he later referred to as "mutilated and worthless" (to Carl Björkman, November 11, 1957, SL p. 234)—destroyed. He wrote to the publisher that his perusal of the second attempt "plunged me into despair":

> While I appreciate your effort to improve the translation and note that many passages omitted in your first edition have been restored, I am distressed to say that the translation remains a sorry mess. In its present condition it would take weeks to correct it and there is hardly any sense in my pointing out to you its innumerable errors, blunders, mistranslations—and, alas, remaining omissions... All in all, you certainly could not call this 'an authorized' translation, or even a 'translation approved by the author'. I emphatically disapprove of it. I probably cannot prevent you from publishing it— under the express condition that *all* the omissions are reinstated, in this second volume as well as in the first volume, where a whole chapter is missing and innumerable passages and paragraphs are omitted... Fortunately I do have the right to insist on the complete reinstatement of the entire English text..." (ibid.)

85 **Lolita.** New York: Putnam's, (1958).

8vo.; paper-covered boards, cloth spine; dust-jacket, lightly rubbed and foxed.

First American edition, with minor textual revisions made from the first edition, expanded with a postscript. Juliar A28.2. A presentation copy, with a delicate, intricate and imaginative butterfly from the Blue group, on which Nabokov was a world authority, rendered on the half-title in pale shades for Véra—it is named *Verina verae* Nab.—and docketed *August 1958, Ithaca.* Johnson notes that "it is perhaps significant that Nabokov draws this species with short hindwing tails and a hint of orange color along the wing margins. Of all the Blues Nabokov named from the West Indies, one—*Pseudochrysops bornoi*—was known as the Antillean Tailed Blue. It is very rare, occurring in desert areas of Hispaniola and Puerto Rico. Although looking quite like this, the real butterfly lacks the pointed forewing which Nabokov appears to have drawn here only on the left."

The first book VN published with Putnam's inaugurated the tradition of a white dust-jacket printed with the title and VN's name in black, with a burst of color rising behind. Evidence suggests that VN himself designed the jacket: tracing paper sketches of the cover for *The Gift* elsewhere in this collection, and for *Speak, Memory* in the Berg Collection at the New York Public Library, as well as published correspondence. He wrote to Walter Minton on March 7, 1958:

> ...I would rather not involve butterflies. Do you think it could be possible to find today in New York an artist who would not be influenced in his work by the general cartoonesque and primitivist style jacket illustration? Who would be capable of creating a romantic, delicately drawn, non-Freudian and non-juvenile, picture for *Lolita* (a dissolving remoteness, a soft American landscape, a nostalgic highway – that sort of thing)? There is one subject which I am emphatically opposed to: any kind of representation of a little girl...(SL p. 250).

And six weeks later: "I want pure colors, melting clouds, accurately drawn details, a sunburst above a receding road with the light reflected in furrows and ruts, after rain. And no girls. If we cannot find that kind of artistic and virile painting, let us settle for an immaculate white jacket (rough texture paper instead of the usual glassy kind) with *Lolita* in bold black lettering" (April 23, 1958, SL p. 256).

86 **Lolita.** New York: Putnam's, (1958).

8vo.; paper-covered boards, cloth spine; bumped and lightly frayed; dust-jacket, lightly used, spine browned.

First American edition. Juliar A28.2. An annotated presentation copy, inscribed to Véra with a note in Russian, *Véra's duplicate* on the half-title, with a butterfly drawn in pencil with an eyespot, complete with eyelashes, in each of the four wing sections, in blue and green with red highlights in the two top sections. These eyelashes, Johnson notes, may be the lepidopteral equivalent of Lolita batting her lashes at Humbert: "There are in fact some Hairstreaks, of the genus *Macusia*, with the eyelash like 'hairs' along the front margin of the wing but, in reality, those eyelash-like structures are 'hair pencils' – part of an apparatus that puts a scent into the air to attract a mate." He continues, "That aside, the rest of the butterfly is imagined, but perhaps not completely. Its large eyespots are quite like those of the well-known European Peacock butterfly, one of Europe's most colorful butterflies and well-known to Nabokov. Its name conjures the image of the magnificent eye-spotted tail feathers that bird uses to attract a mate."

VN labeled the front cover in heavy black marker, *Vé/corrected*, reflecting the nine emendations made throughout the text, listed by page number on the front endpaper in pencil and black ink, along with the note: *The locking of rooms. NB in Part II, ch. 35 should be revised in accordance with Russian version.* With additional markings to four pages.

87 **Lolita.** New York: Putnam's, (1958).

8vo.; lightly shaken; paper-covered boards, cloth spine, lightly rubbed, minor wear to extremities.

First American edition. Juliar A28.2. VN's "official" corrected copy, labeled in black marker *V* on the cover, *Corrected* in blue marker underneath, and *author's copy* on the half-title. Eight corrections, in ink and pencil, listed by page number on the front endpaper, are labeled *1969* with the note: *all transferred to Vé's and bound copy* (referring to the copy inscribed to Véra and the publisher's presentation copy). Additional emendations appear on the copyright page (docketed *August, 1958*) and page 119 ("rubous" to *rubious*), and there are marginal lines and ticks on approximately 2 dozen pages (several of these are partially erased).

This copy contains several butterflies: a pastel tissue-paper specimen affixed to a white paper fragment, clipped to the front endpaper. Four pencil butterflies of various sizes superimposed on each other at different angles in grey, white, and shades of red, are on the half-title — on which VN wrote *Lolita* three times in the katakana alphabet (once vertically and twice horizontally, under which he wrote *Lolita in Japanese*). On the title page he incorporated the printed device into a pinkish-colored butterfly. Johnson identifies all four of the butterflies aswirl on the half-title as probably all from North American species — "consistent with the journeys of Lolita and Humbert." The top one is likely a stylized Variegated Fritillary; the second from the top, with the rows of eyespots along both wings, alludes to the Appalachian Satyr, "a species Nabokov sought for many years around Cornell University until finding it in the McLean Bog near Ithaca, New York." The third "lep" down looks like North America's Tortoise Shell butterflies, "which Nabokov not only greatly admired but collected regularly on his expeditions to the West." The one on the bottom is "a very common kind of Metalmark, some of which occur in the American West and which have 'maplike' designs on their wings resembling criss-crossed roads and highways." Johnson pursues this, noting that "in the tropics these Metalmarks can get quite grand, colored not only orange and yellow but pinkish as well."

88 **Lolita.** New York: Putnam's, (1958).

8vo.; gilt-tooled dentelles; top edge gilt; satin ribbon; full brown morocco, stamped "V. N." in gilt on the front cover.

First American edition, second impression, so stated. Juliar A28.2. A specially bound publisher's presentation copy, a Christmas gift from the publisher to VN with a card inscribed with holiday greetings from Walter Minton loosely inserted. Docketed on the binder's first blank by VN: *Corrected, 1969* in pencil; with VN's emendations to six pages, all also made in his "desk copy" and in the copy corrected for Véra.

89 **Lolita.** Translated from the English by E. H. Kahane. (Paris): Gallimard, (1959).

12mo.; photographically illustrated wrappers; light wear.

First French translation of the complete text, trade issue; preceded by a deluxe edition limited to 80 numbered copies, six lettered. Juliar D28.7. Kahane's translation – reviewed and revised by VN – was used for two subsequent editions: a paperback in 1963 (Paris: Livre de Poche) and a cloth edition in 1966 (Lausanne: La Guilde du Livre). VN wrote to Girodias on May 14, 1957 of the presence of Kahane's annoying blunders appearing in proof, in his estimation, at the rate of "at least three on every page" (SL p. 219).

A presentation copy, inscribed on the first leaf: *for Verochka/ VN/ Sept. 1973/ Montreux.* With a lovely butterfly in profile, colored in pastels with an eye on a lower wing – *Trozrachna verae Nab.* – flying past a green leafy stalk. Johnson writes: "This drawing offers convincing evidence that Nabokov was thinking of real butterflies when he rendered many of the Véra drawings. The green plant behind the butterfly can be seen through the transparent wings. This characteristic, along with the large eyespot, clearly indicates Nabokov was thinking of the groups of transparent-winged Satyr butterflies that occur in South America, in which opaque color often occurs only toward the base of the wings and the hindwings are marked with large and colorful eyespots, including shades of yellow, orange, pink, and blue."

90 **Lolita.** Translated from English by the author [Perevel S Angliiskogo Avtor]. New York: Phaedra, (1967).

8vo.; pink cloth; dust-jacket; one-cm closed tear to front panel.

First Russian translation, with English title page and verso; expanded with a new Russian postscript and glossary, both composed specially for this edition; second issue, in pink cloth (the first was in white wrappers), with the three cancels called for by Juliar. Juliar A28.7.

The dedication copy, inscribed *To my Verochka/October 1967/Montreux* on the front endpaper in Russian, and *Vérochka's* in Russian on the dust-jacket; with three permutations of VN's signature on the front pastedown: *V. Nabokov, Vl. Nabokov, Vladimir Nabokov*, opposite which he drew for her a spectacular butterfly on the front endpaper: *Colias lolita* Nab. (female), with the wing shape and pattern of a true female *Colias*, and lavender shades completely unknown in this group. "At most, some northern and high mountain Sulphur butterflies tend to dusky green or grayish, but the idea of a vividly purple and blue *Colias* is grand indeed" (Johnson).

The debate surrounding VN's translations of his own works is of long-standing. Issues of textual fidelity and revision are subsumed by the larger question of how many new works VN sacrificed to the task of bringing his Russian novels into English and, in the instance of *Speak, Memory* and *Lolita*, vice versa. In a 1964 interview for *Playboy* he offered the following partial explanation:

[I]t occurred to me one day – while I was glancing at the varicolored spines of *Lolita* translations into languages I do not read, such as Japanese, Finnish or Arabic – that the list of unavoidable blunders in these fifteen or twenty versions would probably make, if collected, a fatter volume than any of them. I had checked the French translation, which was basically very good yet would have bristled with unavoidable errors had I not corrected them. But what could I do with Portuguese or Hebrew or Danish? Then I imagined something else. I imagined that in some distant future somebody might produce a Russian version of *Lolita*. I trained my inner telescope upon that particular point in the distant future and I saw that every paragraph, pockmarked as it is with pitfalls, could lend itself to hideous mistranslation. In the hands of a harmful drudge, the Russian version of *Lolita* would be entirely degraded and botched by vulgar paraphrases or blunders. So I decided to translate it myself.

After failed attempts by his brother and sister, at the end of January 1963 VN began translating the first few chapters for publication in Roman Grynberg's journal *Aerial Ways* [*Vozdushnye puti*]. The task was difficult. He soon discovered that Russian was "a good 'From' language but a terrible 'Into' one," explaining that "[t]he main trouble is with technical terms: they are either longwinded and roundabout or facetious" (to Bertrand Thompson, quoted TAY p. 491). In a later interview he again admitted: "I've lots of difficulties with technical terms, especially with those pertaining to the motor car, which has not really blended with Russian life as it, or rather she, has with American life. I also have trouble with finding the right Russian terms for clothes, varieties of shoes, items of furniture, and so on. On the other hand, descriptions of tender emotions, of my nymphet's grace and of the soft, melting American landscape slip very delicately into lyrical Russian" (Hughes interview, 1965, SO pp. 52–53). In addition to noting the hurdles presented by the individual affinities and proclivities of both Russian and English, in his foreword written specially for this edition he laments that "[t]he history of this translation is a history of disillusionment."

Alas, that "wondrous Russian tongue" that, it seemed to me, was waiting for me somewhere, was flowering like a faithful springtime behind a tightly locked gate, whose key I had held in safekeeping for so many years, proved to be nonexistent, and there is nothing behind the gate but charred stumps and a hopeless autumnal distance, and the key in my hand is more like a skeleton key... the rattle of my rusty Russian strings only nauseates me now. (Sampson, p. 190)

By 1967 VN had translated many substantial Russian works, the largest being Pushkin's Eugene Onegin; and had translated or supervised the translations several of his own novels, most significantly, The Gift. He had also brought Speak, Memory into Russian in 1954. Many critics look favorably on this translation of Lolita, and discount VN's self-deprecating introduction. While still immersed in the project, VN noted: "The book will be published in America or perhaps Paris; traveling poets and diplomats will smuggle it into Russia, I hope" (Hughes interview, 1965, SO pp. 52–53). This would be just one of the rewards; in one letter he referred to the task as "completing the circle of my creative life. Or rather starting a new spiral" (to Katharine White).

91 The Annotated Lolita. Edited, with a preface, introduction and notes by Alfred Appel, Jr. New York: McGraw-Hill, (1970).

8vo.; black cloth; white dust-jacket, lightly used.

First edition, first issue; the second issue was in wrappers. Juliar A28.8. A presentation copy, inscribed by Appel, VN's former Cornell student, with a pun on *Ada* and a butterfly sketch: *To V.N. With deepest Adamiration, as Quilty might say – Alfred Appel August 28, 1970*; with Appel's typed errata list affixed to the front endpaper. VN inserted a notecard with several queries and notes corresponding to underlining and ticks throughout Appel's introduction, and added his own errata directly on the front endpaper including a comment on his change of "named after" to *named by: A describer's name, often abridged as here (Chat.) is placed after the (italicized) name he gave to the insect. Only in popular names of animals or plants, i.e. in English not in Latin, is the describer's name given as it were to the bug "Chateaubriand's mosquito."* He left pencil lines in the margins, question marks, and other notations on several pages of Appel's introduction and notes, and appears to have been especially skeptical of his readings of *Invitation to a Beheading* and *Laughter in the Dark*.

In 1970 Appel organized a festschrift for VN under the auspices of the *TriQuarterly Review*, and contributed his own essay, "Backgrounds of *Lolita*." VN assessed it as "a superb example of the rare case where art and erudition meet in a shining ridge of specific information (the highest and to me most acceptable function of literary criticism" (*Anniversary Notes*, p. 2), likely seeing the essay as the result of his influence during this project. Appel had begun annotating *Lolita* in 1967, gleaning information on internal and external allusions in conversation and correspondence with VN. In a letter containing nearly two dozen responses to Appel's draft, the first will give a flavor of VN's participation: "p. 33, 'Dillingham' has no significance. *A Murder is Announced* on the next page, of course. A Percy Elphinstone did write *A Vagabond in Italy* which I found in a hospital library. The nearest thing to a prison library. The 'Elph-in-stone' is wrong. It is my own random recollection of Percy, a happier vagabond than my man. But it is worth noting that the fairy tale *Lolita* ends in Elph's Stone and begins in Pixie" (May 23, 1967, SL pp. 412–13). Such replies conjure images of James Joyce working with, and perhaps even writing for, the contributors to *Our Exagmination Round his Factification of Incamination of Work in Progress*, a critical anthology organized to promote *Finnegans Wake*. Still, though VN at times asked Appel "to prune luxuriant detail and tone down his irrepressible humor, hardly apropos in scholarly annotations that a publisher would want compactly bound into affordable copies of the novel," at the same time he "delighted in someone like Appel, who did not sit reverently waiting for the master's words but could hold his own and even cheerily characterize himself as a 'Jew d'esprit'" (TAY p. 530).

92 **Lolita: A Screenplay.** New York: McGraw-Hill, (1974).

8vo.; black cloth; white dust-jacket.

First edition of VN's screenplay adaptation. Juliar A45.1. Includes nearly all the text he submitted to Stanley Kubrick for his 1962 film. Though Kubrick ultimately used more than just the "bits and shadows" VN later asserted (Appel interview, 1966, SO p. 90), he filmed only a fraction of the whole script, claiming that as written it would have yielded over seven hours of film. Motivated to bring out this edition by a desire to "give it some kind of form which would protect it from later intrusions and distortions," VN states in the foreword: "I included quite a number of scenes that I had discarded from the novel but still preserved in my desk" (Appel interview, 1970, SO pp. 165–66), making no mention of the dozens of typescript pages he ultimately left out.

The dedication copy, inscribed to Véra—docketed on the dust-jacket in Russian, *Véra's book* (transliterated Russian, Shapiro)—with VN's brilliantly attired hand-drawn butterfly (likely a tropical Brushfoot) on the half-title, cleverly named to make the screenplay a subspecies of the *Lolita* species, of the "Verinia" genus: *Verinia lolita cinemathoides/ V/April 1974*. With a minor typographical error corrected on page 109 and noted on the half-title.

VN wrote seven Russian plays during his career, and adapted one into English; he taught a summer course on drama at Stanford; and his use of visual media in his novels, especially in *Lolita*, seem to lend themselves to screen adaptation—as when Humbert Humbert gives instructions to his audience, "If you want to make a movie out of my book…" (p. 222). But in 1974 he claimed that he and Véra had "virtually not been to the cinema more than two or three times in fifteen years, nor do we have a TV at home" (November 8, SL p. 537). In the early '30s he had been enticed to submit scenarios to Lewis Milestone, the Russian-born producer of "All Quiet on the Western Front" and "The Front Page," and apparently expressed his love of the cinema to Sergey Bertenson, his link to Milestone (TRY p. 376). But *Lolita* was his only complete screenplay.

The decision to go ahead with the project did not come easily or quickly. Stanley Kubrick and Frank Harris approached him early on in 1959 and, after several meetings and much thought, he declined, wary of some aspect of the project that troubled him. By the time of Kubrick's second attempt to win him over nearly a year later he had worked the undisclosed problem out "in an aesthetically satisfying form" according to Véra's letter to the director (December 31, 1959, SL p. 304). Just before the premiere he recalled the process of adaptation in an interview: "Turning one's novel into a movie script is rather like making a series of sketches for a painting that has long ago been finished and framed. I composed new scenes and speeches in an effort to safeguard a *Lolita* acceptable to me. I knew that if I did not write the script somebody else would, and I also knew that at best the end product in such cases is less of a blend than a collision of interpretations...From my seven or eight sessions with Kubrick during the writing of the script I derived the impression that he was an artist, and it is on this impression that I base my hopes of seeing a plausible *Lolita*..." (1962, SO pp. 6–7).

In retrospect, VN was pleased with the result, though Véra admitted to his cousins that it "might have been somewhat different had he made it himself but it certainly was excellent anyway and contained nothing whatsoever that he could find offensive, false or in bad taste" (to Peter and Joan de Peterson, July 24, 1962, SL p. 338). VN, in letters and interviews, never attacked Kubrick's version, but continually lamented the loss of his own artistic vision for the movie. In anticipation of this publication, he wrote:

Although there are just enough borrowings from it in his version to justify my legal position as author of the script, the film is only a blurred skimpy glimpse of the marvelous picture I imagined and set down scene by scene during the six months I worked in a Los Angeles villa. I do not wish to imply that Kubrick's film is mediocre; in its own right, it is first-rate, but it is not what I wrote...I shall never understand why he did not follow my directions and dreams. It is a great pity; but at least I shall be able to have people read my *Lolita* play in its original form. (Gold interview, 1966, SO pp. 105–06)

In the foreword he admits that had he become a playwright or screenwriter instead of a novelist he would have "advocated and applied a system of total tyranny, directing the play or the picture myself, choosing settings and costumes, terrorizing the actors, mingling with them in the bit sort of guest, or ghost, prompting them, and, in a word, pervading the entire show with the will and art of one individual." He continues: "All I could do in the present case was to grant words primacy over action, thus limiting as much as possible the intrusion of management and cast" (ix–x).

A few days before the opening there was a private screening; VN wrote that "Kubrick was a great director, that his *Lolita* was a first-rate film with magnificent actors, and that only ragged odds and ends of my script had been used. The modifications, the garbling of my best little finds, the omission of entire scenes, the addition of new ones, and all sorts of other changes may not have been sufficient to erase my name from the credit titles but they certainly made the picture as unfaithful to the original script as an American poet's translation from Rimbaud or Pasternak..." (xii–xiii). He later considered what he would have done differently if given complete control: "I might have insisted on stressing certain things that were not stressed – for example, the different motels at which they stayed" (Toffler interview, 1964, SO p. 21).

VN was nominated for an Academy Award for the screenplay; he did not, alas, win.

to Véra
Sept. 1960
L.A.

NO. 44

LOLITA
A SCREENPLAY

Verinia lolita cinemathoides

April 1974

VIVACIOUS VARIANTS

Towards the end of his travels with Lolita, Humbert Humbert studies the pictures of several wanted men in the post office of the western town of Wace. Recalling this scene, he tells his readers, "If you want to make a movie out of my book, have one of these faces gently melt into my own, while I look." Humbert's guilt speaks in this projected image, his eager awareness of his crime; but his loneliness speaks too, and perhaps even more movingly. Abandoned by Lolita, unwanted by her, Humbert longs to be, longs to have been, a wanted man in a sense the post office is not likely to understand.

Alas, no one is going to make a movie out of the book within the book that Humbert calls *Lolita, or the Confession of a White Widowed Male*, although Adrian Lyne, with his rather solemn focus on Humbert's woes, recently came very close. This book is a melodrama, all about Humbert, the story of his obsession and sorrows. The book that has now twice been filmed (by Lyne in 1997, by Stanley Kubrick in 1961) is not Humbert's book, but Nabokov's. The two texts are verbally identical, of course, except for a brief Foreword which Humbert cannot have read, but they are quite different, as we all know, in their texture and its meaning. Nabokov's *Lolita* (no sub-title) borrows Humbert's voice and travails, but is not only about him. It also situates and implicitly comments on him, invites us persistently to read between his lines. It is about the *Lolita* he can't see as well as the one he can, and it is about us, the ladies and gentlemen of Humbert's imaginary jury. It is not a melodrama at all, but a darkly glittering antic comedy.

In the summer of 1959, Stanley Kubrick invited Nabokov to write a screenplay based on *Lolita*. Nabokov said no at first, but thought again. He and Véra went to Hollywood early in 1960, and stayed there until October. During that time

Nabokov produced what he called Act One of his screenplay (March 23), Act Two (April 25), various additions to those two acts (June 7), a Prologue (June 17), Act Three (July 9), and some new sequences for that act (July 21 and August 11). On September 8, he sent to Kubrick an "abridged and corrected copy" of the whole work. "You will observe," he said, "that I have not only eliminated several long scenes but have also introduced considerable alterations in the remaining dialogue, changing a number of phrases and spanning with new bridges the gaps between sundered parts. You have thus a practically new version of the play."

All this can be documented from Nabokov's letters, but for the full story of the various versions of the screenplay, we need to turn to Dieter Zimmer, who is about to publish a German edition of the complete work. There are, as Zimmer, stepping cleanly through the tangle, makes beautifully clear, three states or moments of the screenplay: a long typescript (some 400 pages), from which you are about to read some 30 out of 85 previously unpublished pages; a shorter typescript (155 pages); and the book published by Nabokov himself in 1974 as *Lolita: A Screenplay*. The relations among these works are intricate and fascinating, and well worth studying in their own right, but a grateful summary of Zimmer's findings will be sufficient here. The long typescript is everything Nabokov sent to Kubrick between March and August 1960 – it has incoherences and repetitions because it includes old and new versions of certain scenes, and maintains all the different and parallel choices of continuity. The shorter typescript is what Nabokov sent to Kubrick on September 8, 1960, his "practically new version." And the published book – there is an element of Nabokovian conjuring about this very procedure – is the shorter typescript plus a number of sequences restored from the long one. And one entirely new scene. The interest of the long, unpublished version is that it brings us closest to seeing Nabokov at work, caught in the very act of re-imagining an already spectacularly imagined story.

Nabokov was disappointed when he saw Kubrick's film in New York in June 1962. The writer's "first reaction... was a mixture of aggravation, regret, and reluctant pleasure." But then, Nabokov added, Kubrick "saw my novel in one way, I saw it in another." If we allow this generous, apparently casual phrase to take a little stress, it offers a luminous critical insight. Kubrick the movie director saw *Lolita*, and turned what he saw into a film. Nabokov, who had already seen *Lolita* into words, saw it again, and not, I think, exactly as a film-to-be—why would he, when he had spent his whole adult life turning himself into a novelist? What Nabokov saw, and wrote in 1960, was a wonderful, *imagined* film of *Lolita*, the film that runs in our heads as we read—scarcely a filmable script, we may think, but not just a dramatic recension of the novel either. Kubrick was right not to use much of it, and Nabokov was right to think it was a treasure. When Nabokov, glancing at Pushkin (whose narrator in *Eugene Onegin* says "a novel in the old mood" will occupy his "gay decline"), calls his a work"a vivacious variant of an old novel," he is both telling a precise truth and understating his achievement. However literal and practical his intentions in writing the screenplay, Nabokov ultimately invented a subtle new genre: the implied film, the work of words which borrows the machinery and landscape of film as a dazzling means to a literary end. His written camera slides, glides and shudders, catches the "gesticulating black trees" of a violent storm; his written soundtrack reproduces the "hot moist sound" of Lolita's whisper; and when "we dissolve briefly to Lolita's cry of joy," we are going well beyond the reach of the technical term. We shall not see and hear and enact these things in the cinema; but then we don't need to. We are already seeing Lolita in "another" way.

The following passages from the long typescript allow us to watch Nabokov at his double task: writing a film for Kubrick which is already a "vivacious" new book for himself. I have chosen them because they read very well as dramatic sequences, and require relatively little contextualizing for their comprehension. And also because they give us a very strong sense of Nabokov's feeling for mischief, his delight in the additional detail or afterthought. Thus Lewis Carroll, alias Charles Dodgson, makes an impish appearance not permitted to him in the novel, and Humbert's nervousness is suddenly echoed in a desperate memory of Edgar Allan Poe. More generally, Nabokov's satire of American manners here translates exceptionally well into dialogue form.

The first set of scenes comes from the end of Act One, which takes the story up to the moment of Charlotte Haze's sudden death. Humbert discusses Lolita's future with Charlotte; visits a doctor and gets some sleeping pills—his plan is to drug both mother and daughter, and fondle one sleeping beauty while the other snores. We hear the sound of the ambulance which seems to be weirdly, prophetically, on its way to an accident that hasn't happened yet. Then there are two alternative endings to Act One. In the published version it ends with a scene in a police academy, where students are shown a photograph of the scene of Charlotte's death. The photograph then comes to life, and all the pictured people move. In the first unpublished ending Humbert manages to persuade the Farlows that he is Lolita's father, and the act ends with the splendidly melodramatic (and bogus) revelation: "John, John, don't you understand? Lolita is Humbert's daughter." The second unpublished ending shows the excruciating encounter with Jack Beale, the driver of the car which killed Charlotte—Nabokov mentions this scene in his letter to Kubrick of June 7, 1960. Here we see the apparently distraught Humbert indulging in his favorite activity: the insolent baiting of the brainless.

The remaining passages are from Act Three. We see Humbert and Lolita continuing what looks like an old sad quarrel; we get the hilarious encounter between Humbert and Miss Pratt, already brilliantly staged in the novel, but here turned into full-blown verbal farce; and we catch a glimpse of the ape-like Quilty, aptly chosen winner of the Poltergeister Prize, and the faintly sinister Vivian Darkbloom. Our last sight here is Humbert and Lolita on the road, far into the American West, pursued by the mocking Quilty. Lolita smiles her "junior Gioconda smile," and shortly afterwards vanishes from the hospital in Elphinstone. The comedy continues, but Humbert's helplessness has increased considerably, the ruthless baiter is now the ruthlessly baited. In these pages, even more clearly than in the novel and in the published screenplay, the jokes and the plot have turned on him. The dreadful headmistress and the monstrous Quilty seem to be in cahoots, but only because Humbert's whole world has become a vast mirror-world of signs, hints of conspiracy and of Lolita's imminent defection. "Very good," he says in tribute to Quilty's ingenuity—although of course he doesn't know yet who his tormentor is, and things could hardly be worse. *Lolita* has "no moral in tow," as Nabokov insisted, and what we are seeing here is something more complicated than Humbert's comeuppance. But the imagined film has allowed Nabokov to add new levels of darkness to the old dark glitter.

In all versions of the screenplay, published and unpublished, Humbert's eye falls on a shop window in Wace where unclothed mannequins are being rearranged. The implied or imagined film is at its most eloquent here: "On the floor, where the employee crawls, there lies a cluster of three bare arms and a blond wig. Two of the arms, not necessarily a pair, happen to be twisted and seem to suggest a clasping gesture of horror and supplication. Humbert, tense and bitter, his face twitching, points out these details to sullen Lolita."

Seeming to suggest: the whole art of fiction in any form. But then, as you will remember, this brilliantly realized piece of film already appears in the novel.

Michael Wood
Princeton University

LOLITA

Verina verae Nab.

Aug. 1958
Ithaca

LOLITA

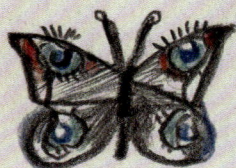

Взрочки
дубликат

B.

LOLITA: A SCREENPLAY

Unpublished excerpts from Nabokov's original typescript, courtesy The Henry W. and Albert A. Berg Collection of English and American Literature, the New York Public Library, and the Estate of Vladimir Nabokov.

I

Humbert, brooding in his study, sits examining a Child's Encyclopedia. Charlotte saunters in. She rubs her cheek against his temple.

CHARLOTTE	Am I interrupting?
HUMBERT	Yes.
CHARLOTTE	Is there anything special my lord would like for dinner. Jean and John will be dropping in later.

Humbert examines Camping in Scandinavia.

CHARLOTTE	Say, by the way, why is that suitcase locked? It's empty, isn't it?
HUMBERT	It isn't.
CHARLOTTE	But what do you keep there?
HUMBERT	Old love letters.
CHARLOTTE	Oh, Hum! *(pauses)*. How is your neuralgia today? Shouldn't you see Dr. Byron again?
HUMBERT	At the moment I'm trying to work.
CHARLOTTE	But it's a book for children. Oh, you funny person.

Cut to:

Dinner. Humbert and Charlotte.

CHARLOTTE	Hum, I've taken a very amusing decision *(eyes him fondly over a spoonful of soup)*. This fall, after Lolita is off to that boarding school we two will go to Europe.

Humbert swallows his spoonful, carefully wipes his lips, clears his throat.

CHARLOTTE	Hummy approves?
HUMBERT	And I have taken an even more amusing decision. Lolita is not going to that boarding school. Don't touch me!
CHARLOTTE	Why! What's the matter, dear? We discussed it the other day and you agreed.
HUMBERT	I did not say a word. On the contrary, I've thought it over and I disagree.
CHARLOTTE	But, my darling –
HUMBERT	Now shut up. I'm going to talk for the nonce. Even in the

most harmonious of households as ours is not all decisions are taken by the female partner. No, wait a minute. The present matter is largely incidental. I'm concerned with general trends. When you wanted me to spend my afternoons on the lake instead of in the study, I gladly gave in and became a bronzed glamour boy for your sake. When you lead me to bridge and bourbon with the excellent Farlows, I meekly follow. When you – when we – when we decided to marry, you made it a condition that I'd be a father to your child. I accepted. This is now our joint responsibility.

CHARLOTTE   My dearest, I'll do anything you say.

HUMBERT   First stop doing what you are doing now. Louise may come in.

CHARLOTTE   It's not her day.

HUMBERT   Well, it's not my day either. Now referring to this matter of our daughter. I want her to return to Ramsdale. I want to teach her French. I want to take her to Europe if we decided to go.

Cut to:

STAIRCASE. Humbert comes out of his room; stops; and, unbuttoning his coat, returns to his room. Charlotte, face up, hand on banisters. Humbert emerges again buttoning up his coat.

HUMBERT   Do you want me, my dear Charlotte, to put the car into the garage when I come back from Dr. Byron's?

CHARLOTTE   I want you, my dear Humbert, to leave it in the driveway. I'll go to the hairdresser's after lunch. No parting kiss? That's better. Please, don't forget to ask the doctor if he thinks you should see a specialist about your neuralgia.

Humbert, humming, locates his sunglasses in the hallway.

CHARLOTTE   Oh, wait a second. I've been carrying about a postcard I wrote her three days ago. Ah, yes. It's in my bag. Will you mail it before you drive off. Otherwise you're sure to come back with it. Oh-rev-war, lovey.

Cut to:

Humbert crosses the street and walks to the mailing box. On the lawn slope above, Jung's collie stands wagging his tail. Humbert reads the postcard before mailing it.

"My dear Lo: I'm very much displeased that you lost the blue sweater. That rain won't last so will you please cheer up. What is this nonsense about rag weed? Little girls simply do not have hay fever. Write when the spirit moves you. Your affectionate mother."

Humbert glances back at the house and rapidly adds in pencil: "Love, kisses, loads of kisses and love from Dad."

Cut to:

Humbert presses the door bell next to the name: Melville Peabody Byron, M. D. End of interview. Dr. Byron is writing a prescription.

HUMBERT	They should be exceptionally strong, those tablets. Ordinary ones are no match for my insomnia.
DR. BYRON	Here's something that will really work.
HUMBERT	Are they harmless? I mean, if a child swallowed one –
DR. BYRON	Well, no pills should ever be left lying around. One of these at bedtime is quite safe – and very effective. When my Margaret sprained her wrist and could not go to sleep I gave her half of one tablet and she snored through the loudest thunderstorm we ever had in Ramsdale. Yes, that's my lass.

Humbert inspects her photograph.

DR. BYRON	She goes to school with your daughter, I mean your step-daughter. I guess I'll come out with you. I have to go to the hospital.

Humbert and Dr. Byron walk.

DR. BYRON	Quite warm today.
HUMBERT	Yes, I'm jolly glad I discarded my waistcoat.
DR. BYRON	I've not worn one for the last thirty years.

(The clamor of an ambulance)

HUMBERT	What – a fire again?
DR. BYRON	No, ambulance.

Dissolve to:

342 LAWN STREET. Clamor of ambulance.

Charlotte tidying up Humbert's room is about to put away a vest lying on a chair when a small flat key slips out of its pocket. She smiles, hesitates, tosses her head – and unlocks the forbidden suitcase. Still smiling, she examines the small black diary. Her smile fades.

Dissolve to:

SIDEWALK NEAR DR.'S HOUSE.

DR. BYRON   It's the siren of an ambulance.

Humbert and Dr. Byron part company. Humbert crosses to the pharmacy. He comes out whistling softly. He drives on Main Street. Near the bank, a big, expensive, old-fashioned car is being clumsily parked by a fat-faced driver (McFate's nephew). He nearly backs into Humbert's car which abruptly stops. The limousine is jerked back and forth by its perspiring operator.

THE DRIVER OF THE LIMOUSINE

I'm very sorry. I have to park here to pick up my uncle. Mr. McFate.

Humbert patiently waits and presently is driving down Lawn Street.

HUMBERT   *(rhythmically)* Pills, pills, beautiful pills. "Your daughter" *(chuckles)*. My sleeping beauty! Mr Dodgson, please, tell me a bedside story.

Jung's dog races Humbert's car.

II

Evening of the same day. 342 LAWN STREET. Humbert and the Farlows in the living room.

JOHN FARLOW *(lighting his pipe)* I still think that the child should be right here tomorrow for the funeral.

JEAN FARLOW But he says he telephoned and they've gone away on a three-day hike.

HUMBERT   Yes. I telephoned. And the caretaker told me they were all camping out in the back country.

JOHN   Back country my foot! One would think it's Tibet. Back country, indeed. A potato patch! I've been there. The local police would contact them in five minutes. When did you call the camp?

HUMBERT   Are you checking on me?

JOAN [sic]   Now, now. Please, Humbert. Let us discuss all this as civilized people. You don' [sic] care to have her come for the funeral. Right?

HUMBERT   She's a nervous highstrung child. Why expose her to a distressing tradition.

JOHN   Death considered as a tradition. That's a curious angle.

JEAN   Well, John, perhaps he is right, perhaps it might create in her some complex, some block mechanism.

JOHN	Yah. Only she does not look a block mechanism to me that kid. What are you going to do about her anyway?
HUMBERT	I'll do what is thit – what is fit. Then after the funeral I'll go and fetch her at that camp. Then we'll drive around a bit, I'll take her to some resort or something. And then we'll head for Beardsley where I have that job.
JOHN	I see.
JEAN	There's a nice school for girls in Beardsley.
JOHN	Yah. Of course, we are aware, aren't we *(puffs at pipe)*, that Lolita has not a single relative left in the world; but we also wonder if legally she is your adopted daughter.
JEAN	Well, does not a stepfather automatically become a guardian in such cases?
JOHN	Ah, that's the point. What I mean is –

Humbert realizes that this is the crucial moment. The tape recorder is heard again as a crazy and capsizing echo, muttering the garbled phrases from Edgar Poe's letter to Mrs. Clemm ("they are taking –taking–taking her away–lost–everything lost– "). Humbert now speaks up very forcibly.

| HUMBERT | All right. Let us settle this question once for all. There's a secret involved and I'll disclose it. Tell me: Do you really imagine that a Ramsdale housewife, a widow, a rather shy woman – do you imagine that in one month's time she could grow so enamored with a chance lodger, with a stranger from Europe, to marry him? Don' [*sic*] you think it's rather singular? Now will you please examine this little document. |

He shows the little snapshot Charlotte inscribed for him: "To chéri Humbert April 1936." With autograph note in typescript: "Check year; changed from 1946."

JOHN	Well, I certainly was not aware that you've known her for fourteen years. Jean and I met Charlotte only two years ago when they came from Riskey.
HUMBERT	Yes. Interesting, isn't it. In 1936 she was engaged. I had a wife in Europe. But wait, this is not all.
JOHN	I still don't quite see what bearing it has on –
HUMBERT	There was a brief romance, a fantastic love affair. And then I returned to France.
JEAN	John, John, don't you understand? Lolita is Humbert's daughter.

END OF ACT ONE

III

HUMBERT'S STUDIO. He is packing. Louise the maid enters carrying a dress in a cellophane bag on a hanger.

LOUISE	There's a gentleman downstairs to see you, sir. And this has come from the cleaners. It's Mrs.'s party dress. Shall I hang it up in the closet?
HUMBERT	Hang it up in the closet.

Cut to:

LIVING ROOM. Humbert enters.

THE VISITOR	I am Jack Beale.
HUMBERT	You are Jack Beale.
BEALE	Yes. Mr. McFate's nephew. I was driving him to a family reunion when that tragic thing happened.
HUMBERT	When that thing happened.
BEALE	May I sit down for a moment?
HUMBERT	Yes – sit down for a moment.
BEALE	My two eldest, Jack and Mary, are in the same grade as your Lolita.
HUMBERT	My Lolita.
BEALE	Mrs. Beale asked me to extend her sympathy – she is deeply – *(flounders)*
HUMBERT	What is it exactly you want? Because you want something, don't you?
BEALE	*(more happily)* Well, yes. Is it all right if I remove this ash-tray? Mr. McFate and me have prepared this – chart *(unrolls it on the table).* This is the diagram of the drama. It has been signed, as you see, by several eye witnesses. Here you can follow the tragic – the trajectory followed by Mrs. Haze – I mean, Mrs. Humbert – from this point to this – across the street – from sidewalk to – well, sidewalk.
HUMBERT	Illustrated. Who are these ladies? Air hostesses?
BEALE	Oh, just outline figures. I happened to cut them out of some statistical survey. Each represents a given position.
HUMBERT	Career girls, judging by the briefcases.
BEALE	Yah. Just career girls, I guess. You see, we stuck them all along this dotted line like so to show your wife's erratic progression across the street.
HUMBERT	You have not shown the dog.
BEALE	Oh, I have. Here he is – this red triangle, a Greek D. And that

	of course is the limousine. Well, anyway if you study the chart carefully you'll see from it that the accident was entirely her fault.
HUMBERT	"She" being this multiplied silhouette?
BEALE	Yes. This pedestrian. Technically, it was the pedestrian's fault, not the driver's.
HUMBERT	Technically. Yes, I believe you are right. I have no quarrel with you.
BEALE	*(much relieved)* So you exonerate me completely?
HUMBERT	Show me your hands.
BEALE	My hands?
HUMBERT	Yes. Knuckles and palms.
BEALE	Smudge of red ink on this finger tip.
HUMBERT	On this flat finger tip. Thank you, Mr. Beale. I just wanted to touch a link – a cuff link – in the chain of events. Something more tangible than your outline figures.
BEALE	*(casting a last look at the chart which he is about to roll up again)*. Yes, I know. Maybe, I should have tried to find profile figures – shown running. Like, you know, symbols of children, at play, school signs, that sort of thing. Well, it was good seeing you. I mean, it was so good of you to be so sympathetic. My little Mary joins Mrs. Beale and me in transmitting to your Lolita –
HUMBERT	She is not here. She's at summer camp.
BEALE	The funeral is this afternoon, isn't it?
HUMBERT	She won't attend. Her group is camping out in the mountains and cannot be reached.
BEALE	Oh, that's a shame. Look, Mr. Humbert, maybe I could –
HUMBERT	You could nothing. I'm going to drive there tomorrow and take her away from all this.
BEALE	No, no, what I meant was – you have been so generous about the whole matter, I was about to suggest that – maybe you would allow me to pay the funeral expenses. Well, I must be on my way now.
HUMBERT	Yes. Thank you. I think you should do that.
BEALE	Excuse me?
HUMBERT	I said yes – I accept your offer.
BEALE	You do?
HUMBERT	Yes.
BEALE	You want me to foot the bill?

HUMBERT	That's what you said.
BEALE	I see. Of course, I shall have to consult Mr. McFate about it. We'll get in touch with you.
HUMBERT	Don't forget your beautiful diagram.

Exit Beale.

END OF ACT ONE.

IV

HUMBERT	...Now come along, I want you to help me straighten the rooms. We are positively drowning in dirt. Next week I'll have that Mrs. Cowan come to tidy up—if you promise you will not chat with her.
LOLITA	Some day.... Some day you'll be sorry.
HUMBERT	I know it's all very simple really. You don't love me. You never loved me. Isn't that the main problem?
LOLITA	Will you let me act in the play?
HUMBERT	Do you love me just a little, Lolita?

She looks at him, mysterious and meretricious, pondering whether to get what she wants by granting or by refusing.

Cut to:

THE OFFICE OF THE HEADMISTRESS AT BEARDSLEY SCHOOL. A secretary ushers in Humbert.

HUMBERT	Could you tell me why the headmistress wishes to see me?
SECRETARY	I wouldn't know. Make yourself comfortable. Miss Pratt will be here any moment.
HUMBERT	*(uneasily)* The invitation was rather sudden. Has Dolores been naughty? Some pecadillo? No?
SECRETARY	Oh, we all think a lot of your Dolly. Here's Miss Pratt.

A bulky old woman with smooth hair and somewhat hippopotamic features shakes hands with Humbert. The secretary leaves.

MISS PRATT	So glad you managed to come, Mr. Haze—I mean, Mr. Hum.
HUMBERT	*(clearing his throat)* Humbert.
PRATT	Sit down, sit down. Cigarette? I want to have a little chat with you. To begin let me... *(lights up)* Let me clarify our general approach.

After a pause, wrinkling her brow in phoney concentration.

	As you know, Mr. Humbird, we are not particularly concerned with having our students become bookworms or be able to reel off all the capitals of Europe which nobody knows anyway. What we *are* concerned with is the adjustment of the child to group life. We stress the three C's: community, communication, and common sense. And the three D's: Dramatics, Dating, and Dance.
HUMBERT	*(attempting a weak joke)* But not dunce, I hope?
PRATT	Well, there are dunces and dunces, Dr. Humburg. A wit might say that we teach our girls to smell well rather than to spell well. But joking apart we *are* more interested in communication than in composition. Oh, naturally, we have to stick to some teaching techniques: without the alphabet no child could use the telephone book. We pay due respect to Shakespeare and – and others, but we want our girls to leave the musty old libraries and plunge into the world of people.
HUMBERT	Dolores thought you wanted to see me about her report.
PRATT	Yes, we are coming to that. But it is not the scholastic side that bothers us. You see, Professor Hummer, we think in organismal and organizational terms. Your delightful Dolly will presently enter a group age where dates, dates dress, date book, date etiquette mean as much to her as to you business, business connections, golf, and lunching with your boss.
HUMBERT	I teach literature at Beardsley College, Miss Pratt.
PRATT	Bully for you. But do you realize that in Dolly Hummer's case medieval dates are of less vital interest than *(twinkling)* weekend ones? We live in a world of things, not thoughts. For us words without experience are meaningless. What on earth can Dorothy Hummerson care for Greece and the Orient with their harems and girl slaves?
HUMBERT	What, indeed? But to return to Lolita–
PRATT	We call her Dolly, ye know, a plainer and more wholesome cognomen. Now let me ask you a blunt question. Here I have reports concerning –concerning, wait a moment–no, that's right: Dolores Haze,–from Miss Redcock and Miss Cormorant. Now, here's my question: you are an old-fashioned, continental father, aren't you, Mr. Haze?
HUMBERT	She's my stepdaughter, really; but–well, yes: I'm what you might call loosely, conservative.

PRATT | That's what I suspected. I shall endeavor to explain the situation in simple non-progressive terms. Dolly Haze is still shuttling *(gesture)* between the anal and the genital zones of development. Fundamentally, she is a lovely child. But the onset of sexual maturing seems to give her and us trouble. Now let me be more specific *(rummages among her papers).* Here is one special research report: "Enjoys singing with group in class though mind seems to wander. Crosses her knees and wags her left leg to rhythm." Let me see…"Handles books gracefully. Nose unobstructed. Feet high-arched." Ah, here we are. "Antagonistic, dissatisfied, cagey. Impudent with Miss Redcock. Simulates eyestrain to get away with scholastic incompetence. Tennis form excellent to superb. Metabolic efficiency superfine. Sexual education—" attention, now!—Miss Cormorant feels that fourteen-years-old Dolly remains morbidly uninterested in sexual matters. Miss Redcock is positive that Dolly represses her curiosity in order to save her ignorance and self-dignity. We all wonder if anybody in the family has instructed the child in the process of mammalian reproduction. Her poor mother apparently did not? We feel the best course would be if you had the family doctor tell her the facts of life.

HUMBERT | Well…

PRATT | Unless, of course, you'd prefer to have our psychiatrist talk to her. Ponder this, Dr. Hazer. Another approach is this. When we questioned her about her troubles, Dolly refused to discuss the home situation. But we know from her friends that you are opposed to the natural recreations of a normal child.

HUMBERT | *(with a show of last-ditch jauntiness)* Do you mean, sex play?

PRATT | *(displaying her dentures in a genial grin)* Well, I certainly welcome this civilized terminology. No. What I have in mind is simply more leniency, more flexibility on your part. For example, we think that you should allow her to enjoy the company of her friends' brothers at the Junior Club, or in The Reverend Rigger's organization, or at the lovely homes of our parents.

HUMBERT | She may meet boys at her own lovely home.

PRATT | Splendid. But there is one other thing you must do for her— and for us. Promise?

HUMBERT	If it's reasonable—
PRATT	It's like this, Mr. Haze. At the end of the term our school is putting on a little play. We are all busy rehearsing it. It is called *The Hunted Enchanter* and was written by my old friend, Mr. Clare Quilty. You know, the man who got the Poltergeister prize last year.
HUMBERT	I think I met him the other day on the campus.
PRATT	A handsome man and a lovely person.
HUMBERT	I'm afraid I did not pay much attention. Fat little fellow?
PRATT	Oh, gracious, no! A big elegant gentleman. I'm sure some of those bawdy Elizabethan poets looked like that. I'm lunching with him today. He lectured last night on the Art of Love —or was it the Love of Art? No matter. But it was marvelous —in the course of the whole lecture he did not make one single dry scholarly remark and had the students in stitches all the time. Well, this little play of his is a kind of children's classic, and we want your Dolly to participate in it.
HUMBERT	She's very shy, very nervous.
PRATT	The words "shy" and "nervous" are practically meaningless in modern psychiatry. If your child is too shy, as you say, to engage in school theatricals, then there is a very bad block somewhere, and she must be analyzed by our Dr. Cutler at once.
HUMBERT	Analyzed. Oh no. Not that. I'm against that. A doctor does not have the moral right to force confessions from a patient.
PRATT	It's either or, my dear man.
HUMBERT	I don't know...Perhaps, after all I'm wrong, and she might enjoy acting.
PRATT	That's better.
SECRETARY	*(opening the door)* Mr. Quilty and Miss Darkbloom have come to fetch you, Miss Pratt. They are waiting for you outside.
PRATT	All rightee. Coming. Well, Mr. Hazert, it has certainly been a pleasure chatting with you.

Cut to:

THE SCHOOLYARD. The secretary is seen advancing toward Quilty and Vivian Darkbloom, and Humbert is seen exiting from the school along an adjacent path. Vivian is archly sitting in the swing. Quilty is hanging by one hand from a high horizontal bar, quite still, a little bored, in a grotesque ape-like position, two inches from the ground.

SECRETARY	She'll be down in a moment.
VIVIAN	*(chin pointing at receding Humbert)* I think that's somebody we know.
SECRETARY	He is the father of one of our girls—Dolores Haze, Lolita.
QUILTY	*(who has ripely dropped to the ground and is rearranging his clothes)* Never heard of her.
SECRETARY	Lolita is a very graceful and not very happy child.
QUILTY	Nope. Don't know any such girleen.

Vivian glances at him with a twinkle of sly wonder.

V

A ROADSIDE PICNIC GROUND IN A COTTONWOOD GROVE ON A HOT WINDY AFTERNOON IN SAGE BRUSH COUNTRY. Humbert takes out of the car provisions bought on the way and arranges them on the sun-flecked table. He and Lolita eat in silence for a while.

LOLITA	There should be pickles in a separate bit of paper. You threw them away with the bag, you dope.
HUMBERT	No, I have them here.

A pause. Cars pass on the highway.

HUMBERT	*(spreading out a map)* We have traveled about 250 miles today and should make as much more before we stop for the night.
LOLITA	*(indicating a point on the map)* There is a good motel off Highway 17. I looked it up in the tour book.
HUMBERT	With one thing and another, I have decided not to put up in a motel but sleep in the car.
LOLITA	*(grimacing)* What?
HUMBERT	We'll park in some permitted spot and start tomorrow at dawn.
LOLITA	You're crazy.
HUMBERT	My motto is meekness and unobtrusiveness. Tomorrow we shall cover at least 600 miles, rest for a couple of hours and drive on so as to reach Borderton after-tomorrow before noon.
LOLITA	I thought *I* was to plan this trip.
HUMBERT	Well, we are following the itinerary you traced.

At this moment Quilty drives by, slows down, cries "bon appétit!" and proceeds merrily on his way.

Cut to:

A TRAILER PARK AT NIGHTFALL IN GRANTCHESTER. It is a second-rate place with primitive plumbing and poor lighting. There is an agglomeration of some ten trailers of different types. Two or three have taken root and evolved small gardens. Children are being hollered for and put to bed. Radios are playing. The wind that has been spinning dust devils in the surrounding wasteland all day gradually subsides. Humbert pulls up and talks to the trailer court manager.

Cut to:

SAME PLACE AT DAWN. Lolita is fast asleep in the backseat of the parked car. There is a kind of junior Gioconda smile on her lambent lips in the early light. Humbert walks around and between trailers in search of a lavatory. On the other side of a lane, a cafe has just opened. He returns to the car, finds a thermos bottle in the back (Lolita is now sleeping with her face buried in a traveling pillow, the morning light on her hair) and walks toward the cafe, letting the coffee dregs trickle out of the thermos as he goes. Just beyond, there is a motor court (Monarch Motel). "No Vacancy", and "Sorry, Pardners" – and Humbert recognizes his pursuer's rather special car.

Cut to:

A SIGN: "LEAVING GRANTCHESTER". THE ROAD GOES UP A MOUNTAIN PASS AND THEN DOWN.

HUMBERT   *(looking at a car in the rearview mirror)* That convertible is much too close for comfort on a winding road.

        Lolita laughs. The car passes. The driver is Quilty.

HUMBERT   Oh, that's what it is. Different car. Must have rented it at Grantchester. Very good, very good.

Cut to:

WACE. (THURSDAY). A BLAZING MORNING. A sign says "Welcome to Wace." Main Street with a vista of mountains and a W formed of white stones on a steep talus. Humbert stops at the supermarket. Lolita and he go into the store.

ADA

Верочке

моою лучшую бабочку

Vladimir Nabokov

Christmas

1969

Mont Reux

NO. 123

93 Spring in Fialta and other stories [Vesna v fial'te i drugie rasskazy]. New York: Chekhov Publishing House, 1956.

8vo.; raspberry printed wrappers; one light crease.

First edition of this collection of fourteen short stories, written between 1931 and 1939, that VN was planning to publish upon its completion when the war intervened; ultimately brought out under his pen-name "Sirin." Juliar A29.1. A presentation copy, inscribed for Véra on the first blank with a lovely pencil, red and blue butterfly named in Russian, *My darling*, with this name incorporated into an inscription: *to you/ My darling/ Nab./ 28.iii.56.*

According to Boyd, VN wrote the title story during a brief respite from *The Gift* in Berlin in 1936, and it "always remained one of his favorite stories."

An émigré recounts a chance meeting in the seaside resort of Fialta...with a glamorous woman who has often streaked through his life like a bright but giddy comet. He relives his whole bizarre relationship with her over fifteen years...Deeply haunted now by all their repeated meetings and partings to the dance of time, Vasily tells her he loves her—and retracts it when he sees her frown. Half an hour later, driving out of Fialta with her husband, Nina is killed when their car crashes into a circus truck...Never has Nabokov conveyed better the richness mortality bestows on time's incidentals, never has he imparted a more vividly haunting personal force to time's designs. (TRY pp. 426–27)

94 Spring in Fialta and other stories [Vesna v fial'te i drugie rasskazy]. New York: Chekhov Publishing House, 1956.

8vo.; printed raspberry wrappers; three light creases; top edge foxed.

First edition. Juliar A29.1. VN's working copy, evidently used in preparing the translation of two of the stories into English: "The Circle [Krug]" and "Lips to Lips [Usta k ustam]." There are marginal translations in pencil on 31 pages, including the index, totaling about 650 words. A number of notes have been crossed out or erased in the process of critical review, but many remain legible. (A quick comparison with the English-language versions of both of the corrected stories, published in *A Russian Beauty* (1973), shows that VN revised his translation further prior to publication.)

95 Collected Stories [Gesammelte Erzahlungen]. Hrsg. Von
Dieter E. Zimmer. (Reinbek bei Hamburg): Rowohlt, (1969).

8vo.; steel grey cloth; dust-jacket, tape on front flap.

First edition of the German "collected stories"; including Zimmer's
translations from *Spring In Fialta* (Rowohlt, 1966) as well as nine more.
Juliar D29.3. A presentation copy, inscribed: *For Véra/from V/Jan. 5,
1970/Montreux*, with a magnificent butterfly from the tailless *Polydamas* Swallowtail group, named by VN *Adorata adorata*, wings spread,
climbing a green stem. There are several varieties of *Polydamas* Swal-
lowtails, "but all share this wing shape and the dentate hindwing margins. In nature some species are duller and some brighter, particularly
along the edge of the wings, but Nabokov has chosen to portray one in
his usual dark iridescent shades of bluish black" (Johnson). The dust-
jacket is labeled in ink: *Véra's copy 1970*, and either VN or Véra divided
up the stories listed in the table of contents with the designation *D* or *VN*,
and totaled the pages: *DN: 157*; *VN: 171*—likely to resolve translation
copyright issues between father and son.

96 Pnin. Garden City: Doubleday, 1957.

8vo.; broken type on pages 10, 12, 45, 168; orange topstain; black cloth,
spine stamped in yellow and orange; dust-jacket, few nicks to extremities.

First edition of VN's first National Book Award nomination; dust-jacket
variant A, with "46946" printed under the price on the front flap. Juliar
A30.1; 1991 update. Four chapters ran in *The New Yorker*—one at the
end of November 1953, and three in 1955—widening VN's audience and
increasing his popularity. In a 1967 interview he claimed to have completed an eighth chapter in his mind, to be inserted between the fourth
and fifth chapters of the published book, but "a combination of chance
circumstances in 1956 prevented me from actually writing that chapter,
then other events intervened, and it is only a mummy now" (Appel
interview, SO pp. 84–85). *Pnin* went into a second printing within two
weeks of publication. Edmund Wilson attempted to explain its success,
writing VN that he "may at last have made contact with the great American public.... the reviews I have so far seen all say exactly the same
thing: this shows that no one is puzzled, they know how they are meant
to react" (March 17, 1957, NWL p. 309). Perhaps surprisingly, Kingsley
Amis was appalled by the novel; he wrote: "That this limp, tasteless
salad of Joyce, Chaplin, Mary MacCarthy [*sic*] and of course Nabokov

(who should know better) has had delighted noises made over it by Edmund Wilson, Randall Jarrell and Graham Greene is a mystery of some dimensions" (*Spec*, Sept 27, 1957; quoted in *The Chelsea House Library of Literary Criticism*, vol. X, p. 2790).

A presentation copy, inscribed to Véra in Russian: *To my darling from V. 8.ii.1957 Ithaca*. With a darkly detailed butterfly named *Vanessa verae* that, Johnson notes, more closely resembles the genus *Araschnia*: "It may represent what Nabokov would have liked to have seen in *Vanessa* if he would have had his way with nature." With a handful of spelling and punctuation emendations, all noted by VN on the second half-title in blue and grey pencil, suggesting two readings.

Clearly concerned that he would never find a publisher for *Lolita*, and that, if he did, his position at Cornell might be jeopardized, VN embarked on *Pnin* with the hope of lucrative serial publication and a book deal. Though when it came out Cornell's own Marc Szeftel was identified as a primary model for Professor Pnin, the star-crossed Russian émigré lecturer at an American university, VN had drawn from his own experiences and ample experiences with similar types, and Pnin embodied bits of all of them.

Ironically, given VN's intent to strive for publication and popularity, two chapters of *Pnin* were rejected by Katharine White at *The New Yorker*: one apparently on the grounds that it was "unpleasant"; and another for its political undertones and clear antipathy to Stalin and Lenin. Upon its serial completion VN had as hard a time as ever in securing a book publisher for it—then titled *My Poor Pnin*—despite the fact, as he told Cass Canfield, the president of Harper's, that he had "never had so much fan mail from readers with my other stories as I had with the four Pnin chapters" (December 8, 1955, SL p. 182).

He wrote to Pascal Covici at Viking: "When I began writing *Pnin*, I had before me a definite artistic purpose: to create a character, comic, physically inattractive—grotesque, if you like—but then have him emerge, in juxtaposition to so-called 'normal' individuals, as by far the more human, the more important, and, on a moral plane, the more attractive one... What I am offering you is a character entirely new to literature—a character important and intensely pathetic—and new characters in literature are not born every day" (September 29, SL p. 178). He later described the protagonist to White: "He is not a very nice person but he is fun" (TAY p. 225). Two months later he told Canfield that Pnin was "[a] man of great moral courage, a pure man, a scholar and a staunch friend, serenely wise, faithful to a single love, he never descends from a high plane of life characterized by authenticity and integrity. But handicapped and hemmed in by his incapability to learn a language, he seems a figure of fun to many an average intellectual, and its takes a Clements or a Joan Clements to break through Pnin's fantastic husk and get at his tender and lovable core. It is this combination of the grotesque and the gentle that makes him so pleasingly bizarre. And this is also what apparently endeared him so much to the readers of the *New Yorker*" (December 8, SL p. 182). Though VN altered his plot—which originally saw Pnin through a fatal heart attack—apparently on Covici's advice, both Viking and Harper's rejected *Pnin* for want of length.

Epstein accepted it for Doubleday, and went immediately into production. After a first attempt at a dust-jacket design elicited groans from him, VN was moved to detail just how Pnin should look. He sent Epstein photographs of "Pnin-like Russians, with and without hair, for a visual appreciation" (October 1, 1956, SL p. 190) and a detailed critique of the first round art proposal. His suggestions were taken seriously. His response to the next version was overwhelmingly positive: "The jacket is absolutely splendid—I never imagined that an illustrator could render an author's vision so accurately" (November 13, 1956, SL p. 192). When Doubleday suggested Pnin should hold a book, VN added that the title should be *Pnin* and the author, V. Sirin, in Cyrillic. He was likely pleased to receive Wilson's note: "By some miracle, the picture on the jacket is excellent" (March 17, 1957, NWL p. 309). The "miracle" was performed by Milton Glaser. One of the founders of Pushpin Studios, Glaser had already established himself as one of the most innovative graphic designers of the day. He would later achieve greater accolades and public recognition as one of the designers associated with the '60s psychedelic graphic revolution. With Pushpin Studios and independent of them, Glaser established an acceptable vernacular of bold design associated with hallucinogenic states, giving a palatable correlate to the extravagant colors associated with the LSD experiences. Through his graphic, an unsuspecting public embraced a design idiom more familiar to a disaffected culture "tuned in, turned on, and dropped out."

97 **Pnin.** Garden City: Doubleday, 1957.

8vo.; orange topstain; black cloth; light wear to extremities; dust-jacket, heavily worn, extremities chipped; internally mended with wide, heavy, dark brown tape, glue stains showing through.

First edition, dust-jacket variant A; broken type on pages 10 and 45. Juliar A30.1; 1991 update. VN's corrected copy, so labeled on the dust-jacket, with seven emendations throughout and his errata list on the front endpaper. These textual revisions were not incorporated into Doubleday's second printing of the novel. With a loosely inserted slip in Véra's handwriting bearing a quotation from Horace with special reference to *Speak, Memory*; and a tear-sheet from *Notes and Queries* explicating the use of the croquet term, "Hong Kong," in *Pnin*. It is noteworthy that the article on "Hong Kong" cites a definition from the 1863 book *Croquet* by Mayne Reid, whose *Headless Horseman* VN translated into French Alexandrines when he was in his teens.

98 **Pnin.** London: Heinemann, (1957).

8vo.; black cloth; extremities gently bumped; white dust-jacket; five small closed tears repaired with tape, spine bumped.

First English edition, incorporating two of the corrections made on page 56 of VN's copy of the first edition (see previous entry). Juliar A30.2. A presentation copy, inscribed in pencil on the front endpaper: *Véra/Oct. 1957/ot* [Russian, "from"]/ *V*. With a Hawkmoth in yellows and pinks, named *Svingidka verae*.

99 **Pnin.** Translated by A. E. Bayer. Baarn: Hollandia, 1958.

8vo.; red cloth; a few dents to edges; mustard dust-jacket; edgeworn, spine lightly creased.

First Dutch edition. Juliar D30.1. A presentation copy, inscribed to Véra in Russian on the title page in a minute Nabokovian hand, translated by Dmitri: *A little butterfly for Véra/from V*. dated September 1958. With a tiny, prettily decorated butterfly.

100 **A Hero of Our Time.** By Mihail Lermontov. Translated from the Russian by Vladimir Nabokov in collaboration with Dmitri Nabokov. Garden City: Doubleday Anchor Books, 1958.

12mo.; green cloth, wrappers trimmed and bound-in.

First edition, with a translator's foreword by VN, map, author's introduction translated, Lermontov's work translated, notes; and wrappers illustrated by Edward Gorey. Juliar A31.1. The copyright page notes: "Typography by Edward Gorey. Map by Raphael Palacios adapted from an original by Dmitri Nabokov." A presentation copy, inscribed on the half-title, *Véra*, with a butterfly whose black ink outline bled through the page, obscuring a few words of the biographical introduction to Lermontov. VN noted in pencil a misprint on page 175 and made this correction, as well as minor emendations, underlining, and marginal ticks on thirty other pages. This was Dmitri's first translation project with his father, who coaxed him into the task with a retrospective eye to his own first translation – of Romain Rolland's *Colas Breugnon*, which had resulted from a discussion VN had had with his own father about that French text. Boyd comments that VN looked even "more certainly with a prospective eye to Dmitri's subsequent translations."

The biographical sketch of Lermontov reveals the basis for which VN might have felt a spiritual and artistic kinship, and merits quoting in full:

Mihail Yurievich Lermontov was born in Moscow in 1814. At sixteen he entered the University of Moscow but two years later switched to the School of Cavalry Cadets in St. Petersburg, and in 1834 received a commission in the Hussars of the Guard. In 1837 he was transferred to the Nizhegorodski Dragoons and sent to the Caucasus as punishment for the composition and circulation (in MS.) of a violent poem directed at the Court clique responsible for driving Pushkin into fighting his fatal duel (January 1837). He was back in the Guards by the end of the year. Between [1838] and 1841 he wrote his best verse and prose and was acclaimed by the reviewers as Pushkin's successor. An incident at a St. Petersburg ball in the spring of 1840 resulted in a duel with the son of the French Ambassador. Lieutenant Lermontov was transferred again, this time to an infantry regiment in the Caucasus, where he took part in dangerous expeditions against the natives. A trivial quarrel with a fellow officer, one Martinov, led to another duel. The meeting took place on July 15, 1841, near Pyatigorsk, and Lermontov was shot through the heart at the first fire.

VN mentioned the idea of this translation to Pascal Covici at Viking in January 1955, calling the three extant English editions with which he was familiar "execrable" (January 23, 1955, SL p. 155). A month later, he sent an all-out pitch, clearly with the promotion of Dmitri's career in mind: "*The Hero of Our Time* is an exciting novel, always fresh and readable. It is part of every course in Russian literature, and this alone should help to sell it. But it also should appeal to the general public if properly presented in English...My young friend [Dmitri] could not undertake a translation unless something definite can be worked out before. I would like you to mark that this is a very special offer on my part for ordinarily I do not revise other people's work gratis" (February 22, 1955, SL pp. 155–56).

Ultimately Epstein undertook the project for Doubleday; VN sent
approval of the cover text on October 13, 1957 (SL p. 230) and the book
came out in March 1958—in time for VN to use it once during his final
semester at Cornell.

101 **Nabokov's Dozen.** A collection of thirteen stories. Garden City: Doubleday, 1958.

8vo.; black cloth; dust-jacket, very light edgewear.

First edition of this favorably reviewed collection of stories, three of
which were translated from Russian and one from French. Juliar A32.1.
The dust-jacket, appropriately printing a dictionary advertisement on
the rear flap, notes that "Mademoiselle O." and "First Love" are the only
autobiographical tales in the collection, and quotes VN: "I am no more
guilty of imitating real life than real life is responsible for plagiarizing
me." A presentation copy, inscribed on the front endpaper to Anna
Feigin: *To my dear Anuta from Vladimir/ Sept. 1958.* With a simply
drawn butterfly in blue ink.

This was VN's second collection of English stories, preceded by New
Direction's *Nine Stories* in 1947; this includes those stories plus four
more, with "Double Talk" retitled "Conversation Piece, 1945." Because
VN was still enjoying the spotlight from the American publication of
Lolita, Barabtarlo writes, this collection "garnered considerable attention, even if nothing in the way of serious analysis" (p. 102). Perhaps
with this attention in mind VN wrote in a tone of consternation not
unusual for him to Doubleday mid-December 1958 requesting ten
copies, and adding a commercial note: "It is the ideal Christmas present. I am frankly distressed by your not advertising it" (to Pyke
Johnson, Jr., December 16, 1958, SL p. 270).

102 **Nabokov's Dozen.** Thirteen Stories. London: Heinemann, (1959).

8vo.; blue cloth, light wear to extremities; dust-jacket, light wear to
head and heel.

First English edition. Juliar A32.2. A presentation copy, with a butterfly
drawn for Véra on the front endpaper—the cover is labeled *Véra's*, with
the title—named *Verina verae* (female) *April 1959.* With three of VN's
emendations on page 152 noted on the half-title: *misprints p. 152 (3).*
The dust-jacket prints text identical to that of the American edition,

with the dictionary ad replaced by excerpts from a *New York Times* review of VN; the rear panel quotes praise from several critics, most prominent among them Rebecca West, Pamela Hansford Johnson, and, likely to VN's chagrin, Edmund Wilson.

103 Nabokov's Dozen. A collection of thirteen stories. Freeport, NY: Books for Libraries Press, (1969).

8vo.; brown cloth.

"New American edition," part of the Short Story Index Reprint Series; from the 1971 reissue – possibly issued without a dust-jacket – by the Lifetime Library. Juliar A32.7. VN noted in pencil on the copyright page *Received January, 1971.* A presentation copy, inscribed on the half-title: *for Verochka/Jan 19, 1971/Montreux.* A large, detailed, vibrant butterfly, *Brenthis dozenita* Nab., is poised on an electrifying purple flower, under which VN has written in Russian "the pre-zenithal mother-of-pearler" (Shapiro). Johnson sketches VN's personal and literary history with this butterfly:

The modern name is *Fabriciana*, a European genus of Fritillaries. Nabokov mentioned Fritillaries often. They are one of the hardest butterflies to rear from egg to adult, something that fascinated him in *Ada*. In fact, throughout America's Rocky Mountains Fritillaries are often seen nectaring on big purple thistle blooms. This would have been common where Nabokov collected in Colorado, Wyoming, and Utah. Nabokov also knew the European Fritillaries well and was a regular correspondent and close friend of the world authority on Fritillaries, the late L. Paul Grey, of Lincoln, Maine. Many letters in his files are to Grey and concern speciation and the status of "subspecies" and "forms" in this pretty genus. The underside is fanciful to a degree but closely resembles European species which show large green-to-chartreuse spotbands on their hindwing undersurfaces. His drawing is closest to the real species *Fabriciana childrena* and *Fabriciana zenobia*.

104 Poems. Drawings by Robin Jacques. Garden City: Doubleday, (1959).

8vo.; light blue cloth, stamped with a gilt butterfly; some stray gilt to cover; gently bumped; white dust-jacket, lightly soiled with a few creases at edges.

First edition, variant B with "A26" printed in lower right corner of page [44] instead of "A25," as found in variant A; collects the fourteen poems VN wrote in English between 1942 and 1957. Juliar A33.1. A presentation copy, inscribed to Véra on the title page, in Russian: *To you, my darling, V. July 26, 1959/Beverly Hills Hotel/L.A.* VN colored the black and white printed illustration so that a blue and red butterfly alights on a rock amid green grass. The inscription dates to his first consultation in Los Angeles with Stanley Kubrick and Frank Harris over the possibility of a VN screen adaptation of *Lolita*. (For the dedication copy of *Lolita: A Screenplay*, see item #92.)

Though VN's poetic output in English is no match in quantity for his Russian verse, some have suggested it is the language in which his best poems were written. Barry Scherr writes that the English poetry is an improvement over the Russian verse not because VN was a better poet in English than in Russian, but because "his English poetry nearly all dates from his more mature period, when he wrote less but had found his own voice as a poet" (p. 623). But VN, throughout his career, vehemently championed the superiority of his Russian verse. In his 1970 collection, *Poems and Problems*, he would include 39 Russian poems with English translations, but only 14 English poems, claiming in the foreword that "[s]omehow, [the English poems] are of a lighter texture than the Russian stuff, owing, no doubt, to their lacking that inner verbal association with old perplexities and constant worry of thought which marks poems written in one's mother tongue. With exile keeping up its parallel murmur and a never-resolved childhood plucking at one's rustiest chords."

After seeing the final book he wrote to his editor: "I am delighted . . . It is very pretty and quite substantial despite the limited number of pieces, and the butterfly, as finally evolved, is right lepidopterologically" (August 16, 1959, to Pyke Johnson, Jr., SL p. 297). The butterfly he mentions had been a while in the works. In March he had sent a lengthy response to the sketches forwarded him by his publishers. In part:

I like the two colored butterflies on the jacket but they have the bodies of ants, and no stylization can excuse a simple mistake. To stylize adequately one must have complete knowledge of the thing. I would be the laughing stock of my entomological colleagues if they happened to see these impossible hybrids . . . the body should look as in the sketch I am enclosing, and not the way they look in your artist's drawing, and the wings should be attached not to the abdomen but to the thorax. I like the texture and tints of these two insects, and the lettering is admirable.

Now, turning to the title-page butterfly, its head is that of a small tortoise, and its pattern is that of a common Cabbage White butterfly (whereas the insect in my poem is clearly described as belonging to a group of small blue butterflies with dotted undersides), which is as meaningless in the present case as would be a picture of a tuna fish on the jacket of *Moby Dick*. I want to be quite clear and frank: I have nothing against stylization but I do object to stylized ignorance.

I suggest therefore either of two courses: 1) Not to have any butterflies, or any pictures, at all or 2) To provide the insects depicted with butterfly bodies and butterfly heads and (in the case of the title-page butterfly) with a different pattern.

If you look up my correspondence with Jason [Epstein] regarding the *Pnin* jacket, you will note into what hideous trouble the otherwise excellent artist got in his first sketch. I think there were some fourteen mistakes. (to Johnson, March 15, 1959, SL pp. 284–85)

A month later, Johnson sent more acceptable sketches, eliciting the following plea from VN:

The title-page butterfly is now charming—a very natural and stylish little lep in comfortable surroundings. The binding-design swallowtail lacks antennae but otherwise is presentable. The jacket is well drawn but the choice of models (two popular European insects, the Galatea Marbled White and the Machaon Swallowtail) is not apt, and the whole arrangement looks like the jacket of some popular insect book for your collectors. I beg you to give up the idea of a lepidopterological jacket. Let us have it quite plain, with no drawings at all, or perhaps just a duplicate of the title-page lep. (April 15, 1959, SL p. 287)

105 **Poems.** London: Weidenfeld and Nicolson, (1961).

Slim 8vo.; blue cloth, spine gently bumped; white dust-jacket, lightly soiled with some wear to the top edge.

First English edition; reproduced from Doubleday's edition. Juliar A33.2. VN's reading copy, with two poems written out by him in the rear: two quatrains from "The Swift" (a poem from *The Gift*) in both English and Russian on page [45], with this introductory note: *In one of my old novels transliterated into Russian as The Gift. The poem by the young man in the novel* ... On the next two pages is "Wanted, Wanted," a 13-stanza love poem composed by Humbert in *Lolita*, with the explanation: *written by Humbert Humbert after Lolita's disappearance*. The text of this poem differs in one significant point from that of any published version, changing "Dolores" in the last stanza to *Lolita*. This alteration was made in pencil after VN copied out the text in ink. He significantly altered one of the printed poems, as well, restoring the original final line of "On translating *Eugene Onegin*" (p. 38), *dove-droppings*

They varnished the stump, put up railings and signs.
Restrooms nestled in roses and vines.

Mrs. Longwood, retouched, when the children died,
Became a photographer's dreamy bride.

And now the Deforests, with four old men,
Like regular tourists visit the glen;

Munch their lunches, look up and down,
Wash their hands, and drive back to town.

July 6, 1957

2 mm.

Ласточка
(The Swift)

Yu One of my old novels
The GIFT translated from the
Russian
The poem by the young
man in the novel
The English version first.

One night between sunset and river
On the old bridge we stood, you and I.
Will you ever forget it, I queried,
—That particular swift that went by?
And you answered, so earnestly: Never!

And what sobs made us suddenly shiver
What a cry life emitted in flight!
Till we die, till to-morrow, for ever,
you and I on the old bridge one night

Now the Russian text:

Ласточка

Однажды мы под вечер оба
Стояли на старом мосту
Скажи мне, спросил я, до гроба
Запомнишь — вон ласточку ту?
И так отвечала: еще бы!

И как мы заплакали оба,
как вскрикнула жизнь на лету,
До завтра, навеки, до гроба,
— Однажды, на старом мосту

45

44

next page
Mental Worlds

on your monument. The New Yorker had made him change it to the more palatable "The shadow of your monument," which he regularly readjusted by hand on printed copies. The version published in *Poems and Problems* (1970) contains the correct "dove-droppings" line. While teaching at Cornell, VN was frustrated by the lack of a competent transliteration of *Eugene Onegin*. Therefore he undertook the project himself, devoting a decade to preparing a text for press, and nearly another ten years revising the first edition of his version. In 1966 he defined the centrality of Pushkin's work, writing: "Pushkin's blood runs through the veins of modern Russian literature as inevitably as Shakespeare's through those of English literature" (Appel interview, SO p. 63). The restoration of this self-deprecating line in the commemorative poem is a significant and appropriate tribute to a major influence.

VN further annotated this copy for performance – the spine is cracked in several places, permitting it to lay flat; the cracked hinges are strengthened with tape – with alterations and vocal stresses in pencil throughout and the reminder to *pause* after reading each title. In some instances he docketed the reading time at the head of a poem (10 minutes for "An Evening of Russian Poetry"; 4 minutes for "The Room" (p. 25); 2 minutes for "Lines Written in Oregon" (p. 33); 1 minute for "Rain" (p. 39); 6 minutes for "Ballad of Longwood Glen" (p. 41), which he considered his best English poem; and an arrow and cue to the next reading, at the foot (*p. 33 Lines written in Oregon* on page 26; *p. 39 Rain* on page 34; *Pale Fire p. 11* on page [44]; *Next page: Wanted Wanted* on the first blank page in the rear, page [45], which VN filled with "The Swift" in English and Russian). A lengthy introduction to "An Evening of Russian Poetry" (p. 19) has been heavily smudged and partially erased.

106 Poems [Poesie]. Translated by Alberto Pescetto and Enzo Siciliano. Milan: Il Saggiatore, 1962.

12mo.; blue and black paper-covered boards, extremities rubbed.

First Italian translation of 16 Russian poems from *Stikhotvoreniia 1929–1951* and 14 English poems from *Poems* (1959), with the original texts facing the Italian translations. Juliar D27; D33. Boyd reports that Véra "mastered the rudiments of Italian grammar" for the express purpose of checking the translations in this edition "word by word against the dictionary" (TAY p. 420); the presence in their library of her Italian grammar gifted by VN while still at Cornell suggests her studies had already begun before they left Ithaca in January 1959. A presentation copy, inscribed on the front endpaper *To Véra/from V. Nabokov*, also signed with his two pseudonyms: *V. Sirin, and Basilio Šiškov/April, 1962/Montreux.* With a small butterfly in pink, blue, and grey, that Johnson writes is representative of both "small blue-black Metalmarks of this shape" from Latin America and "similar looking Hairstreak butterflies in Africa." However, "given Nabokov's general knowledge it's most likely he was thinking of the Latin American Metalmarks. As Nabokov shows, the wing colors can be finely mottled with iridescent blue and black; some species also show brilliant metallic flecks of gold along the wing margins."

VN's annotated copy (labeled twice by him on the cover, *Additions*), with previous and later publication information added to the English poems; he placed a pencil "x" to the top of nearly every page on which a Russian poem begins, numbering the lines of three poems; made formatting corrections to several pages; added textual notes or translations to two pages (one erased); provided the places and dates of other publications for each entry in the English poem section; and made the well-known alteration to "On translating 'Eugene Onegin,'" restoring *Dove-droppings on your monument* as the last line.

107 **The Song of Igor's Campaign.** An Epic of the Twelfth Century. Translated from the Old Russian. New York: Vintage, (1960).

12mo.; wrappers illustrated with a map depicting the lands bound by the Baltic and Black Seas; disbound and reglued.

First edition; not issued in cloth. Juliar A34.1. Apparently a photographic model, disbound for shooting and reglued. A presentation copy, inscribed on the half-title: *to Véra/from/V/Sept. 1960/LA.* (In February 1960 VN and Véra had returned to Los Angeles to resume discussion with Kubrick about the *Lolita* screenplay; on September 8, he sent the director his final version of the complete script.) With a lovely blue and pink butterfly with a pencil outline. An emended copy, with VN's pencil list inside the cover, of eight pages (two are crossed out beyond recognition) bearing mistakes – primarily of line numbers cited in the text – and with two index cards inserted: one with his cryptic pencil note: *other copy from C3 mailed to McGraw*; and one with his or Véra's list of the errors noted in this copy.

VN's idea of publishing a translation of *Igor* – the epic medieval Russian tale of three princes, led by Igor, who set out to defend their homeland against invaders – had been festering since the late forties; he contacted Roman Jakobson, who had just brought out a study contributing to the scholarship dating the manuscript (with Henri Grégoire and Marc Szeftel) in 1949 to discuss a potential collaboration. In 1952 he outlined a book to Pascal Covici at Viking along the following lines: "1. The basic Slavic text (about 25–30 pages), 2. My translation (about 40–50 p.), 3. My notes (about 40 p.), 4. Historic and linguistic commentaries by Prof. Jakobson of Harvard Univ. and Prof. Szeftel of Cornell Univ. (about 100 pages)" (May 16, SL pp. 132–33). Soon after, he contracted with the Bollingen Press for the project. Five years later, after VN's antipathy to Jakobson's leftward leanings had hardened, he wrote to his intended collaborator: "After a careful examination of my conscience, I have come to the conclusion that I cannot collaborate with you in the proposed English-language edition of the *Slovo*. Frankly, I am unable to stomach your little trips to totalitarian countries, even if these trips are prompted merely by scientific considerations" (April 14, 1957, SL p. 216).

By 1959 VN had finished the project on his own, and told Edmund Wilson: "I once translated [it] but now have completely revamped [it]. The commentary to it has inherited a Eugene [Onegin] gene and is threatening to grow into another mammoth... Russia will never be able to repay all her debts to me" (March 2, 1959, NWL p. 327). Though he and Jason Epstein at Doubleday had agreed on an anthology comprised of translations of works by several Russian poets as well as the *Song*, VN had expended much more effort than he had expected before even tackling the other translations. He offered to withdraw the manuscript – comprised of a foreword "explaining the discovery of the *Slovo* and describing its structure... an Index of the princes, a genealogical chart and a map... The *Song* itself... a Commentary including notes to the Foreword and notes to The Song" (June 6, 1959, SL p. 291) – and to return Doubleday's advance. Epstein apparently agreed, and Vintage brought it out the following year. Though he suffered several delays as the project developed and bounced from publisher to publisher, VN taught from the manuscript for one semester at Cornell, and left a copy on reserve at the library for the students' use. Pirated copies "circulate[d] at Harvard and Columbia for the rest of the decade until his new translation was published in 1960" (TAY p. 217).

The original text, *Slovo o polku Igoreve*, dates to 1187, though the 1800 first edition was based on a faulty 16th-century transcription. The editors of that edition, according to VN, "separated the words (sometimes incorrectly), introduced modern punctuation and rather haphazardly paragraphed the text. They also printed *en regard* a modern Russian version which abounds in all kinds of inaccuracies, pseudoclassical paraphrases, and glaring blunders." He meant his own edition to improve on previous attempts by dividing the original of "about 2850 words" into 860 lines of literal translation:

I have ruthlessly sacrificed manner to matter and have attempted to give a literal rendering of the text as I understand it. Each page (except the first, the last, and one in the middle) of the lost original contained presumably an average of 310 letters (arranged in about twenty lines of about the same length each). I have preserved on each page of my English translation the amount of material corresponding to what I think was that amount on each given page of the lost MS (or, more correctly, of an earlier MS on which Musin's MS was based); but the breaking up of these batches into lines is arbitrary and only meant to provide easy reference.

108 **The Song of Igor's Campaign.** An Epic of the Twelfth Century. Translated from Old Russian. London: Weidenfeld and Nicolson, (1961).

12mo.; errata slip tipped to verso of title page; grey cloth; green dustjacket; two tape repairs, lightly creased, one small chip to the front panel.

First English edition, reproduced from the Vintage edition. Juliar A34.2. A presentation copy, inscribed on the front endpaper: *For Véra/ from author* [sic]/*with love/Jan. 26, 1961*, with a small, colorfully decorated butterfly. VN made one emendation, adding *Miniver* to correct his notation of a species name on page 112 and noting the change on the front endpaper. This is the only correction made to the first edition that was not included on the errata slip tipped into this English edition, though it is clearly marked in VN's copy of the first edition.

109 **Pale Fire.** New York: Putnam's, (1962).

8vo.; black cloth; dust-jacket; light wear, single tape repair to spine.

First edition of VN's second National Book Award nomination. Juliar A35.1. The dedication copy, inscribed to Véra on the dedication page: *From V/Montreux/April 23 1962*. With an intricately drawn butterfly in blues and greys named for a species making its debut in the title poem of *Pale Fire*: *Vanessa incognita*. (The narrator's derivation of that name is explained in the commentary, in his note to line 270: "It is so like the heart of a scholar in search of a fond name to pile a butterfly genus upon an Orphic divinity on top of the inevitable allusion to *Van-homrigh, Es*ther! In this connection a couple of lines from one of Swift's poems (which in these backwoods I cannot locate) have stuck in my memory: 'When, lo! Vanessa in her bloom/ Advanced like Atlanta's star.'.") Johnson is more precise: "*Vanessa* is a genus of colorful Brush-foot butterflies that occur in many parts of the world, commonly known as Painted Ladies. Nabokov's imagined species 'incognita' portrays the wing shape of this group very accurately. However, it is the final of four drawings in this collection – *Vanessa verae, Colias verae* and *Colias lolita* are the others – where Nabokov adopts blues colors which would not appear in these groups in nature."

There is an additional butterfly – a simple pencil "lep" – on the half-title, where VN noted a misprint on page 53, and added: *for other misprints see my hard copy* (that "hard copy" is item #111). The only other annotation in this copy is some underlining on page 67.

Like so many of VN's novels, *Pale Fire* expands the definition of what a novel can be; he called its form "specifically, if not generically, new" (Appel interview, 1966, SO p. 75). Comprised of a foreword, a 999-line poem in four cantos, accompanying "commentary" of some 300 pages, and an index, its form has been identified by Sergej Davydov as at least in part a nod to Pushkin's verse novel *Eugene Onegin* (p. 483). The foreword, similar to the forewords VN wrote for many of his other works, explains the history and composition of the text – but it is written by the narrator, the supposedly mad critic Charles Kinbote. The poem he edits is by the fictional deceased poet John Shade – once referred to by VN as "by far the greatest of *invented* poets" – and through a line-by-line "commentary" and index Kinbote reads into this poem the history of Zembla.

VN noted in his diary on December 4, 1961: "Finished *Pale Fire*, begun a year ago, 29 November (in its present form)" (quoted in TAY p. 424). That "in its present form" is telling. In reality, he had been mulling the fundamental plot – without the complex narrative structures – since as early as 1939, and "actively planning" it from 1956 (TAY p. 379), but progress was slow. By summer 1959 his confidence had waned, and he wrote to Doubleday that he had put off the novel's completion – though soon after, on the boat to Europe, he jotted an outline of the four parts of the novel in a diary. He took it up again in earnest the following fall, with a vision of the narrative apparatuses that would become its hallmark – beginning, as with *The Gift*, with the hardest part first: the 999-line poem at the core of the novel, originally entitled "The Brink," which he later claimed was "the hardest stuff [he] ever had to compose" (1965, SO p. 55). By spring of 1961 the novel was still incomplete, but he offered the poem to *Esquire*, calling it "racy and tricky, and unpleasant, and bizarre" (to Rust Hills, March 23, 1961, SL p. 329). (*Esquire* rejected it on the grounds that they did not publish poetry.) When the completed novel was published the following April, it sold briskly, thanks in part to Walter Minton's ingenious publicity campaign, likely engendered by VN's vehement reaction against his initial plan. He had bristled at Minton's suggestion that Zembla and its inhabitants be more clearly defined for readers and reviewers; Véra sent a letter listing objections, and followed it up weeks later with the caveat: "'A distant Northern land' has poetry, nostalgia, almost a heartbreaking sob in its sound. If we say 'a non-existent Northern land' it becomes a label on an empty bottle" (quoted TAY p. 464). In response, Boyd reports, Minton sent reviewers advance copies "only after [they had committed] themselves to disclosing nothing before publication day. The strategy worked, and newspapers clamored for information" (ibid.).

By the summer *Pale Fire* was a best-seller, despite the complexity of the narrative and the fact that "few reviewers realized what it was really about" (to Peter and Joan de Peterson, July 24, 1962, SL pp. 338–39). In the *New York Times* George Cloyne wrote that *Pale Fire* "is one more proof of Mr. Nabokov's rare vitality. Unluckily it is not much more than that...the fantasy never gets off the ground" (May 27, 1962). Mary McCarthy was unequivocally positive, and heralded *Pale Fire* as "one of the very great works of art of this century" (TAY p. 465). (She reconsidered this opinion when, in 1969, she read *Ada*, which repelled her.) Boyd's own estimation is that "[i]n sheer beauty of form, *Pale Fire* may well be the most perfect novel ever written" (TAY p. 425); he calls it "a dazzling technical tour de force, a comic delight, an imaginative treat, a study of life and death, sanity and madness, hope and despair, love and loneliness, privacy and sharing, kindness and selfishness, creativity and parasitism, and above all a thrilling ride of discovery" (TAY p. 456).

110 **Pale Fire.** New York: Putnam's, (1962).

8vo.; dust-jacket bound-in; top edge gilt; gilt-tooled dentelles; satin ribbon; full burgundy morocco, stamped in gilt and blind; stamped "V. N." in gilt on the front panel.

First edition. Juliar A35.1. A specially bound publisher's presentation copy (with the dust-jacket bound-in at the rear), with VN's corrections

on nine pages and a dried leaf in the shape of a butterfly pressed between the leaves.

111 **Pale Fire.** New York: Putnam's, (1962).

8vo.; five Asian characters rubberstamped onto the last leaf; black cloth; spine cocked; light shelf wear.

First edition, second printing. Juliar A35.1. VN's "hard copy," with underscorings scattered throughout, emphasizing questionable words and passages; over a dozen additions and emendations to the index; an interlinear Russian translation of lines 653–661 of the poem; minor emendations to spelling and punctuation, and the addition line numbers, on 12 pages, all listed on the front endpaper, one in Véra's hand: she emended "hare breath" to *hair breadth*.

112 **Pale Fire.** New York: Lancer Books, (1963).

12mo.; pages 41–50 detached; printed wrappers.

First paperback edition, with an excerpt from Mary McCarthy's review on the cover. Juliar A35.3. VN's reading copy, used for an event at the Poetry Center at New York City's 92nd Street Y: his note on the title page reads *Copy used for reading at Poets Center with marked passages.* Accordingly, he indicated sections of text to be read, underlining occasional words and phrases for emphasis, and adding additional performance notes such as: *I shall now read a passage of two-hundred lines from Shade's poem. Shade is speaking of his dead daughter* (p. 31); and *I shall now recite a ten-minute poem . . .* (p. 36). He docketed this copy on the cover *corrected*, and under his hand-drawn pencil butterfly on the first leaf wrote *see corrections next page*, where he listed two misprints.

113 **Vladimir Nabokov: Bibliographie des gesamtwerks.** By Dieter E. Zimmer. (Reinbek bei Hamburg): Rowohlt, (1963).

12mo.; pale red printed wrappers.

First edition of the first VN bibliography; in German. VN's copiously annotated copy, labeled *Corrected Master Copy, 1964* on the front panel in pencil. The margins of about half the pages are packed with his minor corrections to the primary entries, with numerous holograph additions to the lists of foreign translations and later editions. That the notes were made in pencil, blue and green ink suggests VN's continual review. With four small leaves of graph paper bearing several additions and notes clipped to the half-title. A sample: about the Berkeley paperback edition of *Pale Fire*, he asks: *Had Putnam's the right to publish it (probably, yes).* He follows up: *Copyright – by Putnam's? (probably, no).* His third *Pale Fire* reminder is simply: *misprints.* Below these questions and answers are several issues he raised about the next edition of this bibliography: *A. Field: German title translation in the first § of each entry are not necessary. 2) Doubleday problem. 3) list permissions.* The fourth note is a reminder to add forthcoming publications, and contains "Remarks" written about various works. On another leaf he suggests adding various interviews; on a third, he questions Zimmer's transliteration, as well as the spelling inconsistencies resulting from the German translation; on the fourth, he lists queries about the publication status of pending translations and contracts.

Zimmer, the editor of Rowohlt's 23-volume German annotated edition of VN's works, began this bibliography for Rowohlt, who had begun to publish VN's earlier books with occasionally inaccurate publication information. He writes that "[i]t was compiled under difficulties that would seem daunting today," including the lack of Xerox machines, effective interlibrary loan and efficient international phone service, and the fact that many libraries and catalogues had been destroyed. "The search soon took on an impetus of its own, and when Ledig Rowohlt saw what I had assembled he took pity on it and had it printed and distributed free as a Christmas gift among the friends of the house." When the booklet came to the attention of the Nabokovs, they forwarded useful corrections and emendations. "Seeing my predicament that all of that would be lost now, Ledig took pity again and had another edition printed, a revised one. Like the first one, it was never for sale, and I would say there were just a few hundred copies of both."

114 Vladimir Nabokov: Bibliographie des gesamtwerks. By Dieter E. Zimmer. (Reinbek bei Hamburg): Rowohlt, (1963).

12mo.; pale red printed wrappers.

First edition. A presentation copy, inscribed on the cover in ink: *for Véra*, with a simple butterfly outline. Labeled *more or less corrected* in pencil on the cover, with VN's copious marginal X's and question marks throughout – with his key to the annotations on the title page in Russian and English: *unauthorized edition marked 'xx' / copyright checked – marked '?' / misprints – marked 'x' / needed addenda – marked 'add.'* On page 19 he noted in Russian, *for translation/already translated; into English apprv'd [by] V.*; and on page 40: *Opyty, NY 196 ... [another poem ...] both in San Remo 1959.* Shapiro notes: "It seems that VN's memory failed him here: the poem "Kakoe sdelal ia durnoe delo" ["What is the Evil Deed I Have Committed"] was first published together with another poem, "Minuty est': ne mozhet byt', bormochesh'" ["There Are Such Moments: 'It Can't Be,' You Mutter"], under the rubric "Dva stikhotvoreniia" ["Two Poems"] in *Vozdushnye Puti* [*Aerial Ways*], No. 2, 1961, 184–85 (see Juliar C5769–70), and not in *Opyty* [Experiments]."

115 Notes on Prosody. From the Commentary to his translation of Pushkin's *Eugene Onegin*. An offprint from Bollingen Series LXXII. (New York: The Bollingen Foundation), (1963).

12mo.; stiff grey printed wrappers.

First separate edition, presentation issue; 200 copies (30 of which were sent directly to VN, *gratis*); off-printed from VN's four-volume *Eugene Onegin* translation – which included a commentary, two appendices (*Notes on Prosody* was the second), an index, and a reproduction of the 1837 second edition, the last Pushkin saw through press himself. VN expected his edition to appear by the end of 1963, but waited over twelve months for its release. It seems plausible that Bollingen off-printed *Notes on Prosody* as a gesture of good faith, in recognition of the unusually long and taxing delays. A trade issue of 3500 copies was issued with a slightly revised text and a different jacket, paginated from [1] to 104, six months after the four-volume set, capitalizing on the furor VN's translation had aroused. Juliar A36.1; 1991 update.

A presentation copy, inscribed on the first blank: *For Véra/ April 22, 1963/ Corsica.* VN had originally signed the presentation in Montreux – the erased letters are visible beneath "Corsica." With an elaborately rainbowed Hawkmoth (or Sphinx Moth) named *Deilephila raduga Nabokov* (female), cobbled together from several sources. "The antennae are what typify the genus *Hyles*. The big body is typical of the genus *Sphinx*. The wing colors are typical of the group *Zygaenoidea*, a group of micromoths with very outstanding colors like this." Johnson speculates, "Nabokov may have wanted to imagine what those colors would look like on a much larger moth." Docketed by VN on the cover in pencil: *came out: April 22, 1963, 5:15 PM/Clarke & Way*, a graphic and poignant testament to the pains of the process.

G. S. Smith has noted that VN "dealt with the theory and practice of Russian versification in a number of his writings"—naming the Edmund Wilson correspondence, the versification theories of his protagonist in *The Gift*, and chapter 11 of *Speak, Memory* as worth special notice—but rightly calls *Notes on Prosody* his "most substantial single work on the subject" (p. 561). In a fairly balanced review, he acknowledges the contributions made by VN's "acute ear, his own refined taste in two languages, and great accuracy and consistency of observation," and his "captivating" historical notes of "considerable practical interest"; but he critically notes that VN writes in a "private language," uses "arcane methodology," and ignores relevant scholarship, ultimately providing a system of analysis that "remains essentially a solipsism" (pp. 564–65). His conclusion offers an astute explanation, if not necessarily a defense:

Nabokov's choices resembled those made by other émigré poets of the interwar period, with the marked exception of [Marina] Tsvetaeva. For them, as for all Russian poets, verse form was an ideologically semanticized area: formal innovation was characteristic of those poets who stood politically to the left, who accepted the Revolution of 1917, and remained in Russia or soon returned to it. For Nabokov, this rendered them unacceptable; and the formal choices that he made indicated very graphically his nostalgia for a time before the spirit of innovation had changed Russian poetry and Russian society. His theoretical views were similar: he chose to ignore the work in versification that was one of the most genuine and lasting achievements of Soviet scholarship in the humanities, remaining faithful to the memories of his youth. (pp. 565–66)

116 **Eugene Onegin.** A Novel in Verse by Aleksandr Pushkin. In four volumes. (New York): Pantheon Books, Bollingen Series LXXII, (1964).

4 vols., 8vo.; red satin ribbons; blue-grey cloth; spines rubbed and faded; publisher's cardboard slipcase; a well-read set in very good condition.

First edition; 4282 copies, the entire edition, published in June 1964; one of only a handful with the red ribbon book marks (this is the second copy we have encountered); includes VN's translation, commentary, two appendices ("Abram Gannibal" and "Notes on Prosody"), index, and reproduction of the 1837 second edition, the final text Pushkin saw through the press. Juliar A37.1. The second appendix had been off-printed a year earlier as a presentation issue for VN.

The dedication copy, inscribed to Véra on the front endpaper, with two butterflies—one in pencil, the other, in red and grey set on a pink and grey background. VN aggressively edited this copy over the course of several years for the revised edition which appeared a decade later, with the note at the head of the *Notes on Prosody* section: *Reprint this from the separate volume published in 1964 Boll. LXXIIa 1964 Pantheon Books where there are some minor corrections.* (This appendix had been inexpensively published in wrappers, with a few minor revisions, a special note, index, and new preliminaries, six months after the full edition.) With his notes on the same page in blue ink, grey pencil, and red pencil: *Published: June 1964. Corrected 1967 (conforms to typescript sent Boll.) Added corrections 1971 in red to be included in proof*, and docketed the printed label on the cardboard slipcase: *Corrected set revised Jan. 1967.* The large note scrawled in pencil on the front paste-down—*See p. 88*—refers to instructions he added for the typist.

In 1952, VN wrote in his plan of study submitted to the Guggenheim Foundation, "Eugene Onegin is as great a world classic as *Hamlet* or *Moby Dick*, and the presentation of it will be as true to the original as scholarship and art can make it" (SL p. 131). In his aggressive defense, "Reply to My Critics," he stated that he had already begun work on a second, revised edition, to be "even more gloriously and monstrously literal than the first" (SO p. 124); he felt that his first edition "[fell] short of the ideal crib," and wrote: "It is still not close enough and not ugly enough. In future editions...I think I shall turn it entirely into utilitarian prose, with a still bumpier brand of English, rebarbative barricades of square brackets and tattered banners of reprobate words, in order to eliminate the last vestiges of bourgeois poesy and concession to rhythm" (SO p. 243). This is the copy he used for the task. Nearly every page of the poem has been revised in this uncompromising spirit, with at times entire stanzas retranslated in the margins. The second and third volumes, printing his commentary, bear notes to the excerpted poetry, and occasional additions and clarifications to his explanations. Among the more substantive of these is an updated explanation in Eight: XXVI. In attacking Olga Oom's edition of the diary of her grandmother, Anna Olenin, he had originally asserted that she misread the Russian of "Jack Rover" (a contemporary actor) as "Red Rover," and that she "anachronistically [lent] it a political sense." In this copy he crossed out that ensuing explanatory paragraph and added in the margin that "Red" had been correct: *She nicknamed Pushkin Red Rover (the title of a novel by Fenimore Cooper as Mr. Carl R. Proffer* [founder of Ardis Press and early VN scholar] *tells me in a letter of Oct. 4, 1966). Miss Oom, who provided me with the wrong reference [ ] me in my 1964 ed., anachronistically lent a political [ ] to "Red."* In the 1975 edition VN eliminated the accusatory tone, and simply corrected the reference: "She dubbed Pushkin 'Red Rover' after the hero of James Fenimore Cooper's novel *The Red Rover* (written in the summer of 1827 in a village near Paris). This is the name of a pirate ship flying a blood-red ensign and it is also the nickname of her captain, William Heidegger..." (p. 202). The index, in the fourth volume, bears this note: *Index not corrected*, and the photographic reproduction of the Russian *Onegin* text bears his translations on the first several pages.

In a lecture delivered in 1937, the centennial of Pushkin's death, VN claimed that reading Pushkin was "without a single exception...one of the glories of earthly life" (quoted in Davydov, "Nabokov and Pushkin," p. 489). By this time he had christened both *The Empyrean Path* and *Mary* with epigraphs from Pushkin; created characters whose fates can ultimately be traced to their knowledge of, and faithfulness to, a Pushkinian aesthetic (in *The Defense*, *Despair*, and *Invitation to a Beheading*); and attacked the leading exponents of anti-Pushkin sentiment, notably Georgy Adamovich and Georgy Ivanov. In 1937, too, he published *The Gift*, whose protagonist's artistic development "loosely parallels the path Russian literature took after the Golden Age of poetry in the 1820s...Entire sections of the novel are written in verse form, overt and concealed, which makes *The Gift* a generic cousin to Pushkin's experimental 'novel in verse,' *Eugene Onegin*" (ibid. p. 490). And though VN had the last paragraph typeset as prose, it unmistakably preserves the rhyme and meter of the *Onegin* stanza. Later he would complete "The Water Nymph," a verse play Pushkin had left unfinished, and would spend as much time in translating, publishing, and revising *Eugene Onegin* as Pushkin had spent writing it. (Davydov, pp. 482–495)

When he started teaching Russian literature at Wellesley in 1946, VN repeatedly expressed frustration at the lack of an adequate literal translation of *Onegin*. (Alexander Dolinin has noted that "'free translations' of Pushkin's greatest work inadvertently albeit inevitably reduce him to a lesser Byron" (p. 119).) According to VN, Véra eventually suggested he prepare his own since he had already begun translating excerpts for class use. In 1952 he won a Guggenheim Fellowship to pursue the project, which he had optimistically hoped would be completed "within a year or so." He defended his choice of subject in his Plan for Study as "the first and fundamental Russian novel: Its general atmosphere, the logical and harmonious development of its plot from the essential features of the characters, the retrospective and introspective rambles of the writer's thought, are rightly considered by critics to have 'given the cue and pattern to the great Russian novelists of the XIX century' (Mirsky, *History of Russian Literature*)" (To Henry Allen Moe, April 5, 1952, SL pp. 131–32). He further noted that his would be the first edition in any language—including Russian—to include "the exhaustive commentaries that the text should have for adequate understanding and enjoyment"; that previous verse translations into English "transformed one of the most brilliant works ever composed into a vague, lame, third-rate concoction with rhymes of the 'pleasure-leisure', 'heart-part' sort"; and that "[s]ince there is no way of transforming the complex Russian structure of the piece into adequate English verse, I propose to offer not only a literal prose translation but to accompany it by profuse notes explaining as thoroughly as possible the musical impact of the Russian line and various points of Pushkin's technique." He also outlines "notes on Russian customs, literary events, and other matters referring to Pushkin's time"; an introductory biographical sketch of Pushkin "and an evaluation of the novel's place in West European literature"; and "fragments and new readings of various passages" that have cropped up over the years.

Almost six years after the composition of his Guggenheim proposal of a year-long project, VN wrote to Katharine White that the "monster" had "grown far beyond whatever I planned originally," and optimistically asserted that "[i]t is not only going to make 'Eugene Onegin' accessible to the foreign reader but will also give the American reader, and the English-reading Russian, a unique and exhaustive work on the subject" (February 16, 1957, SL p. 201). A month later he told Edmund Wilson: "I have at last discovered the right way to translate *Onegin*. This is the fifth or sixth complete version I have made" (March 24, 1957, NWL p. 311). At the end of summer he admitted more confidentially to his sister: "I hope that I can finally, finally finish my monstrous Pushkin . . . I am tired of this 'bookish exploit' . . ." (to Elena Sikorski, September 14, 1957, SL p. 227).

In 1958 the completed manuscript—without the index—was accepted by the Bollingen Foundation, which was about to inflict on him an entirely different breed of publishing difficulties from those he had recently suffered for *Lolita*. The editing process was a long one, though he willingly accepted critique from his "meticulous and brilliant" editor Bart Winer (quoted TAY p. 463). After editing was completed, the project was stalled for a full year, VN claimed, because of "inefficient preparation of copy on the part of an inexperienced member of the Bollingen staff." By the end of 1962 he had finished the index begun by Dmitri, which VN had conceived of as a reflection of the translation and commentary, "its virtues and its shortcomings, its tone and personality (as I have proved in *Pale Fire*). It should be an afterglow and not a yawn" (to William McGuire, quoted in TAY 470).

All along VN had been anxiety-ridden lest his publication be preëmpted by the work of another scholar—a fear that proved to be well-founded. Perhaps in an attempt to mollify him, Bollingen issued his second appendix, *Notes on Prosody*, that June in an offprint edition, limited to 200 copies and distributed *gratis*; it is clear from this offprint that the plates were set by March or April at the latest; from his prefatory note we know that he fully expected to see the complete text by the end of the year. But he had not yet heard from Bollingen's legal department. In a letter signed "Vladimir Adamant Nabokov" he contentiously tackled fifteen instances in his text where, they felt, he set them up for lawsuits by attacking previous translations and editions of Pushkin's work (SL pp. 347–49). In the mean time, Walter Arndt published a translation of *Onegin* at the end of 1963—and, somewhat maddeningly, won the Bollingen Prize for poetical translation; VN trashed the work in a *New York Review of Books* piece on April 30, 1964; publication of his own edition was still half a year away.

The relief VN experienced at publication was almost immediately shattered by Wilson's caustic review, "The Strange Case of Pushkin and Nabokov" (July 15, 1965, *New York Review of Books*), which engendered a series of rebuttals, qualified retractions, and counterattacks, and effectively terminated their quarter-century friendship. Bollingen had been eager to send the work to Wilson prepublication to allow him ample time to compose a strong review. They did this with VN's very reluctant permission. He warned William McGuire that Wilson was an "envious ass," and that his Russian was "primitive, and his knowledge of Russian literature gappy and grotesque" (August 27, 1964, SL p. 358), though as early as the summer of '42 he had suggested Wilson translate

The Gift into English and almost 17 years earlier had suggested they collaborate on "a scholarly prose translation of *Eugene Onegin* with copious notes" (September 3, 1948, NWL p. 205). Though that never came to pass, they indulged in a correspondence frequently tackling issues of Russian and English translation, prose, and poetry. In May 1949 VN had even warned Wilson: "I am quite certain I am not going to do any *rhymed* translations any more—their dictatorship is absurd and impossible to reconcile with exactitude, etc." (May 23–25, 1949, NWL p. 227).

Wilson's criticisms were substantially based on his belief that a translation should be written in "idiomatic and recognizable English," a view diametrically opposed to VN's own. Offering the defense that "[s]ince Mr. Nabokov is the least modest of men, I do not hesitate to urge my own rival claims against him," he also censures VN's "addiction to rare and unfamiliar words"; his "Russianisms"; his "actual errors of English"; and even his failure to adhere to his mantra of "scrupulous literalness." In addition, "The commentary, the appendices, and the scholarly presentation suffer in general...mainly from a lack of common sense," as well. The appendix, *Notes on Prosody*, is "tedious and interminable," the system expounded in it, "ridiculous." The commentary is "overdone." Finally, VN's interpretation, we are told, is flawed. In one particular instance, "Nabokov has simply not seen the point." At the end of the third page (of four), Wilson begins assessing "the positive side," a survey he completes with heavy qualification. "The commentary, if one skips the *longueurs*, does make very pleasant reading, and it represents an immense amount of labor," but VN "underrates Pushkin's knowledge of English and quite disregards the evidence." "There is a good deal of excellent literary criticism" and some "excellent little essays," but their author is more often "merely snide and silly." He acknowledges VN's contribution in his detailed exegesis of Pushkin's "texture and rhythm of writing, to the skill in manipulating language, for the rendering of varied effects." He also praises the level of detailed historical and cultural contextualization, and concludes that ultimately, in spite of "his queer prejudices," of the fact that his theory of prosody is flawed, and of the fact that "when he tried to translate *Onegin* 'literally,' what he writes is not always really English," VN "serves a useful function of cross-fertilization...his sense of beauty and his literary proficiency, his energy which seems never to tire, have made him a virtual live wire which vibrates between us and that Russian past which still provides for the Russian present a vitality that can sometimes inspire it and redeem it from mediocrity." Wilson's final paragraph praises the physical attractiveness of the volumes, which won awards for typography.

On August 26, 1965, the *New York Review of Books* printed VN's response, addressing seven specific points of the critique, and suggesting that "Wilson's didactic purpose is defeated by the presence of such errors (and there are many more to be listed later) as it is also by the strange tone of his article. Its mixture of pompous aplomb and peevish ignorance is certainly not conducive to a sensible discussion of Pushkin's language and mine." Wilson admitted, in a reply printed in the same issue, that upon reflection he "felt that [his article] sounded more damaging" than he had intended. Letters from readers were mixed, some agreeing with Wilson, others siding with VN. Outside the *Review*, John Bayley and Elena Levin praised the commentary for its indispensable scholarship, other critics joined Wilson in attacking VN's ugly and awkward turns of phrase. Boyd offers a perspective on the growing debate: "[I]n the letters columns, review pages, and editorials of the *New York Review Of Books*, the *New Republic*, *Poetry*, and elsewhere, others continued to join in the fray, and Nabokov was vexed that many who knew no Russian or missed the point of his translating the way he did took Wilson's side and hissed at the hideousness of a translation he had never tried to prettify" (TAY 497).

In "Reply to My Critics," published in the February 1966 issue of *Encounter*, reprinted in *Nabokov's Congeries* (1968) and, in a slightly revised form, in *Strong Opinions* (1973), VN singled Wilson out for writing "the longest, most ambitious, most captious, and, alas, most reckless, article." He began somewhat gently: "Unlike my novels, EO possesses an ethical side, moral and human elements. It reflects the compiler's honesty or dishonesty, skill or sloppiness. If told I am a bad poet, I smile; but if told I am a poor scholar, I reach for my heaviest dictionary" (February 1966, SO p. 241). Soon he launched a frontal attack: ...The mistakes and misstatements in [Wilson's review] form an uninterrupted series so complete as to seem artistic in reverse, making one wonder if, perhaps, it had not been woven that way on purpose to be turned into something pertinent and coherent when reflected in a looking glass... A patient confidant of his long and hopeless infatuation with the Russian language and literature, I have invariably done my best to explain to him his monstrous mistakes of pronunciation, grammar, and interpretation... From our conversations and correspondence in former years I well know that, like Onegin, he is incapable of comprehending the mechanism of verse – either Russian or English... In his rejoinder to my letter of August 26, 1965, in *The New York Review*, Mr. Wilson says that on rereading his article he felt it sounded 'more damaging' than he had meant it to be. His article, entirely consisting, as I have shown, of quibbles and blunders, can be damaging only to his own reputation—and that is the last look I shall ever take at the dismal scene. (SO p. 266)

The intellectual brouhaha did, however, focus attention on an important work that had long been neglected in the States. Despite accusations that VN "distorts English deliberately and transparently" to his own ends (Steiner); that he uses obscure, or made up, English words; and that he confusingly "persisted in retaining the meter, and at times only the semblance thereof" (Gerschenkron); most acknowledge that VN was writing a work to be studied, not read, by a specific audience: an English-reading public whose view of Russian literature had been distorted by the paucity of Pushkin available in translation, and who needed a grounding in the "notes on Russian customs, literary events, and other matters referring to Pushkin's time" that VN had projected in his Guggenheim Plan for Study. And Dolinin, at least, acknowledges a debt to VN's "unrivaled discoveries" of Western European literary sources. "For instance, he was the first to identify many reminiscences, quotations, and clichés of eighteenth-century French poetry missed by his predecessors; he read attentively all the texts mentioned or alluded to by Pushkin, and his witty, very amusing synopses of the long-forgotten novels and plays elucidate their connections with *Eugene Onegin*; he studied French prose translations of Byron and proved beyond any doubt that Pushkin owed much more to these 'mediators' than to the English originals" (p. 125). (VN admitted in a letter to Harry Levin that in preparation for the task he had, indeed, read "all the books Pushkin refers to in 'E. O.'. Even Burke. Even Gibbon. Of course, Richardson and Mme Cottin. [*sic*]. And moreover, I have read all the stuff (Richardson, Shakespeare, Byron) in French, since this is what Pushkin had done" (May 2, 1953, SL pp. 136–37). This is the procedure he had followed in composing the "Life of Chernyshevski" chapter of *The Gift* in the 1930s—reading all of the work that his protagonist, the writer Fyodor, would have needed to read to produce that biography.)

Even as he rigorously defended his translation, VN was also assiduously revising it, in an attempt to bring it ever closer to the ideal form of translation he advocated in his critical writing. (Boyd makes the point that, had VN's translation been printed as an interlinear text with Pushkin's Russian—as a true literal translation should be—the noise made over its publication would likely have been considerably quieter.)

By the end of 1966, the new translation was almost complete – he labeled this copy *Corrected 1967*, noting that it conformed to the typescript sent to Bollingen. In fall 1969, when their second edition was still not ready, he sent the manuscript to McGraw-Hill; he still had a few books to go to fulfill his contract with them, and suggested a briefer edition of his *Onegin*. He included a note: "I am now through with that diabolical task forever. I feel that I have done for Pushkin at least as much as he has done for me" (TAY 573–74). But he was not yet done; he had to wait for the Princeton University Press – who had taken over Bollingen – to get their new edition out, a task that, somewhat inexplicably, took them six years. An additional note in this copy reads *Added corrections 1971 in red to be included in proof*. (By then McGraw-Hill had turned down the chance to publish it.) VN includes in his list of delays: "a strike by electrical employees, a printer's slowdown, a mismatched inking job, and more" (quoted in TAY 587). Boyd assesses the final edition in light of its potential to serve as the basis for a future version:

Nabokov followed Pushkin's lineation exactly, even at the cost of a wrenched and unnatural word order in English. To Gleb Struve [who had written the first and most comprehensive survey of émigré literature, and had introduced VN to his English readership] he wrote that his text had now become "ideally interlinear," yet even this revised version fails to provide an interlinear, transliterated, accented Russian text. When someday Nabokov's translation is published in this fashion, I expect every reviewer who knows Pushkin in the original and who has preferred verse translations over Nabokov's uncompromising literalism will recant. (TAY p. 330)

117 **Eugene Onegin.** By Aleksandr Pushkin. [New York]: Bollingen Series/Pantheon Books, (1964).

8vo.; blue cloth, spine stamped in red and gilt; dust-jacket, light wear.

First edition of volume I of the four-volume set; an unrecorded variant, possibly done up as a sort of proof. The binding is of a thinner stock of board, covered in a smoother baby blue cloth than regular copies; the endpapers are of an entirely different stock of paper and the printing of the text itself appears noticeably darker. The dust-jacket also differs in several respects from regular copies: a cooler cream color has been used for the background on the front panel and flaps; the rear panel is pure white, rather than uniform with the rest of the jacket; and the rear flap copy differs from that on ordinary copies in its omission of *The Collected Works Of Paul Valéry* from the list of Bollingen projects in progress. A cursory examination reveals no textual variations, although it is possible that some may have eluded our eyes. Juliar A37.1. The dust-jacket is labeled by both VN and Vé: *separate volume* and *Separate Volume (March, 1964)*. The spine is also labeled by VN, *Separate volume I.*

118 **Notes on Prosody.** From the Commentary to his translation of Pushkin's *Eugene Onegin*. An offprint from Bollingen Series LXXII A. (New York): Pantheon Books, (1964).

12mo.; stiff white and tan wrappers.

Second separate edition, first offered for sale; 3500 copies published over a year and a half after the presentation issue, with a slightly revised text, new preliminaries, pagination from [1], and an index. Juliar A36.1. The new author's note states that "[a] few corrections, chiefly typographical, have been made for this reprinting. There was not space for a footnote that I should have liked to add, on p. 47, asterisked to the phrase 'monosyllabic adjectives' in line 4 of paragraph 2, to wit: 'Not counting, of course, the monosyllabic predicative forms – adverbish mongrels, really – of disyllabic adjectives, such as *glup*, 'is stupid,' from *glupïy*, or *bel*, 'is white,' from *belïy*" (this footnote is present in VN's autograph in his annotated copy of the 1964 edition, see previous entry). Though copy on the dust-jacket flap justifies this edition of VN's second appendix, by "its special interest to poets, students, and teachers," it is likely that Bollingen was capitalizing on the controversy surrounding the work. A presentation copy, inscribed on the cover in pencil, *For Véra*, and again on the first blank in Russian along with an unpublished quatrain signed, *V. Sirin*, with a small ink and pencil butterfly: *To Verochka: When the world was not old / How fond were we / Of the marmoreal cold / Of winter in Italy. / V. Sirin Abano, 7 January 1965.* The poem, translated by Dmitri Nabokov, likely refers to their winter stay in Abano, near Padua, from the end of December 1964 to the start of January 1965.

119 **The Waltz Invention.** A Play in Three Acts. [New York]: Phaedra, 1966.

8vo.; blue cloth, extremities lightly rubbed; dust-jacket, extremities worn, with several small chips and closed tears repaired with tape.

First English translation, first edition, of VN's last play, written in the

'30s, and the only one of his seven plays translated into English in his lifetime (he wrote no plays in English, except *Lolita: A Screenplay*); variant A, with the first signature printed on acid-free paper and the rest on a cheaper stock, given to browning, and in the first state red, black, and white dust-jacket. This translation by Dmitri, heavily reworked by VN to appeal to his vision of an English-reading, 1960s audience, came nearly 30 years after the Russian-language serialization in *Russkie zapiski* (No. 11, November 1938, pp. 3–62). Juliar A19.1. This copy bears Véra's note on the front endpaper: *Author's copy/Please return to Vladimir Nabokov/Montreux Palace Hotel/Montreux, Switzerland.* A few of Dmitri's discrete pencil x's locate points in the text where corrections were to be made—he wrote out two emendations on a loosely inserted card. Since no other edition of this play has since been published, the errors remain uncorrected. The second of three VN titles brought out by Phaedra, who had published *The Eye* in 1965 and would issue his Russian translation of *Lolita* in 1967.

The Waltz Invention is the final installment in what Boyd sees as a series of artistic attacks on the growing threat of Nazism, beginning with the story "Cloud, Castle, Lake," chapters 2, 3, and 5 of *The Gift*, and another story, "Tyrants Destroyed" (TRY p. 489). Boyd states: "Nabokov was writing *The Waltz Invention* after Hitler had swallowed up Austria and was about to take his first bite at Czechoslovakia...He comes far closer here than in 'Tyrants Destroyed' to suggesting a Hitler, a Lenin, a Stalin, when he shows that the lunatic, the tyrant, and the poet are of imagination all compact" (TRY p. 492). This assessment, playing off a line in *A Midsummer Night's Dream*—"The lunatic, the lover, and the poet/Are of imagination all compact"—is reminiscent of VN's encapsulation of *Bend Sinister:* "The scholar, the poet, the scientist and the child —these are the victims and witnesses of a world that goes wrong in spite of its being graced with scholars, poets, scientists and children."

After the December 1938 Paris premiere of *The Waltz Invention* was cancelled when the director quit, VN waited over 25 years to see his "lightweight nightmare, a study in insanity, a succession of comic one-liners and dramatic sight gags, and a fable about the puerility of political or any other dreams..." performed (TRY p. 489). He had shown an English translation of it to Wilson in 1943 (we have not been able to determine the identity of the translator; VN wrote simply that "it was translated in England some years ago"), but received a negative response from him and Mary McCarthy; Wilson wrote:

Mary and I have both read it and think it not one of your best productions. I doubt whether you could get it produced. The first scenes amused me, but I don't think there is enough to the idea to make it last through three acts — also, the unreality of everything gets on the reader's nerves before he understands that it is all a fantasy in the madman's mind; when he does find that out, he feels sold. (April 1, 1943, NWL p. 99).

Diment, too, feels this is "perhaps, the weakest of his longer plays" (Diment p. 594). Nonetheless, when the William Morris Agency in 1964 suggested VN stage one of his plays, he put Dmitri to work on this translation that summer, and subsequently revised it himself in proof. Though Boyd comments that some of these changes "were far from last-minute flourishes, deriving as they did from ideas that had taken shape in 1939 as he began to prepare the play for a performance that was subsequently cancelled" (TAY p. 504), Diment suggests that VN, fearing he'd be "identified" with the anti-Vietnam movement if he published his play as it was, "attempted to downplay the political overtones" (Diment p. 596). The play had its English-language premiere in Hartford, Connecticut, in January 1969; it followed the world premiere of the revised Russian-language version, which had incorporated VN's recent changes to the English text, staged in March 1968 by Oxford University's Russian Club.

120 **Nabokov's Quartet.** London: Weidenfeld & Nicolson, (1967).

8vo.; red cloth stamped in gilt; front endpaper creased; dust-jacket, lightly rubbed.

First English edition of this collection of four stories: "An Affair of Honor," "Lik," "The Visit to the Museum," and "The Vane Sisters." Juliar A38.2. Preceded by Phaedra's 1966 edition. The first three stories, printed in various émigré periodicals in the '20s and '30s, were translated by Dmitri; the final story, written in English, was rejected by *The New Yorker* and ultimately published in *The Hudson Review* and *Encounter*. Though in his foreword VN states that he composed it in February 1959, Barabtarlo claims it had been written eight years before its publication (p. 112). VN's corrected copy, with his emendations on two pages, and his explanation of the changes in a six-line pencil note on the half-title; in part: *a reversed mark of admiration leaving its position (not 'an exclamation mark leaving its ordinary position.* [*sic* no closed parenthesis] All three changes noted are to "The Vane Sisters."

121 **Nabokov's Congeries.** Selected, with a critical introduction, by Page Stegner. New York: Viking, (1968).

8vo.; black cloth; dust-jacket, light wear to rear panel.

First edition of this anthology, including eleven stories, eight essays, ten poems; *Pnin*, and excerpts from *Despair*, *The Gift*, *Invitation to a Beheading*, and *Speak, Memory*. Juliar A39.1. With a loosely inserted index card on which VN jotted the title of his most contentious essay, *Reply to My Critics*, written in response to the attacks leveled against him – especially by his erstwhile friend Edmund Wilson – for his translation of *Eugene Onegin*, and previously published in the *Evergreen Review*. In a letter to the editor, Page Stegner, Véra conveyed VN's approval or veto on the items listed in Stegner's projected table of contents. Of "Reply to My Critics" she wrote: "The inclusion of this piece V.N. considers very important because Mr. Wilson furtively continues his personal attacks" (February 20, 1967, SL p. 403). VN's series of pencil corrections to its text (pages 300–324) were incorporated into the essay before it was reprinted in *Strong Opinions* in 1973; one note provides the conclusion to that version: *Completed on January 20, 1966 and published in February of that year in "Encounter." One or two forced peeps did come after that "last look." The essay was reprinted in "Nabokov's Congeries," Viking, N.Y. 1968*. In addition to word substitutions, the addition of foot notes and the revision of transliterated Russian words, several significant remarks directly address Wilson's critique: *For reasons having nothing to do with the subject of this essay I subsequently changed the translation, exact in tone but not in syntax, of those two lines* . . . (p. 311). One note addresses Wilson's article in the *New York Review of Books*: *This is the text readers should consult. It is reprinted in an abridged, emended and incoherent form in Edmund Wilson's "A Window on Russia," Farrar, Straus & Giroux, N.Y., 1942*.

122 **Nabokov's Congeries.** Selected, with a critical introduction, by Page Stegner. New York: Viking, (1968).

8vo.; three-quarter black calf stamped in gilt, top edge gilt.

First edition. Juliar A39.1; 1991 update. A specially bound publisher's presentation copy, inscribed to Véra on the binder's first blank, in Russian, *V. from V, Montreux, Dec. 12, 1968*. With a large-winged butterfly in flight, named for the volume, *Congeria verae* Nab.

123 **Ada, or Ardor.** A Family Chronicle. New York: McGraw-Hill, (1969).

Large 8vo.; three-quarter morocco, top edge silver.

First edition, fourth printing (so stated) of what is arguably VN's finest English-language novel. Juliar A40.1. A publisher's presentation copy, specially bound without the dust-jacket. The dedication copy, inscribed on the binder's first blank in Russian – *To Vérochka – my best butterfly*, signed in full and docketed *Christmas/Montreux/1969*, with a magnificently colorful butterfly, its peacock-like wings spread. Johnson comments:

This rainbow and stained glass colored butterfly represents the larger wings and smaller bodies that characterize the Brushfoots. Both some Brushfoots and some Metalmarks show such brilliant colors, and rows of eyespots along the hindwing are most like some species of the brilliantly iridescent African genus *Euphaedra*.

Ada had been marinating in the form of a philosophical investigation into the nature of the fourth dimension – clearly inspired, at least in part, by Henri Bergson's work – since 1958. The result of that foray would become part four of *Ada*, "The Texture of Time," a book by the novel's protagonist Van Veen. The fuller novel nagged at him during the composition of *Pale Fire*, the translation of *Eugene Onegin*, and several other publications. By 1963 he had a more concrete sense of its themes and fragments, and in 1964, after the publication of *Eugene Onegin*, was able to attack *Ada* head-on. But he later claimed, "[o]nly in February 1966 did the entire novel leap into the kind of existence that can and must be put into words" (quoted TAY p. 509). Meanwhile, his Russian translation of *Lolita* and his revised memoir were published in 1967, and he continued to revisit his *Onegin* for an edition which was finished between 1967 and 1971, though it did not come out until 1975. And there were the proofs of Andrew Field's biography and the revisions to the Russian *King, Queen, Knave* to contend with. Despite these interruptions, of major and minor proportions, *Ada* was completed by October 1968 and came out soon after, in April 1969.

On the most basic structural level, *Ada* is framed as the work of a philosopher whose primary area of study is the nature of time; it is his memoir of his lifelong incestuous love affair with his sister, and includes some of his own philosophical writing and his correspondence with Ada, along with his reminiscences, in a five-part format which dictates each part achieve only half the length of the preceding one. Veen is writing on Antiterra, while "Terra," our earth, is "the subject of endless debate. Only deranged minds accept the notion of Terra" (Appel, "Ada: An Erotic Masterpiece That Explores the Nature of Time," *New York Times*, May 4, 1969). *Ada* is simultaneously a family epic of the Russian aristocracy, a literary history of Russia, and a meditation on the nature of time, and is easily VN's most difficult book. Dense with games and deceptions, literary, historical, scientific, and cultural allusions, derived from Russian, American, and Nabokovian contexts, in Russian, French, and English, it is his most complex linguistically and thematically. And the subject matter—a contented, incestuous love affair that spans from the couple's youth into their happy old age—is perhaps his most hard to take. In his response to Appel's essay, "*Ada* described" (which appeared in *Anniversary Notes*, brought out by the *TriQuarterly Review* in honor of VN's 70th birthday), he suggested the manifold difficulties the novel presents by claiming that in the first paragraph alone he had "planted three blunders, meant to ridicule mistranslations of Russian classics," and implied that the reader's challenge would not end there. *Ada* continues to serve as a well-spring of VN study, criticism and exploration.

It was considered fairly inaccessible upon publication and received mixed reviews—though Alfred Appel and John Leonard, both in the *New York Times*, were respectively reverent and ecstatic. Others were positive, if perplexed, like Joyce Carol Oates and John Updike. VN noted at the time that "American reviewers have been remarkably perceptive in regard to my most cosmopolitan and poetic novel. As to the British press," he continued, "the observations of a few discerning critics were also most welcome; the buffoons turned out to be less clever than usual…" (Whitman interview, 1971, SO p. 179). Eight chapters from the first part were, perhaps astonishingly, printed in *Playboy*. Columbia Pictures paid half a million dollars for the film rights. *Time* did a cover story on VN coinciding with its publication. But a critical onslaught followed both the initial avalanche of praise and a 20-week stay on *The New York Times* best-seller list; the attack was unexpectedly inaugurated by Mary McCarthy, who was lead to reconsider her previous praise of *Pale Fire*, so abrasively did she react against *Ada*.

But McCarthy's vitriol could not damage the book's reputation; nor could the vehemence with which VN refuted the autobiographical—or, perhaps, anti-autobiographical—strains in the novel as they were pointed out by the press. Boyd's encapsulation of the novel merits quoting:

Ada brings together all that has mattered most to Nabokov: the countries and languages and literatures he loves; first love and last love and family love; memory and time; art and science, art and life; the riches of consciousness, the loss of these riches in death, the possibility of a world beyond loss. And proof of its proximity, if not to the literal details of his personal past, at least to the things he treasured, can be seen in the fact that one of *Ada*'s central motifs, Chateaubriand's line "*Du château qui baignait la Dore*," was Nabokov's suggestion for the French title of his own autobiography. (Boyd, "Ada," p. 12)

124 **Ada, or Ardor.** A Family Chronicle. New York: McGraw-Hill, (1969).

Large 8vo.; black cloth, well-worn.

First edition. Juliar A40.1. VN's copiously annotated copy—he has put his hand to nearly all 589 pages—labeled on the front endpaper: *Author's copy* with a five-word note in Russian: *a book of genius—the pearl of American literature*, an inscription Boyd has traced to a copy of *Madame Bovary* VN's father had given him, with an identical inscription in French, calling it "a book of genius—the pearl of French literature." He speculates that though VN's "echoing" inscription in his copy of *Ada* "may well be a joke . . . there must have been a grain of seriousness to provoke that 'pearl' into being. After all, *Ada*'s long part 1 opens with an echo of the opening of *Anna Karenin* and ends with an echo of the end of part 1 of *Madame Bovary*, as if it were signaling its intention to vie with the greatest novels of the Russian and the French traditions. That, some readers would say, is precisely the problem. Like Van and Ada themselves, Nabokov has become too sure of himself" (Boyd, "Ada," p. 3). VN wrote on the first text page that this is the copy he used in considering the translation of *Ada* into French and Italian, and in envisioning a later edition in English, as well. The half-title is covered with page numbers and corresponding corrections, in pencil and blue pencil, with several of Véra's corrections as well. The facing page is covered with various notes: a lengthy passage about translation, written in French; a few "sample" passages to translate into French, and several phrases in Russian. In addition, VN decoded allusions throughout—to his own works, to other parts of *Ada*, and to a wide range of literary and cultural moments.

This copy is a gold mine for scholars and teachers of VN's work, who may or may not have figured out that "Billionaire Bill" is Shakespeare; that "Sig Leymanski" is Kingsley Amis; that "Dr. Henry" is James; and that "The Weed Exiles the Flower" is derived from line 6 of Melville's short poem, "The Ravaged Villa" (1891). Additionally, VN has helpfully explained various references to flora and fauna throughout, and culturally defined objects which are foreign to most Western readers—such as "stella," a "four dollar gold piece." His frequent "T"s and occasional spot translations in this copy, which indicate patches of text slippery to the reader in English, evince his concern that the novel would pose no end of impossible riddles to the foreign translator, as it continues to challenge the English-speaking reader. He inserted a later magazine clipping depicting a woman in a large hat, jotting on it a reference to *Ada*—"A modern—and much finer version—of the vulgar Toulouse Lautrec poster 'Divan Japonais'... See description of Lucette p. 460–1." The passage conjured by the ad reads: "'Your hat,' he said, 'is positively Lautrec-montesque—I mean, lautrecaquesque—no, I can't form the adjective.'" This clipping, along with VN's multitudinous annotations, reveals that the novel continued to resonate for the author, as well. In a letter to Carl Proffer clearing up some points to be made in his *Keys to Lolita* he makes reference to this clipping: "p. 33. I am not sure you realize that the Kreutzer Sonata picture is the one reproduced in the Taboo perfume ads (in the *New Yorker*, for instance)" (SL p. 433). Also inserted are nine Red Cross Christmas 1969 butterfly stamps; and a one-page typescript on beaver fur, headed "Marina's and Ada's firs," with VN's pencil annotations.

125 **Ada, or Ardor.** A Family Chronicle. New York: McGraw-Hill, (1969).

8vo.; black cloth, tips bumped; dust-jacket, edgeworn.

First edition. Juliar A40.1. VN and Véra together listed, in pencil and ink, seven pages on which minor corrections to spelling and printer's errors were made, with one word substitution; the notes on a loosely inserted index card referencing six passages (these passages bear no markings) are likely Véra's. VN left his marginal marks and characteristic X's at the top each page from 99–101. A comparison with the text of the British edition of *Ada* reveals that some, though not all, of his tentative revisions were incorporated into later printings of the text.

126 **Ada, or Ardor.** A Family Chronicle. (London): Penguin Books, (1970).

12mo.; wrappers; cover creased; light wear to lower panel.

First English paperback edition; appended edition, with "Notes to 'Ada'" by Vivian Darkbloom – the first edition to print the notes. Juliar A40.4; 1991 update. The dedication copy, gifted to Véra (labeled in pencil on the cover *Véra*), with a butterfly on the title page. A corrected copy, with seven page numbers listed in pencil opposite the title page. With minor emendations to all of these pages, and also to page 475. In red pencil VN circled Penguin's erroneous year of his birth, 1901, and added a question mark (he was born in 1899). He had written to Frank Taylor that the proofs of this edition had been "exasperating" (December 9, 1969, SL p. 464), and he was further irritated by the publisher's failure to make all his changes. He exhorted a later publisher to "insist that Penguin fulfill their obligation and destroy . . . all other existing domestic edition copies which still harbor on p. 257 the wretched 'she was pregnant' instead of the correct 'he was pregnant,'" among their other errors (to Miss MacLennan, April 27, 1971, SL pp. 484–85).

As usual, VN imposed as much control on the cover art as possible. Upon receiving a potential design from Penguin he responded, in part:

Your artist's Cyprideum looks like a ghastly vulva, and the Puss Moth caterpillar is all wrong (and, moreover, does not breed on orchids). I am emphatically against this symbolic design. I want three or four non-anatomical genuine orchids, prettily colored, garlanded around "ADA". Why don't you simply use the drawing of the three species I made for you – possibly multiplying and stylizing them (but not freudianizing those innocent blossoms)?

On the other hand, if you cannot reproduce, or don't wish to bother with, the reproduction of an elegant old-fashioned vignette for my elegant old-fashioned novel, with delicate contours and tender tints, then I would prefer you to cancel all idea of a pictorial design, and replace it with plain lettering. Just my name and ADA would be enough. . . . (to Oliver Caldecott, November 17, 1969, SL p. 463).

127 **Poems and Problems.** New York: McGraw-Hill, (1970).

8vo.; marbled endpapers; top edge gilt; three-quarter calf stamped in gilt.

First edition; culls 39 Russian poems, with English translations (constituting "no more than one percent of the mass of verse which I exuded with monstrous regularity during my youth"); 14 English poems (all from *Poems*, A33, and all written after 1940, when the Nabokovs left Europe for the States); 18 chess problems, with solutions (the first, which had appeared in *Speak, Memory*, written days before their emigration in

1940 and 17 composed in Montreux; five of these had been previously unpublished); bibliography of previous publication of the poems (composition and publication information about the problems appears with each). Juliar A41.1. He confessed to his editor that "weariness and various professional worries" kept him from writing an index (to Frank E. Taylor, December 9, 1969, SL p. 464).

The dedication copy, a specially bound year-end publisher's presentation copy, with a Hairstreak drawn for Véra, *Thecla verae* Nab., docketed *Christmas 1971*; the only butterfly we have encountered facing right. The *Thecla* genus, according to Johnson, was the one genus into which lepidopterists placed the vast group of tropical Hairstreaks for over a century. Though he narrows down the possible source butterflies to two genera by wing shape and pattern, in this drawing, he notes, "Nabokov's penchant for blue takes over," replacing the bands of brilliant burgundy found in nature with bands of blue. "The large eyespot near the tails represents what Nabokov knew well as the 'false head,'" a protective ruse employed by the butterfly to fool predators. VN noted on the half-title two emendations: the addition of a pawn to the board illustration on page 192, where he wrote *BP added on e6 preventing cook* and *corrected Nov. 1971*; and its corresponding addition in the notation of the board's set-up on page 207.

Many of VN's most ardent critics are at a loss to evaluate his chess problems, his lepidopteral work, frequently his Russian writing and, perhaps on some level, even his poetry. In this collection he incorporates three of these four challenging elements, defending his inclusion of chess problems with the statement that "problems are the poetry of chess. They demand from the composer the same virtues that characterize all worthwhile art: originality, invention, conciseness, harmony, complexity, and splendid insincerity" (from the foreword). He had paired poems and problems as early as 1918, in a notebook titled in Russian: "Poems and Schemas" (Phillips, p. 168). He had been composing chess problems since his late teens, and published nearly three dozen throughout his life—though his American years saw a hiatus from publishing, if not composing, problems. (He notes in his foreword parenthetically that "the chess manuscripts of the 1940–1960 period have been mislaid and the earlier unpublished jottings are not worth printing.")

Janet Gezari, in a survey of VN's works, reveals that "Nabokov's heroes include a chess grandmaster...and a chess problem composer...; chess games occur in several of the novels; and chess and chess problem language and imagery regularly put his readers' chess knowledge to the test" (Gezari p. 44). She posits the possibility that VN "may have deliberately misdated" problem #1—the one that appeared in *Speak, Memory*—"in order to enable it to mark not just his departure for America but the fulfillment of his autobiographical project" (p. 47). Her run-down of VN's legitimate Caïssan credentials merits quoting:

C. H. O'D. Alexander, a fellow of the British Chess Problem Society and editor of *The Sunday Times* chess column, measured Nabokov's talents against an exacting standard when he described him (in 1970) as "quite a good chess problem composer—not the quality to win a prize, but good sound stuff." The chess problem Nabokov included in *Speak, Memory*, one of his best compositions, merited inclusion in *Chess Problems: Introduction to an Art*, an advanced book by three leading British problemists, who praised its originality. Solvers of the chess problems Nabokov published in the seventies in *The Problemist*, the Proceedings of the British Chess Problem Society, admire his characteristic wit and penchant for "the unexpected." In 1970, Nabokov was invited to join the American team as a composer in future international chess-problem tournaments; a problem he published in 1969 placed third in *The Problemist*'s Intermediate Composing Tourney; and another was a third prize winner in the journal's 1972–73 Selfmates Award Competition. (Gezari, p. 46)

Boyd notes that VN annotated issues of *The Problemist*, to which he subscribed in Montreux, and offers a sampling of his critiques: "'Very poor,' 'difficult but crude,' 'pointless,' 'dull,' 'childish,' 'hideous duals,' 'horrible,' he penciled in a single issue. 'Cooked and recooked.' 'Cannot see any beauty here.'" He notes that "the fellow fanatics who subscribed to *The Problemist* would characterize his problems of the 1960s and 1970s as not necessarily difficult but witty and remarkable for their originality of composition" (TAY p. 575).

VN outlines the development of his poetical voice in the foreword, dividing his Russian verse into five periods:

[A]n initial one of passionate and commonplace love verse (not represented in this edition); a period reflecting utter distrust of the so-called October Revolution; a period (reaching well into the 1920s) of a kind of private curatorship, aimed at preserving nostalgic retrospections and developing Byzantine imagery (this has been mistaken by some readers for an interest in 'religion,' which, beyond literary stylization, never meant anything to me); a period lasting another decade or so during which I set myself to illustrate the principle of making a short poem contain a plot and tell a story (this in a way expressed my patience with the dreary drone of the anemic 'Paris school' of *émigré* poetry); and finally, in the late thirties, and especially in the following decades, a sudden liberation from self-imposed shackles, resulting both in a sparser output and in a belatedly discovered robust style.

He added: "Selecting poems for this volume proved less difficult than translating them." VN had insisted that the English translations of the Russian poems face their originals; bilingual readers will be able to assess the degree to which he remained faithful to his credo of "rigid," "rugged fidelity," keeping in mind that he admitted in his foreword to having indulged himself: "whenever possible, I have welcomed rhyme, or its shadow; but I have never twisted the tail of a line for the sake of consonance; and the original measure has not been kept if readjustments of sense had to be made for its sake." In reprinting the English poems, all of which had appeared in *The New Yorker*, he demanded that the mistakenly capitalized first lines be corrected, noting that "the *New Yorker* did not always respect my habit or I forgot to enforce it" (to Frank E. Taylor, December 9, 1969, SL p. 464). He believed throughout his career that his Russian verse was far superior to his English poetry – he states as much in his foreword: "Somehow, [the English poems] are of a lighter texture than the Russian stuff, owing, no doubt, to their lacking that inner verbal association with old perplexities and constant worry of thought which marks poems written in one's mother tongue, with exile keeping up its parallel murmur and a never-resolved childhood plucking at one's rustiest chords." Barry P. Scherr offers a different, perhaps less biased, take, claiming that by the time VN was writing poetry in English, he had fine-tuned his craft substantially, adding, "Works such as 'Fame' and 'An Evening of Russian Poetry' are indeed minor yet enduring achievements" (Scherr p. 623).

128 **Poems and Problems.** London: Weidenfeld and Nicolson, (1972).

8vo.; maroon cloth, gently bumped; dust-jacket; lightly edgeworn.

First English edition; prints a revised solution to problem 11 on p. 207 that includes a black pawn at e6 per the instructions VN wrote in his own copy – though surprisingly that pawn was not added to the board printed on page 192. Juliar A41.2. The dedication copy, inscribed on the front endpaper in Russian: *To my Verochka. 24–v–1972. V*, with a small, pretty, multi-colored butterfly. With two related note cards loosely inserted, one with both sides covered in French in pencil with VN's translation into French of the first two stanzas of "The Poets" (at the top of that page, 93, VN erased his first attempt at translating the first line, but it is still legible). The other card bears a few words in Russian in Véra's hand.

129 Transparent Things. New York: McGraw-Hill, (1972).

8vo.; black cloth, spine lightly rubbed; silver dust-jacket, light edgewear.

First edition of this National Book Award-nominated novella; brought out after its December appearance in *Esquire*. Juliar A42.1. The dedication copy, with a butterfly drawn for Véra on the dedication page, named *Iridula verae Nab.* and docketed *Montreux/October 16, 1972*. Johnson notes: "*Iridula* is not a real genus, although there are brilliantly colorful groups of lycaenids actually named *Iridana* and *Iridopsis*, the meanings of which refer to the brilliant colors. The wing shape most closely approximates a Blue and, given the wing shape, spotted pattern, and bright colors it is possible Nabokov was embellishing upon the colorful western American group *Philotes*, whose species are light iridescent blue, sometimes with colorful overlays of orange and bronze. Here, however, Nabokov adds the touch of rainbow shades that characterize many of his drawings." The front endpaper is labeled in large pencil block letters, *Véra's copy*, and the volume bears Dmitri's recent light marginal pencil ticks and question marks to a few pages.

Reviewers scarcely knew what to make of this deceptively slim chaser to *Ada*, which had taken him over two years, off and on, to complete, with its complex network of disembodied narrators. It was finished on April Fool's Day, 1971, but not released until the end of the following year. In VN's own words, the reviews "oscillat[ed] between hopeless adoration and helpless hatred. Very amusing" (quoted in TAY p. 608). One such critic called it "an unlovely and unlovable book that begins to touch the reader only the second time around. It is a masterpiece, of course" (TAY p. 608). In a 1972 interview that was ultimately published only in *Strong Opinions* (1973), VN stated its theme as "merely a beyond-the-cypress inquiry into a tangle of random destinies. Amongst the reviewers several careful readers have published some beautiful stuff about it. Yet neither they nor, of course, the common criticule discerned the structural knot of the story" (anonymous interview, 1972, SO p. 194). Boyd's analysis attempts to untie that "knot":

Within the small compass of *Transparent Things* and the bleak life of Hugh Person, Nabokov ruptures the relationship of reader, character, and author more radically than he has ever done, in order to explore some of his oldest themes: the nature of time; the mystery and privacy of the human soul, and its simultaneous need to breach its solitude, the scope of consciousness beyond death; the possibility of design in the universe.

Ada's ebullience and lyricism and color had made it a best-seller. *Transparent Things*, with its squalid world and its heartless characters, seems almost designed not to appeal. But...while the story will not be for everyone it is a masterpiece. (TAY p. 601)

130 **A Russian Beauty and other stories.** New York and Toronto: McGraw-Hill, [1971].

8vo.; teal printed wrappers; duplicating services stamp insider rear cover. In a specially made brown morocco slipcase.

Uncorrected proof of this collection of thirteen Englished Russian stories, likely received *December 10, 1971*, the date VN jotted and initialed on the cover in pencil. According to the foreword, all but one were translated by Dmitri in collaboration with VN (the title story was translated by Simon Karlinsky); however, VN states in the foreword: "I alone am responsible" for the English versions. Juliar A43.1. According to Boyd, Karlinsky initially received only $10 for translating the very short "A Russian Beauty": "a sum he thought so comical he had the check framed for his wall." He later received an additional $40 when news of his action reached the Nabokovs (TAY p. 583). The dedication copy, inscribed *for Véra* on the cover and on the half-title, *for Xmas 1972*, with a vibrant Metalmark in colored pencil. "Of all the Metalmark-like butterflies that Nabokov drew for Véra," Johnson writes, "the color pattern here is least like any of known tropical species. That might explain its rendering as 'A Russian Beauty': the colors, although vivid, are more simple and straightforward, perhaps more appropriate to a fanciful Metalmark from the world's colder, northern regions." VN's heavy black marker butterfly on the cover obscures the "un" in "uncorrected proof," indicating that he made some emendations. In addition to a few pencil alterations to the list of "Books by Vladimir Nabokov" – crossing out *Spring In Fialta and Other Stories*, and changing *Poems* to *Poems & Problems*, he indicated on the copyright page *added corrections* on four pages, in addition to numerous minor corrections throughout. He also added information to the brief publishing history prefacing the title story: *The English translation appeared in ESQUIRE for April 1973.*

131 **Strong Opinions.** New York: McGraw-Hill, (1973).

8vo.; black cloth, lightly bumped and rubbed; black dust-jacket, lightly rubbed with some edgewear, spine nicked.

First edition of this assortment of 22 interviews, 11 letters, 9 articles, and 5 lepidopteral papers; second issue dust-jacket with the title letters filled in cream, but with a noticeably lighter brown outline than all other copies we have examined. Juliar A44.1. The dedication copy, inscribed on the front endpaper: *To Verochka/ from the author* in ink, and labeled in pencil, *Nov. 9, 1973/Montreux.* With a large butterfly, colorfully competing with the orange endpaper. Lightly annotated by VN, with a pencil note on the half-title indicating two emendations he made to the text, in addition to marginal ticks on five pages and two additional annotations: *Misprints:/Melvin J. Lasky p. 275/Korolya Roman, should be italicized p. 39.*

In the foreword, VN makes known his "three absolute conditions" for granting an interview: "The interviewer's questions have to be sent to me in writing, answered by me in writing, and reproduced verbatim." Once these three conditions are met, he writes, "[t]he thing is transmuted finally into a more or less neatly paragraphed essay...that is the ideal form a written interview should take." As a result, many of the interviews herein borrow questions from one another; and they are followed by responses that are, by the last interview, familiar to the reader. Frequently visited topics are VN's writing process, his nationality, his politics, and *Lolita*'s conception and reception. In one response—to the query, "What can (should?) we do about elusive truth?" posed by Israel Shenker June 10, 1971—VN replied: "One can (and should) engage a specially trained proofreader to make sure that misprints and omissions do not disfigure the elusive truth of an interview that a newspaper takes the trouble to conduct with an author who is rather particular about the precise reproduction of his phrase" (p. 182). The "interviews" span a decade, 1962–72, and include the published and unpublished answers to questions by known journalists and "anonymous" questioners that had been prepared for print, radio, or television. Though all have the look of transcripts, only a few actually fit that definition; some of the others had been published only in part or with inaccuracies; others had not been published at all or their fate was unknown to VN. VN contextualizes each interview with a short preface, revealing that most of them are not, strictly speaking, interviews at all. The first interview (June 5, 1962), for example, is comprised of a series of questions and answers typed from notes VN took after "three or four journalists" interviewed him upon his arrival in New York (p. 3); number 19, October 1971, is comprised of a selection of "topics and themes" discussed with Kurt Hoffmann (p. 185); in "interview" number 20, previously unpublished, VN "abridged or stylized" his responses for inclusion here (p. 194). All of the articles and letters included, except one – "On Hodasevich" (*Sovremennye zapiski*, LIX, Paris 1939) – are in their original English, and had been published previously, though some alterations were made to "Reply to My Critics." To our knowledge, the others were reproduced unchanged from their originals.

132 **Look at the Harlequins!** New York: McGraw-Hill, (1974).

8vo.; black cloth; black and white harlequin dust-jacket, light wear.

First edition of VN's last completed novel, another National Book Award nomination, and a Literary Guild "featured alternate" in December 1974. Juliar A46.1. One of two dedication copies, inscribed for Véra (the jacket is labeled in thick black marker, *Véra's* and, in ink, *corrected*) on the dedication page, where VN drew a Metalmark, in profile, with its wings decorated in a playful harlequin costume of alternating white and colored diamonds. He named the creature appropriately, *Arlequinus arlequinus* (female), and signed it *V/ Montreux/ August, 1974.* Johnson writes: "Whether there was a scientific double meaning in Nabokov's reference to Harlequins confounded scholars for years. In the 1990s it was discovered that the common name 'Harlequin' refers only to a few rare Brushfoot butterflies from the West Indies. Since these, although colorful, look nothing like Nabokov's drawing it appears he did not have these actual butterflies in mind."

With Véra's note on the title page: *Mailed by publishers Aug. 28th 1974, received Montreux Sep. 2nd 1974.* The dust-jacket is labeled *corrected,* in faded ink, reflecting VN's nineteen emendations, all listed on the front endpaper by page and line number. Boyd notes that this edition bears an "unusually abundant crop of errors," possibly due to the compressed schedule of composition and revision to which VN had subjected himself (TAY p. 626). The most glaring error corrected in this copy is the repetition of two lines of text on page 116.

Reviews of *Look at the Harlequins!* were mixed; it was "often… deplored" by "keen Nabokov readers but welcomed by hacks who found it less taxing than *Ada* or *Transparent Things*" (TAY p. 651). Richard Poirier opened his somewhat narrow critique in the *New York Times Book Review* with a comparison of Joyce's Stephen and Proust's Marcel, deducing: "there are few reasons to be surprised, and many reasons to be disappointed, by the complicated interplay between Vladimir Nabokov and the narrator of this, his 37th book" (October 13, 1974). Despite such criticism, it was nominated for the National Book

Award but, like *Pnin*, *Pale Fire*, *Transparent Things*, and *Tyrants Destroyed*, did not win.

Still largely overlooked in critical circles, *Look at the Harlequins!* is an important addition to VN's canon for several reasons. Ostensibly it is a fictional autobiography, depicting Vadim Vadimych N. whose life and work resemble VN's superficially, as parodies of the portrait of the artist his public may derive from his fictions and memoirs. It was prompted perhaps in part by the ongoing frustration the Nabokovs were then confronting in Andrew Field's probe into their personal pasts in *Vladimir Nabokov: His Life in Part*: "[T]hree days after beginning to read Field's manuscript, [VN] announced to McGraw-Hill that he would begin a new novel on March 1...On February 6, the day he noted in his diary how appalled he was by Field's 'absurd errors, impossible statements, vulgarities and inventions,' he began to write *Look at the Harlequins!*" (TAY p. 614). But it also recalls a lecture VN delivered in 1937 on the evils of "fictionalized biographies" – while *The Gift* was being published serially and on the centennial of Pushkin's death – called "Pushkin, or the Real and the Plausible." Davydov writes:

In anticipation of the hosts of books written on the occasion of the centennial, Nabokov warns his audience about the genre of "fictionalized biographies." Even the most sincere and well-informed attempt to transform a great poet's life into a biography results in a "monstrous hoax," turning the poet's life into a "pastiche of his art" and reducing the man to a "macabre doll."...Nabokov shows us how easy it is to conjure up plausible vignettes of Pushkin....The impossibility of reconciling the "plausible" and the "real" Pushkin is matched only by the impossibility of translating his verse. (p. 489)

By the time VN came to write *Look at the Harlequins!* he had found a way to circumvent "the impossibility of translating" Pushkin, instead adapting him into transliterated text with commentary; he had confronted Andrew Field's hopelessly wayward biography; he had established "three rules" for conducting interviews, in the hope of keeping his self-statements unpolluted. With this novel, he put himself at the center of a biography detailing the life of a "plausible," but definitely not "real" VN.

In an examination of the final chapter – written, as was the final chapter in *Speak, Memory*, in the second person and addressed to "You" – Boyd refutes this analysis as superficial, discerning the entire novel as a lengthy love letter to Véra:

Nabokov creates Vadim as an inversion of himself not to score points off a character he has made his own inferior, and not to mock misapprehensions about his own life deduced from the superficially heartless worlds of many of his books, but rather to sum up his own impulse to test his art and his happiness against its apparent converse...it is You who helps retrieve Vadim from the realization of his worst fears, You who restores him to his self and who points beyond it...in a very clear sense this You is also Véra Nabokov, the "you" of *Speak, Memory*. A novel that appears terminally narcissistic turns out to be one sustained love song, and no less passionate for all its play. (TAY p. 642)

Perhaps most interestingly, *Look at the Harlequins!* contains a realistic return to Russia that VN never undertook. It seems likely that he did not want to contaminate his idyllic memories; just one example of such a contamination can be found in *King, Queen, Knave*, when Kurt meets Erica on the street eight years after their affair. After they part he thinks: "Now I shall never remember Erica as I remembered her before. Erica number two will always be in the way..." (p. 176). VN may have feared such a lament. But what he stated outright was that he would not associate in any way with totalitarian regimes. He had to settle for adapting details gleaned from friends and family for Vadim Vadimych's homecoming. His sister Elena Sikorski took her first trip to Leningrad in 1969, and made an annual pilgrimage each subsequent summer for ten years. Until then VN had refused to countenance the return of Russian émigrés – he had broken his contract years before to collaborate on the *Onegin* project with Roman Jakobson, who had made a visit, for this reason. In his sister's case he had little choice but to make an exception, and even enlisted her help. Just as Joyce had employed his Dublin-bound aunt Josephine to supply the tastes, sights, and sounds of life in that city, so too VN charged Elena "with a long list of details she was to check out on her travels, from the smells in street and corridor to the patterns on the blinds of Aeroflot planes" (TAY p. 619). A similar service was performed by his friend, one-time translator, and occasional editor Simon Karlinsky. Upon Karlinsky's return from his first visit to Leningrad since his emigration, VN asked for his "very first impression of Petersburg the moment you stepped from your bus" (quoted TAY p. 618). He derived from Karlinsky's response – "Loud women's voices, swearing obscenely" – a scene with his own imagined dialogue.

Having suffered "perilous interruptions" in his composition of the novel, and working at a furious pace in part to fulfill his contractual obligation to McGraw-Hill, on February 11, 1974 VN wrote to his publisher in response to a request for dust-jacket copy: "[T]o produce the description of a book which I have not finished writing is for me no less difficult than the writing about an unread book is for you...I can only say that LATH is a multiple-love story and that during a span of fifty years the scene shifts from my desk to Old Russia, from there to England, from England to France, from France to America and thence to Bolshevisia and back to this lake" (to Frederic W. Hills, SL p. 527). Ultimately the harlequin-checkered jacket stated simply: "A new novel by the author of *Ada* and *Lolita*." Once the book was completed, corrected, and published – VN's diaries, correspondence, and the errors in the first edition suggest, perhaps, too quickly – he was disappointed by the waning enthusiasm he perceived at McGraw-Hill, which had long since ceased hoping for financial success from their most prestigious author. He wrote of his feeling that *Look at the Harlequins!* "has somehow been let down much too soon. I cannot believe that my publisher has run out of enthusiasm and *élan* after the first splendid spurt" (to Hills, February 21, 1975, SL p. 544).

133 Look at the Harlequins! New York: McGraw-Hill, (1974).

8vo.; marbled endpapers; top edge gilt; three-quarter morocco.

First edition. Juliar A46.1. The publisher's presentation copy, and the later of two dedication copies, inscribed on the binder's first blank as a Christmas gift for Véra, with a brightly "stainglassed" Metalmark named *Adorina verae* Nab., most closely resembling the species *Ancyluris latisfasciata* Lathy, "perhaps the most extreme of the rainbow and stainglass-like Metalmarks. They, like Nabokov's creation here, are arranged in window-like 'panes' within thickened black veins resembling the lead dividers" (Johnson). Signed *VN/Xmas/Montreux/1974*. With nine corrections throughout, all minor except for the deletion of the two erroneously reprinted lines on page 116.

134 Tyrants Destroyed and other stories. New York: McGraw-Hill, (1975).

8vo.; black cloth, light wear to extremities; copper dust-jacket, light edgewear.

First edition of VN's second English collection of stories, thirteen in all, six of which were translated by Dmitri in collaboration with VN; six had had previous periodical publication in Dmitri's translations; and one debuted here in VN's original English. Each is preceded by a brief preface by VN. Juliar A47.1. At one point VN had hoped to rearrange the stories in this collection, making "Perfection" the first and title story; this would have been, in his words to Frederic Hills at McGraw-Hill, "more pleasing" (April 13, 1973, SL p. 515). The completion of this collection marked the fulfillment of his contract with McGraw-Hill, as well as his fifth and final failure to top the short list for the National Book Award, for which it was nominated.

The dedication copy, *Received 24.ii.75* (according to VN's note on the verso of the title page), inscribed to Véra in Russian on the dedication page: *Greetings once again, my darling! VN/Montreux/24 Feb. 1975*. With a small, gorgeous Metalmark, "its wing shape typical of any number of South American and African groups, its rainbow colors a grander portrayal of what is seen in one South American species scientists call *inca* (perhaps because of its strong metallic hues)" (Johnson). With VN's pencil notes to the list of "Books by Vladimir Nabokov"—a series of numbers and the note *Fr.* next to several titles, possibly suggesting that they had been—or should be—translated into French.

135 **Details of a Sunset and other stories.** New York: McGraw-Hill, (1976).

8vo.; black cloth, light wear to extremities; sunset-illustrated dustjacket, one faint crease to the cover.

First edition of VN's final collection of 13 Russian stories, all translated into English by Dmitri in collaboration with VN or by VN himself; each with his new introductory preface. Juliar A48.1. The dedication copy, inscribed in Russian in March, 1976 (VN's initialed note on the half title suggests that the book was received in Montreux on March 5) on the dedication page: *to my Verochka. iii.76/Montreux Palace*, with a butterfly whose wings are illuminated by a sunset. Johnson sees two distinctly different possible sources for this imaginative butterfly: "First of all, there are several groups of Blues which have species in which there is a vivid greenish sheen that covers the wing undersurfaces. In collections of Blues these always stand out. But," he cautions, "usually the green sheen does not also occur on the forewing. Perhaps Nabokov imagined it there. However, another compelling suggestion is one of Hawaii's few native butterflies, a lycaenid known as *Vaga blackburni*. Nabokov, and every other lycaenidologist, would have known *Vaga*, one of the Pacific Ocean's great oddities—it's still hard for biologists to imagine where it came from. It is much like the drawing in wing shape, dull bluish on the upperside as shown and, on the underside, a mix of green and brown with few, if any, spot-like markings." With VN's pencil annotations to pages 23 (five single-word French translations) and 25 (a one-word French translation); and with minute pencil checks next to four titles on the list of "Books by Vladimir Nabokov."

VN characterized this collection—at one point entitled *A Letter to Russia*—as "the last raisins and petit-beurre toes from the bottom of the barrel" (to Prof. Gleb Struve, SL p. 548). Though several stories had been translated years before by Struve—a critic who completed the most substantial review of the émigré literary output—VN undertook new translations, explaining: "I had not looked up your versions for many years and now find them not accurate enough and too far removed from my present style in English. Please, don't be cross! Time does not move, but artistic interpretation does" (ibid.). He worked on Dmitri's translations and on his own in grueling tandem with his revisions of the French translation of *Ada* (which ultimately hit #2 on the best-seller list in France). Upon completion it was well-reviewed but made a commercial whimper.

To Véra, Верена мей!

Ⅷ · 76
Montreux Palace

VLADIMIR
NABOKOV
DETAILS OF
A SUNSET
AND OTHER STORIES

PRIMARY SOURCES

Appel, Alfred, Jr., and Charles Newman, eds. *Nabokov: Criticism, reminiscences, translations and tributes.* Evanston: Northwestern University Press, 1970.

Barabtarlo, Gennady. "English Short Stories" in *The Garland Companion to Vladimir Nabokov*, edited by Vladimir E. Alexandrov. New York and London: Garland Publishing, Inc., 1995, pages 101–16.

Beaujour, Elizabeth Klosty. "*Nikolka Persik*," in *The Garland Companion to Vladimir Nabokov*, edited by Vladimir E. Alexandrov. New York and London: Garland Publishing, Inc., 1995, pages 556–61.

Boyd, Brian. "*Ada*," in *The Garland Companion to Vladimir Nabokov*, edited by Vladimir E. Alexandrov. New York and London: Garland Publishing, Inc., 1995, pages 3–18.

———. "Chronology of Nabokov's Life and Works," in *The Garland Companion to Vladimir Nabokov*, edited by Vladimir E. Alexandrov. New York and London: Garland Publishing, Inc., 1995, pages [xxix]–[xix].

———. *Vladimir Nabokov: The Russian Years.* Princeton: Princeton University Press, 1990.

———. *Vladimir Nabokov: The American Years.* Princeton: Princeton University Press, 1991.

Boyd, Brian and Robert Michael Pyle, eds. *Nabokov's Butterflies: Unpublished and Uncollected Writings.* With new translations from the Russian by Dmitri Nabokov and Brian Boyd. Boston: Beacon Press, 1999.

Connolly, Julian W. "*Ania v strane chudes*," in *The Garland Companion to Vladimir Nabokov*, edited by Vladimir E. Alexandrov. New York and London: Garland Publishing, Inc., 1995, pages 18–25.

———. "*King, Queen, Knave*," in *The Garland Companion to Vladimir Nabokov*, edited by Vladimir E. Alexandrov. New York and London: Garland Publishing, Inc., 1995, pages 203–14.

Davydov, "Nabokov and Pushkin," in *The Garland Companion to Vladimir Nabokov*, edited by Vladimir E. Alexandrov. New York and London: Garland Publishing, Inc., 1995, pages 482–96.

Diment, Galya. "Plays," in *The Garland Companion to Vladimir Nabokov*, edited by Vladimir E. Alexandrov. New York and London: Garland Publishing, Inc., 1995, pages 586–99.

Dolinin, Alexander. "*Eugene Onegin*," in *The Garland Companion to Vladimir Nabokov*, edited by Vladimir E. Alexandrov. New York and London: Garland Publishing, Inc., 1995, pages 117–30.

———. "*The Gift*," in *The Garland Companion to Vladimir Nabokov*, edited by Vladimir E. Alexandrov. New York and London: Garland Publishing, Inc., 1995, pages 135–69.

———. "*Lolita* in Russian," in *The Garland Companion to Vladimir Nabokov*, edited by Vladimir E. Alexandrov. New York and London: Garland Publishing, Inc., 1995, pages 321–30.

Gezari, Janet. "Chess and Chess Problems," in *The Garland Companion to Vladimir Nabokov*, edited by Vladimir E. Alexandrov. New York and London: Garland Publishing, Inc., 1995, pages 44–54.

Gould, S. J. "The Hardening of the Modern Synthesis." In *Dimensions of Darwinism*, Marjorie Greene, ed., Cambridge (England): Cambridge University Press, 1983.

Johnson, Kurt, Zsolt Balint, and Dubi Benyamini. "Neotropical 'Blue' Butterflies." In *Reports of the Museum of Natural History* nos. 43–54. Stevens Point: The University of Wisconsin, 1995.

Johnson, Kurt and Steve Coates. *Nabokov's Blues*. Cambridge, MA: Zoland Books, 1999.

Johnson, Kurt, G. W. Whitaker, and Zsolt Balint. "Nabokov as Lepidopterist: An Informed Appraisal," in *Nabokov Studies*, vol. 3 (1996), pp. 123–144.

Juliar, Michael. *Vladimir Nabokov: A Descriptive Bibliography*. New York and London: Garland Publishing, Inc., 1986.

———. *Updates to Vladimir Nabokov: A Descriptive Bibliography*. Privately printed, April 1, 1991.

Karges, J., *Nabokov's Lepidoptera: Genres and Genera*, Ann Arbor, MI: Ardis, 1985.

Karlinsky, Simon, ed. *The Nabokov-Wilson Letters 1940–1971*. New York: Harper & Row, 1979.

Kinsey, A. C., W. B. Pomeroy, and C. E. Marti. *Sexual Behavior in the Human Male*. Philadelphia: W. B. Saunders, 1948.

McGuire, William. *Bollingen: An Adventure in Collecting the Past*. Princeton: Princeton University Press, 1982.

Nabokov, Nicolas. *Bagazh: Memoirs of a Russian Cosmopolitan*. New York: Atheneum, 1975.

Nabokov, Vladimir. *Anniversary Notes*. Supplement to *TriQuarterly*. 17 (Winter 1970), pp. 1–15.

———. *King, Queen, Knave*. Translated by Dmitri Nabokov in collaboration with the author. New York: Vintage, 1989.

———. *Speak, Memory: An Autobiography Revisited*. New York: Vintage, 1989.

———. *Strong Opinions*. New York: Vintage, 1990.

———. *Selected Letters 1940–1977.* Edited by Dmitri Nabokov and Matthew J. Bruccoli. New York: Vintage, 1991.

Newman, Charles, Editor. *Tri-Quarterly Review* 17 (Winter 1970), Evanston, IL: Northwestern University.

Phillips, Rodney, et al. *The Hand of the Poet.* New York: Rizzoli, 1997.

Provine, W. *Sewall Wright and Evolutionary Biology.* Chicago: University of Chicago Press, 1986.

Remington, Charles Lee. "Lepidoptera Studies," in *The Garland Companion to Vladimir Nabokov*, edited by Vladimir E. Alexandrov. New York and London: Garland Publishing, Inc., 1995, pages 274–282.

Robinson, Robert. "The Last Interview." In *Vladimir Nabokov: A Tribute*, Peter Quennell, ed. New York: Morrow, 1980.

Robson, G. C. and O. W. Richards. *The Variation of Animals in Nature.* London: Longmans, Green & Co., 1936.

Sampson, Earl D., trans. "Postscript to the Russian Edition of *Lolita*" by Vladimir Nabokov. In *Nabokov's Fifth Arc*, edited by J. E. Rivers and Charles Nicol. Austin: University of Texas Press, pages 188–194.

Scherr, Barry P. "Poetry," in *The Garland Companion to Vladimir Nabokov*, edited by Vladimir E. Alexandrov. New York and London: Garland Publishing, Inc., 1995, pages 608–25.

Sisson, Jonathan B. *"The Real Life of Sebastian Knight,"* in *The Garland Companion to Vladimir Nabokov*, edited by Vladimir E. Alexandrov. New York and London: Garland Publishing, Inc., 1995, pages 633–643.

Tolstaia, Nataliia and Mikhail Meilakh. "Russian Short Stories," translated from Russian by Maxim D. Shrayer, in *The Garland Companion to Vladimir Nabokov*, edited by Vladimir E. Alexandrov. New York and London: Garland Publishing, Inc., 1995, pages 644–60.

Zaleski, P. "Nabokov's Blue Period." *Harvard Magazine.* July–August 1986, pages 34–38.

Zimmer, D. E. *A Guide to Nabokov's Butterflies and Moths.* Hamburg: Privately published, 1998.

For Véra
from
the captor

Vanessa ataluxticae Nab.

Montreux
23·X·1963

NO. 75

LOLITA

For Vera: Polygonia thaïsoides Nab.

NO. 83

COLOPHON

Typeset in Hermann Zapf's Melior type.

Printed by The Stinehour Press, Lunenburg, Vermont.

Designed by Jerry Kelly.

2000 copies printed, of which 500 have

been cloth bound.

To Véra

Arlequinus arlequinus

NO. 132